I0108646

VENTURE:
THE FRONTIERS OF
FREE METHODISM

By
BYRON S. LAMSON

First Fruits Press
Wilmore, Kentucky
c2016

Venture: The Frontiers of Free Methodism. By Byron S. Lamson

First Fruits Press, ©2016
Previously published by the Free Methodist Publishing House, ©1911
ISBN: 9781621715016 (print) 9781621715023 (digital) 9781621715030 (kindle)
Digital version at http://place.asburyseminary.edu/freemethodistbooks/15/

First Fruits Press is a digital imprint of the Asbury Theological Seminary, B.L.
Fisher Library. Asbury Theological Seminary is the legal owner of the material
previously published by the Pentecostal Publishing Co. and reserves the right to
release new editions of this material as well as new material produced by Asbury
Theological Seminary. Its publications are available for noncommercial and
educational uses, such as research, teaching and private study. First Fruits Press
has licensed the digital version of this work under the Creative Commons
Attribution Noncommercial 3.0 United States License. To view a copy of this
license, visit http://creativecommons.org/licenses/by-nc/3.0/us/.

For all other uses, contact:

First Fruits Press
B.L. Fisher Library
Asbury Theological Seminary
204 N. Lexington Ave.
Wilmore, KY 40390
http://place.asburyseminary.edu/firstfruits

Lamson, Byron S.

    Venture: The Frontiers of Free Methodism / By Byron S. Lamson--
Wilmore, Kentucky : First Fruits Press, ©2016.
124 pages: illustrations, portraits; 21 cm.
Reprint. Previously published: Chicago: Free Methodist Publishing House,
© 1911. Includes index.
ISBN: 9781621715016 (pbk.)

    1. Free Methodist Church of North America -- Missions--History.
      2. Missionaries--Biography. I. Title.

BV2550. W56 2016   266.79

Cover design by Jonathan Ramsay

asburyseminary.edu
800.2ASBURY
204 North Lexington Avenue
Wilmore, Kentucky 40390

First Fruits
THE ACADEMIC OPEN PRESS OF ASBURY SEMINARY

First Fruits Press
The Academic Open Press of Asbury Theological Seminary
204 N. Lexington Ave., Wilmore, KY 40390
859-858-2236
first.fruits@asburyseminary.edu
asbury.to/firstfruits

Venture!

The Frontiers of Free Methodism

by

Byron S. Lamson

Light and Life Press
Winona Lake, Indiana

All rights reserved. No portion of this
book may be reproduced without written
permission from the author. Reviewers
may quote brief passages for articles to be
printed in newspapers or magazines.

Copyright 1960

LIGHT AND LIFE PRESS

Winona Lake, Indiana

Library of Congress catalog card No. 60-11826

Quotations from Copyrighted Sources

Direct quotations from the following copyrighted books have been
included in *Venture!* These quotations are used by special permission of
the publishers.

ADAMS, JAMES TRUSLOW—*Epic of America.* Little, Brown and Company,
Boston, 1931.

ECKARDT, A. ROY—"The New Look in American Piety," *The Christian
Century.* The Christian Century Foundation, Chicago, 1954.

EDDY, G. NORMAN—"Store Front Religion: A Challenge," *The Christian
Century.* The Christian Century Foundation, Chicago, 1959.

LATOURETTE, KENNETH SCOTT—*History of the Expansion of Christianity.*
(*The Great Century in Europe and the United States of America
A.D. 1800-A.D. 1914*, Vol. IV, 1941; *The Great Century in the Amer-
icas, Austral-Asia, and Africa A.D. 1800-A.D. 1914*, Vol. V, 1943; *The
Great Century in Northern Africa and Asia A.D. 1800-A.D. 1914*,
Vol. VI, 1944.) Harper and Brothers, New York.

LUCCOCK, HALFORD E.—"Fire Drill in Church" by Simeon Stylites, *The
Christian Century.* The Christian Century Foundation, Chicago,
1959.

Printed in the United States of America

To

The memory of Mary Virginia

Loving daughter

Radiant witness for Jesus

A continuing reminder of the

Supremacy of the spiritual

Preface

This is not, primarily, either a history of the Free Methodist Church or an account of the founding of its numerous overseas missions. It is rather the profile of a spirit, the delineation of the essential genius of a people called Free Methodists. However, where an account of forces operative in the world and particularly in the parent church that gave rise to the Free Methodist movement leads to a better understanding of this people, such report is given. When the outreach of the pioneers on the western frontier and the overseas missionary venture illuminate the portrait, their story is told. Essentially it is an "inside" job, a story with a purpose, a reminder to Free Methodists of what they are and what they should be doing, now they have come of age. The meaning and purpose of Free Methodism against the background of 1860 is in sharp contrast to the situation a century later. Does this movement still have meaning? Is its essential drive and purpose relevant to the modern world? These are the matters of world-wide concern "inside Free Methodism."

Byron S. Lamson
Winona Lake, Indiana

Acknowledgments

The sources of information for this writing are the Minutes of the General Missionary Board, the early correspondence of missionary secretaries, publishing agents and church leaders, still on file. I have explored the bound volumes of *The Free Methodist* which are stored in the vaults of the Free Methodist Publishing House. Bound copies of *The Earnest Christian* edited by B. T. Roberts have been of inestimable value. My thanks to the Research Secretary, Mabel Cook, of the General Missionary Board office since 1908, and to my wife Freda, for assistance in locating important letters and documents in the early files. The bound volumes of the Conference Minutes were a gold mine of information which was summarized for me by Mrs. Olive Teal. My sincere thanks to the offices that have made available the early issues of *The Free Methodist,* the Minutes of the General Conference, and the *General Conference Daily.* My editorial assistant, Marian Williamson, has made helpful suggestions regarding the organization of material and also assisted me in clarifying in my own mind the thesis of the book. She also prepared the footnotes. Mrs. Lamson arranged the index and many of the paragraph headings. The chronological lists have been prepared and checked by Olive Teal and my secretary, Nellie Jones. I am indebted to Helen Hull, editor of *Light and Life Evangel,* for ideas on procedure and for literary advice.

The entire office staff has taken extra responsibilities to give me maximum release from much of my regular work without which the writing of a book would have been impossible. My early and late hours of writing, together with an almost complete neglect of household responsibilities, have been accepted by my thoughtful wife with rare understanding. The memory of my dear daughter, Mary Virginia, her interest in the book and early helpful suggestions, have been a source of strength and inspiration. I have kept in mind her standards of excellence. Hard and careful work has been the motto. I have striven for accuracy of fact and correctness of interpretation. The point of view expressed and conclusions drawn from facts presented are my own. I believe that they can be supported by factual evidence.

This message is sent out with the prayer that the church and the world may better understand essential New Testament religion as demonstrated by the real genius of Free Methodism at its best. May such understanding lead to repentance and a recovery of the inner spiritual drive of early Free Methodism and of first century Christianity.

February, 1960
Winona Lake, Indiana

Table of Contents

Venture!

"By faith Abraham, when he was called to go out
into a place which he should after
receive for an inheritance, obeyed; and
he went out, not knowing whither he went."
                                                    Hebrews 11:8

". . . I still plan to go . . . leaving my family
and all because Jesus said, 'Go ye,'
and I trust the Lord and the church. . . ."—J. W. Haley

The Frontier,

1860-1900

Section 1—B. T. ROBERTS

A New Day

It is the day of the common man. A new spirit is in the air. Japan has just opened her ports to world trade. Capitalism has resulted in the creation of wealth. A middle class is developing, while labor unions are organizing to promote the interests of the "common man." Charles Darwin has just published his epoch-making *Origin of Species*. The discovery of gold in California in 1848 has only increased the tempo of man's westward trek, already stimulated by the annexation of Texas, the opening of the western states, and the generous offer of free government land. The underprivileged and disenfranchised are getting a hearing.

Hudson Taylor is organizing his non-denominational China Inland Mission. Laymen are prominent in America's mid-century revival, conducting thousands of prayer meetings, visiting in homes, and publicly giving their personal witness to the reality of the Christian faith. The Y.M.C.A. is advocating the cause of foreign missions and the destruction of slavery.

The Victorian Age literature is beginning to have its influence. The *Vanity Fair* of Thackeray, lampooning the follies of the rich, and Charles Dickens' *Tale of Two Cities*, pleading for the rights of the poor, have added fuel to the flame. Count Tolstoy, literary genius and Russian social reformer, is a power in eastern Europe. In 1861 Russia has repudiated serfdom. England has already abolished slavery and America is plunging into a bloody war for the same purpose.

Revivals

Late in the previous century, a mighty movement of spiritual religion had swept over New England, Pennsylvania, New York, New Jersey, Ohio, Tennessee, the Carolinas and Georgia. In New York thousands were reported "praying as never before." Christians began to feel an obligation to carry the gospel to the non-Christian areas of the world. In the wake of this revival, the first foreign missionary society, the American Board of Commissioners for Foreign Missions, was organized in 1810. The American Bible Society came into existence at about this same time. College students were awakened to spiritual reality in remarkable campus revivals. Many of them became concerned with their obligation to evangelize the whole world. The now famous "haystack" prayer meeting of 1806 led to the organization of what later became the Student Volunteers and the sending of thousands of our finest young people as missionaries to the ends of the earth.

Now, a half-century later, the ferment of a second revival has appeared. America's so-called Great Revival with a reported fifty thousand conversions in one week rates front page space in our leading newspapers in 1857 and 1858. The year before, D. L. Moody had started his Sunday school for neglected children in Chicago. "Free seats" make news in the Chicago revival of 1857. "Free" churches, that is, churches for the common man unable to rent his own pew, are appearing in a few of the larger cities.

Roberts

In western New York, the brilliant young Methodist scholar-preacher-writer, B. T. Roberts, champion of the rights of the little man, advocate of free seats in the churches and the elimination of slavery from our national economy, the reformer and statesman, called the church and the nation to repentance and a return to the simple living and faith of the New Testament. His sermons and writings were centered in the life and teachings of Jesus. He took this way seriously. He felt that much church activity was on a sub-Christian level. The real church was more than an efficient organization. Man-contrived efforts to raise money by such means as church suppers, charity sales, bazaars and pew renting were an insult to the founder of the Christian faith who freely gave His life on the cross for the salvation of the world. Such methods testified to the church's spiritual poverty and indicated a lack of genuine commitment to Christ.

He loved his church and sought to bring her back—and he believed it could be done—to the standard of New Testament Christianity. For this he had prepared at Wesleyan University in Middletown, Connecticut. He had seen mighty revivals sweep the campus under such evangelists as Dr. John Wesley Redfield. The president, Dr. Stephen Olin, giant intellect of that day's

12

B. T.
Roberts

Methodism, stood for spiritual religion of the early Methodist type. Mrs. Roberts had lived for many years in the home of her uncle, Rev. George Lane, Assistant Book Agent and Treasurer of the Methodist Missionary Society. At this home in New York Mrs. Roberts had become acquainted with the Methodist leaders who came on business and the missionaries sailing to their fields of service or returning for a needed furlough. The Roberts family knew the leaders of the church and had an insight into the genius and spirit of authentic Methodism.

B. T. Roberts was sacrificially serving the smaller churches of the conference, and with success. Invariably, revivals broke out and large numbers of converts were brought into the fellowship of the church. If success did not attend his labors, he resorted to fasting and prayer, sometimes for an entire night. He had a humble spirit and took the blame on himself for spiritual failure in the church.

He was outspoken. Church leaders and worldly programs were exposed for what they were. He felt called to reform and revive his own conference

13

and the church he loved. He especially called for a return to John Wesley's emphasis on simple living, and the full surrender of the will as a basis for the sanctification of the inner life of the Christian, and the empowering of the Holy Spirit for effective Christian service. Many methods employed by churches of his day seemed to "pronounce Christianity a failure. The gospel possesses," he wrote, "an inherent power that will not only sustain itself, but make its way through all opposition. . . ." The purpose of the church is "two-fold—to maintain the Bible standard of Christianity, and to preach the gospel to the poor. . . . All the seats in . . . houses of worship shall be free. No pews can be rented or sold. . . . The world will never be converted to Christianity when the churches are conducted upon the exclusive system. . . . Free churches are essential to reach the masses. The provisions of the gospel are for all. . . . To savage and civilized, bond and free, black and white, the ignorant and learned, is freely offered the great salvation. . . . The church must follow in the footsteps of Jesus. She must see to it that the gospel is preached to the poor . . . it follows then as a necessary consequence that all arrangements for preaching the gospel should be so made as to secure this object."

Crisis at Buffalo

Soon he was serving an important congregation in Buffalo and promoting an intense evangelistic program, aided by the successful evangelist-friend of his university days experience, Dr. Redfield. At this point he began to meet opposition. Brother pastors of the city and higher officials of the conference successfully broke the influence of the meeting and almost broke young Roberts. Full of faith and hope, however, he presented his position to the General Conference. The General Conference was beset by problems arising out of its own compromise with slavery. Its most influential bishop was sick and had no stomach for a battle with the Genesee Conference leaders in defending the rights and the message of this youthful reformer.

And so, while the Great Revival of 1857 and 1858 swept all around them, his own conference, the Genesee, missed it. They at last expelled B. T. Roberts from the conference—for what? Insubordination? Disloyalty to his denomination?

A Free Church

Thousands of the laymen—the little people, the common folks—who believed in Roberts and his social and spiritual passion, were either dismissed from their churches or deliberately left them to organize "free churches." Here the message of free grace, free seats, the freedom of the Spirit, was freely offered to all. A group of laymen and a few ministers, committed to the Bible and the spiritual teachings of the New Testament, especially as they relate to the doctrine of full salvation in entire sanctification, met in an apple orchard near Pekin, New York, August 23, 1860. Here they sat on the grass to consider the will of the Lord for them. In these humble circumstances, after much prayer, they decided to provide a spiritual home for these persecuted people. Sixty laymen and fifteen preachers on the adjacent campground proceeded to establish the Free Methodist Church. They were loyal to a way of life as taught and lived by John Wesley and the early Methodists, and sought in the newly organized Free Methodist Church polity to preserve this original heritage, and to evangelize the entire world.

It was a great hope.

Section 2—A MISSIONARY CHURCH

That small "apple-orchard" convention of devoted laymen caught the imagination of many who were longing for spiritual reality. From every quarter came urgent calls for camp meetings, revivals and church dedications. Pastors were needed to serve the new congregations being formed both within and beyond the bounds of the Genesee Conference. Laymen, licensed as local preachers, usually cared for the new congregations, while the ordained ministers who had been expelled from the conference, together with those who voluntarily and on principle joined the movement, were assigned to districts, including in some instances an entire state.

These were still the pioneer days of American history. The West was rapidly being settled. The first transcontinental railroad had not been completed. The frontier with its lack of comfort and security, its challenge to the hardy pioneer, the individualist, and the frustrated non-conformist, was all too frequently not only a dangerous place to live, but a sinful one. It was both the enemy of religion and a mission field for the itinerant evangelist or "missionary," as he was usually called.

The new church had made Roberts its first General Superintendent. This church, in his opinion, had no time for denominational quarreling. There should be no rancour, no revenge. The salvation of the world, nothing less, was the objective. In his magazine, *The Earnest Christian*, Roberts kept this high purpose before his readers. His emphasis on plainness of dress and simple church buildings was not an end in itself but a means to an end—the salvation of the world. The Civil War had not yet ended when he declared that with—

"Christians living in a simple, unostentatious style, the supposed necessity for magnificent, costly churches would no longer exist, and the money thus

15

saved . . . (should be) appropriated to the erection of plain churches wherever needed, and to the support of missionaries. In one generation the standard of the gospel would be planted in every quarter of the globe, the banner of the cross would float in every breeze, and all our brethren of the human family would have the opportunity of listening to the glad tidings of great joy."[1]

Use of Wealth

This sense of mission, this concern for the whole world, had earlier led him to apply for missionary service in Bulgaria, and later to volunteer for India and Turkey. In each case Mrs. Roberts' health made the appointment impossible. But at heart Roberts, the missionary, was aflame with a passion for the salvation of the lost of earth. In the great succession of Jesus, Paul and Wesley, he declared that riches peril the soul. Christians, he said, are forbidden to accumulate wealth as an end in itself. It was impossible, he thought, to be supremely devoted to gaining wealth and serving Christ. The desire for wealth can become an obsession and is dangerous. He urged restitution of ill-gotten gains, the entire consecration of self and property, and strict obedience to the commands of Christ in the use of wealth for the preaching of the gospel and the extension of the blessed influences of the church to every dark corner of this underprivileged, sin-darkened world.[2]

The Common Touch

Roberts' "underdog" psychology is freely admitted. He said: "I was born with a love of freedom . . . as far as I know I have always stood on the side of the oppressed at any risk."[3] While attending Middletown University, he regularly taught a Sunday-school Bible class at the Negro church, subjecting himself to criticism and ostracism in that pre-Civil War day. Even earlier, while studying law, he gave an abolition speech,[4] and was amazed to find segregation practiced in the New England churches! "They have too much of the slavery spirit even here," he wrote to his sister, ". . . to worship the universal Father in the same temple with their sable brethren."[5] This concern for the least, the lowest, the lost, is basic in Roberts' crusade for "free churches." He was more concerned with this, if possible, than with merely the growth of his own denomination! He thought "God wants free churches in all our cities . . . not a Free Methodist church, but a free church."[6] His broad views and sympathetic insight are confirmed in his statement that—

> "The experiences through which I have passed have had a good effect in many ways. They have cured me of sectarian bigotry. I have lost my denominational zeal. I feel a deep sympathy with every enterprise that has a tendency to promote the Kingdom of Christ in its purity."[7]

16

So this was really the main drive of his life—not denominational bigness, but bigness of spirit in reaching all men of whatever condition with the gospel of Christ. And his "free churches" in every city have been abundantly realized. In this he was pre-eminently right.

Free seats in Free Methodist churches was a natural. The gospel is for all. All must hear. ". . . all the arrangements . . . should be so made as to secure this object."[8] Therefore, the seats are forever free, a symbol of concern for all men regardless of color or social condition. The validity of this position was grounded in the character of God.

> "It is our mission to *seek the salvation of all classes*. . . . We start with the system of *free seats* and open our doors alike for the rich and the poor, the black and the white, the educated and the illiterate. . . . All men equally need redemption in Christ. As God is no respecter of persons, why should we be?"[9]

Roberts' concern for the underprivileged was basic in his sacrifices to establish and "publish a revival journal" of "Experimental Religion . . . and Christian Holiness" where "the claims of the neglected poor, the class to which Christ and the Apostles belonged, the class for whose special benefit the gospel was designed . . ." would be "advocated with all the candor and ability we can command." To promote this revival among "those not reached by the regular churches," Roberts advocated the "necessity of plain churches, with the seats free, of plainness of dress, of spirituality and simplicity in worship."[10]

Seeking and Saving the Lost

So Roberts gave himself pre-eminently to the work of "soul-saving." Authorized by the first Eastern Convention (Genesee) to employ "ten other preachers" (there were fourteen) still this only partially supplied the new congregations calling for pastoral supervision. He could use a hundred "men full of faith and the Holy Ghost, who seek not their own ease or profit, but the salvation of souls. . . ."[11] He was concerned with the great cities. Buffalo especially attracted his attention. By great personal sacrifice, he secured property in a strategic location, and in October, 1860, "a plain, unpretending brick building, pleasantly and commodiously fitted, and capable of seating from five to six hundred people" was dedicated. A few months later Roberts preached at the Buffalo church where he found the society "all united and walking in faith and love. They enjoy a constant revival," he reported.[12] The church was crowded, gallery, aisles and porch, and "hundreds go away unable to find standing room."[13] He realized that a second church must be opened just as soon as this one was cleared of debt. Roberts was exceedingly

17

careful at the point of personal finance, and this characteristic was reflected in his policies regarding church finance.

So Roberts and the early preachers associated with him were, above all else, men of passion for world redemption. The Buffalo pastor preached on the docks to all who would hear. Roberts gave himself to evangelism in the Albion, New York, jail and in the slums of Buffalo. He raised funds for the Water Street Mission in New York City. In Illinois, the district chairman, J. G. Terrill, reported that on "sabbath I rode on horseback forty miles and preached twice. Last Friday, I rode forty-five miles in an awful snow storm . . . the happiest day I ever experienced."[14] He needed several men to supply new places calling for preachers. They could work "night and day."

A revival meeting started at West Kendall, New York, on New Year's eve. More than fifty conversions were reported the first two weeks. The membership doubled the first year in Illinois, with new churches dedicated at St. Charles, Clinton, Ogle and Belvidere. One Illinois preacher had "during the year walked sixteen hundred miles, visited and prayed with a thousand families, and received thirty dollars."[15]

This was a movement of God. At Marengo, Illinois, the revival closed "every saloon."[16] At Belvidere a vacant Congregational Church was rented, but soon was too small for the crowds. A church of "fifty or more" was organized.[17] A second meeting was held at Marengo in the Metropolitan Hall, the largest in town. A society of over one hundred members was organized. E. P. Hart, youthful pioneer preacher, was appointed pastor. They built a commodious stone church, but says Hart, "This was the only circuit I ever was appointed to which had not been raised up under my own labors."[18]

In this pioneer day camp meetings were an important feature. Roughnecks tore down tents at the Laughlin Grove Camp. Late at night drunken rowdies with "clubs and stakes . . . came on for a general attack." One, Newell Day, who was acquainted with some of the men, quietly talked with them. "They were beyond reasoning." A pointed stick hurled by one ruffian hit Day in the eye, gouging it out! Groaning with pain, he returned to the camp. The men quickly dressed, seized the ringleaders, who were brought to trial. They escaped prison by enlisting in the army.[19] The Civil War was then in progress.

A Missionary Society—1862

To give assistance in planning and financing the extension activities of the young church beyond the borders of Illinois and western New York, the first General Conference in 1862, in its last Tuesday afternoon sitting, enacted a most important and significant measure in what was otherwise quite a disappointing conference. It was—

"Resolved that the following brethren, to wit, B. T. Roberts, Joseph Travis,

Thomas Sully, be a committee to draft a constitution for a Missionary Society of the Free Methodist Church: And to secure its incorporation by the legislature of New York . . . to receive legacies in different states; . . . The General Superintendent was elected president, Rev. Orson P. Raper, secretary, and Brother C. T. Hicks. . . ."[20]

The work of the Missionary Society was primarily that of what we now call evangelism and church extension. Twelve years later, the General Conference enlarged the society and changed its name to General Missionary Board. A Committee on Missions consisting of B. T. Roberts, J. Travis and E. P. Hart[21]—"Recommend a General Missionary Board to look after and provide for the general missionary work among us." The duties of the Board were approved as follows:

"1. The General Superintendent or Superintendents of the Free Methodist Church, with William Gould, E. Owen, T. S. LaDue, Joseph Mackey, E. H. Winchester, shall constitute the Missionary Board of the Free Methodist Church, of which a superintendent shall be chairman.

"2. Officers: Secretary and Treasurer. Their usual duties.

"3. To hold office until the next General Conference or until their successors are elected, unless they cease to be members of the Free Methodist Church. Vacancies to be filled by the Board.

"4. Duties:

a. Have charge of all monies raised for General Missions in the several annual conferences.

b. Make appropriations for the *foreign missions* or to the several annual conferences for home missions within its bounds as in their judgment the cause of God can best be promoted.

c. This Board shall make a full report to each annual conference at their respective sessions, of all monies received and disbursed by them and the results of such appropriations so far as can be ascertained."[22]

Foreign Missions—Premature?

This is the first mention of "foreign missions" in the General Conference legislation. The year is 1874. William Taylor, Missionary Bishop of the Methodist Church, is with Bishop Thoburn in India, holding successful evangelistic campaigns and establishing his so-called "self-supporting" missions as he had already done in Africa and South America. Taylor's appeal for the "Christians in the United States to send missionaries" and the generous impulses of a British official led to the establishment of a mission station in Berar, Central India. This became the first station of what was eventually the Christian and Missionary Alliance work.[23] J. Hudson Taylor of the China Inland Mission was praying for more missionaries while B. T. Roberts was reading the exciting story of Livingstone's travels and explorations in Africa.[24] Roberts was on the committee that prepared the outline of duties for the new General Missionary Board. Ever alert to the movements of history, he made his influence felt in this first "foreign missions" legislation.

But the action was premature. Four years later, the General Conference again revised the rules of the General Missionary Board by excluding all reference to "foreign" missions, simply stating that "money . . . collected shall be appropriated to General Missionary Work."[25] What was "general missionary work"?

Missions—Church Extension

Pioneer evangelists sent to open new work in areas where no church of the sending denomination existed were called "missionaries." This was common practice in most churches. The 1882 appointments of the Iowa Conference listed "Northwest Mission" and "California Mission."[26] The same year Illinois Conference appropriations provided missionary funds for Galva District, Cable Circuit, Crown Point, Wheaton and Abingdon.[27] The Michigan Conference raised $70.76 to send Missionary Vaughn to Southwest Missouri.[28] Pioneer preacher E. P. Hart, laboring in Michigan to establish a new conference, explained that he received "no missionary appropriation." General Superintendent Roberts had charge of all missions outside the recognized bounds of the annual conferences.[29] The early records of the Missionary Board are almost wholly concerned with "General Missions," which meant what we today call "evangelism and church extension."

The 1874 Book of Discipline provided that—

> "It shall be the duty of each preacher in charge of a circuit to hold one or more missionary meetings on his circuit during the year, and to take collections and circulate a subscription for the support of missions within the bounds of his annual conference."[30]

A portion of these missionary funds was sent to the General Missionary Board for new work not cared for by the conferences. Superintendent Roberts was authorized to appoint missionaries to such fields of labor and request the Missionary Board to assist in their meager support. Frequently the collections were small, if taken at all, and often the churches were slow in sending their offerings.

The Free Methodist published urgent pleas concerning this fund. Roberts explains the missions fund as both for the conference church extension program and the work sponsored by the General Missionary Board. He is especially concerned for the Mission at Philadelphia. The General Conference has requested an amount equal to one "cent per member per week"! So Roberts concludes his appeal for Philadelphia, and then, as if to add extra urgency to his request, he says: "There are some foreign missions on the voluntary plan deserving our assistance. . . . Dear brethren, please act with promptness and energy, and put this plan in operation."[31]

Frontier Days

The life of these "missionaries" was rugged. James Mathews, an appointed missionary to Kansas in 1868, reports that—

"My appointment as missionary is no sinecure. We are constantly at work, and the calls multiply. The country through here is new . . . sparsely settled. . . . None of the streams are bridged. . . . It is impossible to go on foot, and most of the time we go on horseback. The people share their meal and potatoes with us with a free heart."[32]

He reports a flood of rain outside and a time of salvation inside. After the service Mathews and his host, a Father Hanby, became lost on the prairie in the soaking rain. Finally, a glimmer of light was seen in the distance. At length they found a log house filled with others who, like themselves, were unable to reach home. They sat by the fire all night enjoying a service of worship. Mathews confesses that "a piece of johnny cake without butter tasted good . . . about midnight."

The first organized churches and conferences, hardly able yet to adequately support themselves, caught the missionary spirit, giving in some instances beyond their ability to establish new conferences on the western frontier. Moses N. Downing, district chairman, urged the Susquehanna Conference to raise its fifty cents per member for General Missions. Thousands of dollars are needed, he wrote, for the new churches recently constructed, and for the work in Philadelphia.[33]

And besides, the 1874 General Conference had voted that "Each annual conference may from time to time by vote, appropriate of its missions funds such sums to the General Missionary Board as in their judgment they may deem proper."[34]

A General Board

As ultimately developed, church extension became primarily the function of the annual conference with a minimum of personnel and finance available on a general church basis. This is in contrast to the foreign missions work which, by its very nature, seems to require centralized planning, finance and control. The denominational program of foreign missions came late, the leaders of the church being spurred to action by the churches and conferences who conscientiously felt that there should be such a program. The nature of the operation, the required finance, the complications involved in operating missions in foreign countries, and the experience of other church boards, all helped in determining the development of centralized denominational administration.

At the 1882 General Conference at Burlington, Iowa, new legislation was drafted, providing, among other things, for the election of a Missionary Secretary by the Conference. They also for the first time provided for General Evangelists. These were to be appointed by the General Superintendents. They were to open new fields, organize new churches, place temporary pastors in charge of the same, and have general oversight of the evangelists laboring with them. They were to receive support from the General Missionary Board on the recommendation of the General Superintendents.

The year 1882 is frequently given as the date of the organization of the General Missionary Board. It would seem that 1862, or at least 1874, would be more correct. However, the first foreign missionaries were appointed during the 1882-1886 quadrennium.

The Home Base

Adapted to the needs of a foreign program, the General Missionary Board served effectively in the early days of the denomination as the vehicle of its outreach. The board meeting minutes tell the story of a young church attempting the impossible! At its second meeting, October 12, 1882, the new Missionary Board authorized a "call" for $400.00 through the columns of *The Free Methodist*. On the strength of this call they appropriated $25.00 each to four evangelists for work in Texas.[35] In November $150.00 was approved to send a General Evangelist to California. The Southern California district chairman, C. B. Ebey, writing about the token appropriation of $15.00 per month says: "I hoped the Board would have helped me so I could have gone ahead but as it is, I cannot."[36] The treasurer reported on February 15, 1883, receipts of $68.68; paid out, $87.50; due the treasurer, $19.12. At this meeting action was taken to appropriate "missionary money only for those in mission work."[37] In July the treasurer reports additional receipts of $120.25 and the deficit reduced to $5.68![38] Three general evangelists working in Wisconsin were given an allowance of $50.00 monthly. Board member J. G. Terrill offered to write a book on Home and Foreign Missions, featuring the India work of Rev. and Mrs. E. F. Ward, Free Methodist missionaries working there on an independent basis. The profits from the book were pledged to the India mission work.[39] At its September 6 meeting reports were received from General Evangelists W. G. Hanmer, W. M. Kelsey and Philip C. Hanna, and $15.00 per month was appropriated for the Philadelphia missionary.[40] Funds were meager and wholly inadequate for the new and expanding program. Accordingly, the treasurer was instructed to pay all appropriations on a pro rata basis.[41] It was decided to use collection boxes to secure funds for the "independent" missionaries laboring in India.[42]

On the March

The young church was on the march. Free Methodism was a movement. One conference report condemns selfish churches that want all their pastor's time.[43] He should devote a portion of his time to opening new work and laboring as a frontier evangelist. The New York Conference appointments for the same year included Washington Territory District, J. Glenn, chairman; Oregon District, T. S. LaDue, chairman, while the Kansas Conference listed appointments in Missouri and Colorado. Success attended these efforts, inadequate and poorly financed as they were. These were men of prayer. Sacrifice was expected and accepted willingly.

Camp meetings were largely attended. The staid General Superintendent, B. T. Roberts, was reported shouting "Hallelujah" as "waves of glory" swept over the Wisconsin Conference camp.[44] In Illinois, mobs attempted to break up the camp meeting but the effort was a failure. In North Michigan there were seventy-four tents with five hundred in attendance.[45] Two years later twenty thousand attended, with services continuing with great power night and day.[46] Many were converted in these great camps. Kansas had a 40 per cent membership increase the same year.[47] The next year Wisconsin recorded a 25 per cent membership gain with that prince of preachers, Dr. A. L. Whitcomb, joining the conference. He was for many years a General Conference evangelist. He also served as president of Greenville College. Between 1874 and 1882 the total church membership doubled, with the number of conferences increasing from six to fourteen.[48]

Pattern of a Movement

How can we explain such rapid growth in the face of opposition from some of the larger churches, the sinfulness of the times, the smallness of their numbers, their lack of finance, an itinerant ministry of below average educational attainment, preaching an unpopular message that demanded sacrifice and total commitment from the newly won converts? Let us see.

1. *The salvation of men was all important in their thinking, writing, preaching and planning.* Urged Roberts: "Let each minister resolve on seeing a hundred souls converted to God the coming year. Importune the throne of grace, be always abounding in the work of God."[49]

2. *They stressed the necessity of bringing the gospel to all men as more important than building up the Free Methodist Church.* Free churches, not necessarily Free Methodist churches, were required to reach the masses. This crusade was in harmony with Christ and the New Testament, and was per-

tinent to the age of pew-renting churches. They lost themselves for a cause and thus saved themselves. Seeking to save men, God in turn saved their church.

3. *Free Methodism from the beginning was a revival movement.* "The Free Methodist Church had its origin in a special outpouring of the Spirit, so it is natural that she should be endued with a great missionary zeal. The spirit of missions was shown in the beginning of her history by going into the highways and hedges—holding religious services in the schoolhouses, private homes, barns, on the streets, in dance halls and in groves—and compelling people to come to the gospel feast."[50] Such methods were peculiarly adapted to the frontier where the greatest evangelistic successes and membership gains were recorded.

4. *No sacrifice was too great.* In 1865 the Illinois Conference salaries averaged less than $200 for the year ". . . Many had left twice or thrice this, others had refused tempting offers to go elsewhere."[51] These preachers were "called of God." They had a sense of divine Commission. They were not working primarily for the church. They were "in" the church but they were working "for" God. Such men gathered a following wherever they labored.

5. *They were bold reformers, loudly condemning the evil practices of the day.* Slavery, alcohol, tobacco, and secret societies were especially arraigned in their preaching. What some denominations labeled human weakness, these preachers denounced as sin. "These bold reformers in their hatred of and uncompromising opposition to iniquity, soon came to questions involving moral issues, and they were not slow in taking their stand or unequivocal in defending their position."[52]

A new convert in Illinois found that one of her sons occasionally frequented the town saloon. One day, finding her boy there, she led him to the door, then with her broom literally swept the shelves of bottled goods. The destruction was beyond repair. The town lawyer defended her. She was never prosecuted. The late General Superintendent E. P. Hart's comment on the incident was: "I earnestly pray that . . . she may prove to be the . . . herald of the gospel of universal prohibition."[53]

6. *They had a strong faith in the power of the gospel to change men and transform the world.* "The world is to be saved. We ought to be in earnest about saving it. Our friends, children, neighbors, the heathen are perishing. We can do something to save them. . . . The apostles were enthusiastic. The Saviour Himself was filled with zeal."[54] Five years after the Free Methodists organized, Roberts wrote: "This little body, raised up in such a providential manner, was never, to all human appearances, as a whole in so prosperous a condition as at the present time. . . . Preachers and people are receiving a greater baptism of the Spirit for the work of saving souls. The work is spread-

ing, and pressing calls for earnest laborers filled with faith and the Holy Ghost are more numerous than can at present be supplied."[55]

In 1861, Benjamin Winget, later the Missionary Secretary, joined the Free Methodist Church. From early youth he was surrounded by these influences. Writing at a later date, he expresses the real genius of Free Methodism—its faith in the redeemability of the world. He says: "All that is needed in order that our work may increase . . . and that we see even larger results is to have our people more generally and believingly come in sympathy with our Lord in His love and pity for those who are in darkness and in the shadow of death."[56] He feels that those who pray "Thy Kingdom come" should expect "greater things . . . in scattering the darkness of heathen idolatry and superstition and bringing in the glorious light of the gospel."[57]

Pleading for the opening of missionary work in the Dominican Republic, he promises that ". . . if we send out a few workers to the south side of the island . . . the barriers of ignorance, superstition and idolatry may be swept away, and the flood-tide of blessing may come upon the people of that republic, and bring them up to a higher standard politically and religiously." He expects that "the Holy Spirit will so melt and unify His people . . . that they will work together in the fellowship of the Spirit . . . in uplifting and sanctifying the people."[58] Winget also sensed "an increasing spirit of prayer for the coming triumph of the Kingdom of God in all the earth."[59] These were men who did not live on any dim corridor between faith and doubt. They had a great gospel fully adequate, they thought, for the needs of all men everywhere. Such faith inspired preaching and activity that issued in revival and church growth.

7. *They had a sense of mission.* The early numbers of *The Earnest Christian* bristle with this feeling of urgency. "Do not wait for buildings," we are told, "but do as the Methodists did at the first, preach anywhere till God begins to work; preach in rooms, lofts, foundries, wherever there is an empty place available."[60]

Even more concerned is Roberts' own plea: "It will not do for us to wait for the people to come to us. We must go to them. Like the apostle, we must teach them from house to house (Acts 20:20). . . . Not a ward or school district in our vicinity should be unvisited. . . . Will you not get upon your souls a baptism of sympathy for the perishing masses around you? . . . Then go at once. . . . Get the baptism of fire upon your soul and go forth in the strength of the Almighty, weeping over your fellowmen and pointing them to Him who is mighty to save."[61] This sense of mission to the point of sacrifice is pointed up in a letter written to one of the first Africa missionaries, who through some misunderstanding did not receive needed funds and transferred to another mission. The Publishing Agent says: "There is not the slightest doubt in my mind but what your wants will be supplied. .... I feel so deeply over this matter that I am ready to say, if no one else can be found to take the field . . . I am ready to do it. . . . I have not spent as much valuable time as I have at my own expense for the past six years . . . to be willing to let our foreign missions work go by default. . . ."[62] Such devotion to the task compensated for inadequate finance and numerical weakness. "Sense of mission" is a marked characteristic of the pioneers and goes far to explain their extraordinary successes.

8. *The Free Methodists were blessed with strong leaders.* Capable district chairmen and pastors of the largest Methodist churches who sympathized with Roberts' views were either discontinued from conference appointment or voluntarily joined the movement. They were men of clear vision and strong conviction, yielding themselves utterly to the tasks at hand. These became the district chairmen. There were too many lay preachers with meager training. However, they spoke the language of the people, and under the supervision of the district chairmen, they were remarkably effective in their service to the church.

9. *They took seriously the teachings and the example of Jesus.* "The church must follow in the footsteps of Jesus," their Book of Discipline declared. They were faithful to the commands of the Bible, especially those of Christ and the apostles. They exhorted more "sympathy with our Lord in His love" for the lost world. Like Jesus, they chose to suffer rather than to defend their own rights. Warning his readers of a so-called "orthodox" emphasis on salvation by "grace alone" that makes provision for continuing in sin, Roberts says that it is not enough to sing: "Jesus Paid It All." We must repent and forsake sin. Faith issues in good works and is proved by a holy life.[63] In Michigan, faithful ministers that preach the "gospel of Jesus in all its purity," are needed.[64] A Baptist minister, describing the early Free Methodists, said: "The Bible is their textbook, Jesus Christ is their pattern." It is true that they were in full sympathy with John Wesley's teaching on Christian perfection. However, at their best they went to the source that Wesley himself had, the New Testament. They knew their Bibles better than their Wesley. Their preaching was with authority.

10. *This way demanded full commitment.* They read the fine print in the contract. The terrific demands of the gospel were not watered down with any superficial announcement of "cheap grace." For them there was no forgiveness without repentance; no birth without death. This was not a "cut-rate" religion of promises and accepting Christ. They did not amend the enormous demands of the New Testament. They took the way of the cross. An outsider, after attending one of their camp meetings, reported that the "Bible standard of holy living is held up vividly, forcibly; entire consecrated-

ness to God's service, a presenting the body a living perpetual sacrifice. . . . In this glorious work of reformation, of spreading scriptural holiness through the land, God is with them in very deed, smiling graciously on their self-denial and untiring perseverance."

11. *Their message was adapted to the frontier of our country.* The compromises of the churches on slavery and social reform alienated the masses who were ready to hear hard-hitting, Spirit-filled evangelists declare the truth of God without compromise. The times called for a bold stand.

12. *The methods used were well adapted to the frontier.* The announcement of a revival meeting usually filled the school or church. Tent and grove meetings brought the curious as well as the faithful. Many of the former remained to pray and join the movement. Street meetings, band workers, the "protracted" meeting that continued until the "break" came, the itinerant evangelist, the circuit rider—these combined to successfully proclaim the gospel of Christ and lay the foundations of the young church across the nation.

13. *There was little or no competition from other churches in many sections of the country.* Often vacant churches were opened to the pioneer evangelist. In such places people were actually hungry to hear the gospel.

14. *The Missionary Board could appoint workers to the places of greatest need and opportunity,* and make some appropriation toward their support.

15. *There was a great concern for the young people.* Schools were started in various parts of the country. Some did not survive, but they reflect concern for youth. B. T. Roberts was a young man of thirty-seven who gathered other young men about him. It was in some respects a youth movement. Concern for the freed slaves led also to the establishment of missions and schools for their benefit.

16. *They reached the people.* Today the growth of the cults, the multiplication of sects and the rise of store-front churches in our cities seem to indicate that the regular churches are middle class and still unable to communicate with the common people. Early Free Methodist lay preachers and class leaders carried major responsibility for the regular services of the church. It was a movement of the people, by the people, for the people. It was a layman's church. Its most rapid growth occurred during the period of greatest dependence on lay workers. This was a part of the trend of history in the middle of the nineteenth century. The common man, his rights and his needs, were being recognized in labor legislation, increased educational opportunities, and social reform. The movement was relevant to the times.

17. *It was a close-knit organization.* Its members were drawn together by loyalty to a cause. There was little if any "member getting" promotion. Join-

ing the movement was on the basis of conviction. There was a unity grounded in love. When this existed the work grew. In some places legalism, peripheral issues, criticism and censoriousness developed, which invariably paralyzed the movement and hindered the revival.[65] Such a situation was aired in the denominational paper. Comparing the movement with another denomination, the writer affirmed that Free Methodists are more denunciatory and less evangelical. They give too much attention to minor evils to the neglect of the great gospel truths. There is wild fanaticism without sufficient attention to the correction of "unscriptural irregularities, less zeal for the salvation of sinners and too much labor to get the church blest, too much time in the upper room, too much spiritual pride."[66] Doubtless this is a fair criticism of isolated sections of the church. That it was printed in the church paper probably indicates that the conditions mentioned were not typical. It may be noted here, too, that Free Methodists have a tendency to self-analysis and criticism to the point of developing a denominational inferiority complex. Always, less introspection, less attention to "her own internal affairs . . ." more emphasis on "the aggressive power of the gospel . . ." can be recommended to and practiced by Free Methodists.[67] But we must not further demonstrate the weakness we describe. In the main, this fellowship of the like-minded with a strong general organization was able to send and support workers in new areas more effectively than larger churches could do without the central organization and the unity of spirit and purpose of a small but committed group. By scattering, dividing and multiplying, the net result was more churches, more conferences, and more members.

18. *The growth was largest on the frontier.* In 1870 Michigan had almost tripled its membership for the quadrennium while Genesee remained static. It must be remembered, however, that from the original Genesee area other conferences were organized and preachers were sent everywhere to establish new work. It was also here that the difficulties occurred which resulted in the formation of the new church. In no other area were relations with the mother church so difficult. Old wounds heal slowly. Free Methodists were sneered at, persecuted and the entire movement subjected to an unrelenting opposition that is now difficult to understand. But Free Methodist revival meetings and camp meetings had their greatest success on the frontier.

19. *Free Methodists are not contemplative theologians of the ivory tower,* detached and insulated from the real life. They are activists, stressing the importance of *doing* the will of God. They not only believe in "orthodoxy" but also in "orthopraxy." They witness to their faith not only by an affirmation of the mind, but by the witness of a holy life made possible by the grace of God and the empowering of the Holy Spirit. "Do not spend all your time," says Roberts, "in getting ready to do something. Lay the foundation,

and then build upon it. Heat your iron as hot as necessary, and then strike good heavy blows. . . ."[68]

20. *Their supreme emphasis on prayer and the empowering of the Holy Spirit* is unquestionably the fundamental cause of these early successes. Roberts prayed: "I am not idle, and yet it seems as if I accomplish but little. Lord, make me diligent. active, useful, devoted. I want to be 'filled with the Spirit'. . . ."[69] Their utter dependence on God was essentially right.

21. *They were ready to cooperate with other churches in promoting the work of salvation,* since building their own ecclesiastical organization was, in their judgment, secondary to the winning of the lost. Representatives of five denominations "worked in harmony for the salvation of men" at the Rose camp meeting. But such association strengthened rather than weakened their work. A Baptist minister, attending the camp, wrote:

> "Among the number standing boldly for Jesus, going forth without the camp, bearing the reproach of Christ, is a society called Free Methodists, rapidly increasing in the West, a devoted, persecuted people. The Lord is with them, crowning their labors with remarkable success."[70]

The basis for such successful and fruitful cooperation was the message of full salvation. "Holiness of heart and life is common ground on which all true Christians may unite."[71]

22. *The personal influence, spiritual power, organizing genius, sense of mission, penetrating insight, humility and devotion of B. T. Roberts* must never be forgotten in assessing the early triumphs of the church. His shadow falls on every new field. He was a man of large affairs, prodigious toil, remarkable achievement. At one time in his life he was serving as General Superintendent, Superintendent of Missions, editor of *The Free Methodist,* while at the same time he continued to edit and publish *The Earnest Christian,* a monthly holiness journal of high quality. Meantime, he did the work of an evangelist, served as president of the General Missionary Board, maintained an active interest in the school he founded at North Chili, New York, served on important church committees, carried the burdens of all the churches. Withal he was a sympathetic friend, a man of trust and simple faith in God. At heart he was a soul winner, a missionary. He practiced what he preached. Always modest, Roberts felt so keenly the importance of soul winning that in his article, "How to Promote a Revival," he makes bold to refer to his own pastoral experience:

> ". . . We can say, to the praise of God's grace, that we never labored for any length of time in any place without having a revival of the work of God. . . . This is not owing to our abilities as a preacher. . . . It does not require great preaching talents to lead souls to the cross. . . . The care of

souls is as much the work of a minister as the care of the body is of the physician. A minister has no right to fail of success. If none are saved through his instrumentality the responsibility rests upon him. He may have a revival if he will!"[72]

Section 3—EDUCATION

Genius of Free Methodism

In the first number of his journal, *The Earnest Christian*, B. T. Roberts publishes an extended article by Bishop Hamline of the Methodist Church entitled, "The Millenium." The Bishop says:

"Our clerical acquaintances hold, for the most part, that the millenium will be a period of unexampled religious prosperity, in which Christ will have spiritual dominion from sea to sea, and from the rivers unto the ends of the earth. This is our opinion."

The Bishop then explains why he takes this position and reveals the grounds for his belief in a world-wide revival. He says:

"1. The prophecies which relate to Christ's millenial reign are highly figurative in their style.
"2. The personal reign of Jesus on earth is hardly consistent with some portions of Scripture . . . 'Unto them that look for him shall he appear the second time without sin unto salvation.' Here the judgment and the 'second coming' are connected, in a way that precludes the millenial advent.
"3. The passage in Revelation 20:4 speaks not of the bodies but of the souls of them that were beheaded for the witness of Jesus and for the word of God; and they lived and reigned with Christ a thousand years. . . . As Elijah was restored to the world in the person of John the Baptist . . . so the ancient witnesses shall return in the persons of many holy ministers, who shall not count their lives dear unto them . . . Happy church, and blessed period, when a martyr's spirit shall glow in every pious bosom!
"As to the commencement of this happy period, we have little to say concerning it. It is near at hand. . . . In the meantime, what should be the attitude of the church? It should be boldly offensive. . . . If all the church were to assume the attitude of a praying, laboring, suffering witness for Jesus, we need not look far forward to that millenium. We should suddenly find ourselves making our triumphant entrance upon its opening scenes of light and joy."[1]

Why did B. T. Roberts print this article? Certainly not for the sake of theological controversy. In a prefatory note he says:

"The following article . . . is so appropriate to the conflict at present going on in the church between spirituality and formalism, that we conclude to give it entire to our readers."[2]

"Image" of Original Free Methodism

This then is an insight into a view of spiritual religion as outlined by a Bishop of the Methodist Church and which so commended itself to Roberts as being the authentic portrait of the true church that full space is given to it in his magazine with words of commendation. A spiritual church is a "praying, laboring, suffering witness for Jesus." This is the genius of early Methodism and the image of original Free Methodism.

A few months later Roberts asks:

"Why should it be thought strange that those that are full of the Spirit of Christ should be proportionately in their love to souls like to Christ? . . . He offered up His blood for souls . . . (with) strong crying and tears. . . . Such a spirit of love to and concern for souls was the spirit of Christ. So it is the spirit of the church."

Roberts concluded his editorial by asking:

"Have we been rescued from our perilous condition? Do we see others, strangers, acquaintances, friends, relatives, in imminent danger of the same destruction which so recently threatened us? Does the compassionate spirit of Jesus dwell within us? Then how natural, how unavoidable is it that we should manifest, when alive to the condition of sinners, the deepest emotion.

> Did Christ o'er sinners weep
> And shall our cheeks be dry?
> Let floods of penitential grief
> Burst forth from every eye."[3]

Free Methodists believed that the world was lost. They believed and felt this awful "lostness." They were sure that the gospel of Christ was fully able to change the lives of individual men. Society must be changed but this could only be effected through changed men. There was strong preaching—great preaching of the "good news," the "great salvation," Christ was made real in the preached word. The records are clear. The "real Presence" frequently illuminated the preacher's mind, loosened his tongue, clarified his vision, strengthened his grasp on things spiritual and eternal. God became real to the worshiping congregation.

> "And heaven comes down our souls to greet,
> While glory crowns the mercy seat."[4]

Such preaching at its best was thoroughly Biblical. Theology was important, but the servant of experience. It was the function of theology to give sound Biblical interpretation of the great transforming power that had delivered them from the "power of darkness" and had translated them into the "kingdom of his dear Son."[5] This was the glorious fact. It had happened in thousands of lives. Their theology gave them adequate intellectual and Biblical grounds for the mighty transactions of the Spirit that had been effected in human hearts and lives. They stressed nurture and the development of the fruits of the Spirit. The class meetings, prayer meetings, cottage meetings, revival and camp meetings, the love feast, the quarterly meetings, the Sunday school, were all for one purpose—the development of saints.

It is no accident that early emphasis was given to education. It was Free Methodism's fixed purpose to save their youth, nurture them in the Christian graces, and prepare many of them for the full-time service of Christ and the church.

Schools

Four years after the Free Methodists began work in western New York, Roberts visited the campus of Oberlin College. It had been operating for twenty-five years. There were six hundred students. He found a spirit of prayer and revival on the campus. He heard Charles G. Finney speak and pray. The prayer meeting seemed too exclusively devoted to "our national affairs" but in writing to his wife, Roberts confides:

> "I do not know but we are too much taken up with our own personal salvation. . . . We must pray more about our contemplated school, and ascertain what the will of the Lord touching it is."[6]

In 1866 Roberts became financially responsible for the establishment of Free Methodism's first educational institution. He purchased a strategically located farm on what is now a main highway between Buffalo and Rochester,

Roberts Hall, first school building on campus of first Free Methodist school, North Chili, New York

New York. A mortgage of $10,000 was assumed by Roberts. Additional land was purchased to provide 196 acres for the campus. The city of Rochester is now converging on the campus, which is becoming increasingly valuable, a tribute to the remarkable insight of Roberts and an answer to his prayers for "the will of the Lord" concerning "our contemplated school." An overseas missionary program without an educational program could hardly succeed. A missionary church concerned with the salvation of its own youth and the world naturally turned to the establishment of educational institutions for the training of preachers and missionaries where the poorest could obtain an education under genuinely Christian influences. This need was especially apparent in the years following the Civil War.

"Shameful Decade"

The years 1865-75 have been labeled "the most shameful decade in our entire national history."[7] The post-war era in the southern states is a sordid story of the "political shysters," the "carpetbaggers" from the North, helping the "white riffraff" and the ignorant Negroes seize control of state and city governments. Taxes increased ten times, treasuries were bankrupt, while the pockets of the politicians were lined with money. There is "no parallel for the situation in the history of modern civilized nations. . . . The war left the South prostrate; reconstruction left it maddened."[8] The whole country seemed to have lost its conscience. It was an era of bank robberies, stock swindles and business scandals. Even the President and the Ambassador to England were involved in the sale of worthless gold mine stock. "The extraordinary part was that none of them appeared to consider that they had engaged in unethical practices" as across the country "bribery and corruption became general."[9]

The capitalist and speculator fared better than the laboring man. From 1860 to 1866 wages rose 60 per cent while prices increased 90 per cent and rent more![10] Industry was being organized for large-scale production. Great wealth was being concentrated in the hands of a few. Some of the more idealistic founded colleges and universities. John D. Rockefeller established the University of Chicago. "The Lord has prospered me," said Colonel George M. Scott, "and I don't want it to harden my heart."[11] So Scott endowed the Female Seminary at Decatur, Georgia. Carnegie fought the unions, pinched the wages of his employees, and invested millions in libraries. Some cities refused to accept gifts of such money. The Y.M.C.A. was organized in 1869 and expanded rapidly. There was increased immigration from Europe to supply cheap labor for the eastern factories, while many of the earlier immigrants and established citizens were moving west, taking advantage of the liberal homestead laws to secure free government land.

The Missionary Motive

The obvious strategy for Free Methodism in such a world was to insulate itself as much as possible from the evils of the age. Educational opportunities were few. Public schools in the big cities were unfriendly to the ideals of the infant church. In 1885 B. T. Roberts printed a pamphlet entitled *Schools and Crime*. Within seven years there were eleven schools planned or actually established! At Powhatan, Virginia, a mission school for Negroes was founded just two years after the Chili school was opened. The General Conference of 1882 approved a "mission college . . . for the saving and training of colored teachers who shall go out to spread scriptural holiness among their race here, and also on the now heathen continent of Africa."[12]

This is the first official pronouncement by the General Conference on the sending of missionaries to Africa. At that time it was hoped to accomplish this by sending the Africans themselves to evangelize their own people.[13] This was three years before any missionaries actually were sent by the Mission Board. At the Powatan school in Virginia, Rev. John Glen, preacher and teacher, needed his salary. The 1866 General Conference appropriated $500 for his support, which had not been received. An urgent request was made for funds to be sent to H. Hornsby, Perry, New York, for this purpose.[14] A "large school" was reported in successful operation.

The missionary motive was strong in the founding of the church schools. At Seattle, Mr. N. B. Peterson, "a man greatly interested in the cause of foreign missions, said he would donate five acres of ground in the city of Seattle if they would make it a missionary school."[15] This purpose was prominent in founding the college. Greenville College outlined a strong program of missionary training which was approved by the Missionary Board.[16]

The early decades of the nineteenth century witnessed some remarkable college revivals. Graduates often went out to found other colleges, while many volunteered for missionary service overseas.[17] In 1860 there were 166 well-established Protestant colleges in this country. The number had increased to 403 by 1900, and the Free Methodists established their share of them. More than twenty-five educational institutions had been officially approved by conferences, interested groups of ministers and laymen, or boards of trustees. Some were unable to continue. All were inadequately financed. But this urge to organize denominational schools far beyond the needs of its own constituency indicated a major concern that was essentially missionary.

Self-Criticism

Self-criticism voiced by leaders within the movement indicate that the church was alert to the ever present danger of losing its "first love." In 1880 D. W. Abrams sounds a warning. He affirms the fact that plain dress and

34

simple living benefit financially the members of the church and warns of the danger of covetousness. He finds that the missions in Chicago and New York City are receiving "very meager" support. Concerning a Free Methodist church in Oregon wrecked by rain and wind and for which B. T. Roberts had made urgent appeal, Abrams claims that only *one* church responded with financial assistance! He thinks ministers fear to ask the people for money and soon the people think they are too poor to give. He points to the danger of laying up treasures on earth and recommends that each church install a box for "grateful offerings."[18]

At the end of the first decade, Elias Bowen's appraisal of the Free Methodist Church was that "she has not sufficiently availed herself of the aggressive power of the gospel, but has been too well contented to get happy herself, and look after her own internal affairs."[19]

First Steps to Africa

These are the warnings of friends. They indicate the restless discontent of the idealist. The vision of God always transcends human achievement. The Kingdom of God can never be equated with any human manifestation of it in history. These criticisms reveal the presence of the remedy already at hand. The real church always witnesses to an ideal that condemns itself, but there is also an inner power of the Spirit of God at work in the church that makes self-correction possible. Two years later Abrams persuaded the General Conference to include in its printed minutes the history of the "Kansas Mission" for the "colored race." An initial offering had been pledged at the St. Charles camp meeting three years earlier. More than six hundred dollars had been received and his appeals for additional funds for the mission and to establish a "mission college" to prepare "colored teachers" for missionary service in Africa had the approval of the General Conference.[20] Abrams' proposal would achieve four important objectives:

1. Evangelize the thousands of recently freed slaves who have moved to Kansas.
2. Help solve the race problem by sending at least some of the colored race to Liberia.
3. Take the first small step toward the evangelization of Africa.
4. Give the Free Methodist Church a channel for the Christian use of the money saved by simple living, plain dress, and separation from worldly amusements and practices. It is a call to the stewardship of all of life.

Total Commitment—A Cause

Simple living with avoidance of luxury is not the retreat of a monk to some cave for purposes of developing a holiness uncontaminated by the world. It is for a high mission that the soldier of Jesus Christ lays aside the unnecessary. He is engaged in a world crusade. Nothing less than the salvation of the whole world is at stake. Soldiers do not take overstuffed davenports to the "no man's land" of battle. The sincere followers of Jesus lay aside "all superfluous ornaments." They avoid "gold, pearls, and costly array" so that they may the better carry on the "good works." Our gratitude to the Abrams of 1880 and the Roberts of 1860 for this insight into "the aggressive power of the gospel." The Free Methodist rule on simple living then is not an end in itself. Luxury may be an index of pride. It is worse! It indicates lack of insight into world need, unconcern for and lack of faith in the redeemability of a world living in hell now. Free Methodists at their best give themselves, their children, their material possessions, according "to their power . . . yea, and beyond their power"[21] for the cause dearest to their hearts—the salvation of the lost.

Free Methodist Schools—Chronology

1864 June	B. T. Roberts visits Oberlin College and writes of "our contemplated school."
1866	Roberts starts school at North Chili, New York.
1868	Freedman's Mission and school, Powhatan, Virginia.
1869	First building completed at Chili Seminary. Dedicatory address by Dr. M. B. Anderson, President of Rochester University.
1871 September	Michigan Conference approves purchase of school campus and two buildings at Spring Arbor, Michigan. Classes start in 1873.
1880 April 7	Representation of the Illinois and Wisconsin Conference, with B. T. Roberts, organized a Board of Trustees to operate Evansville Seminary, Rock County, Wisconsin.
1882	General Conference approves a "mission college" for colored teachers in Graham County, Kansas.
1883	Orleans Seminary, Orleans, Nebraska, incorporated by the West Kansas Conference.
1885	*Schools and Crime* pamphlet by B. T. Roberts, published.
1886	Louisiana Conference votes to establish a school.
1886	Dakota Conference pledges $1,068.50 for the new school established later at Wessington Springs.
1887	Gerry, New York, school operated by W. A. Sellew.
1887	Iowa Conference votes to establish its own school at Walkes, Iowa.

1888	Gerry School property valued at $7,200 sold to Genesee Conference for $1,500. School, orphanage and retiral home established by Genesee Conference.
1888	Texas Conference takes steps to open a school.
1888	New York Conference appoints a committee to purchase school property. Campus of 568 acres secured at Spotsylvania, Virginia. Efforts to integrate the school defeated by conference vote. A. Beers was the first principal.
1889	Chicago Industrial Home for Children incorporated to carry forward and expand the orphanage work which had been managed by T. B. Arnold in his own house for several years. The "object of the Home" was to provide a home for the homeless, orphaned, deserted, destitute, wayward and dependent children; to educate and instruct them in industrial pursuits.[22] Hundreds of children have found "here good educational advantages, excellent training, wholesome moral and religious instruction . . ."[23]
1889	The Kansas Conference pledged $840 to found a new school at Lawrence, Kansas.
1889	Kansas Conference votes to establish Seminary at Neosha Rapids.
1891	Washington Conference takes steps to start a school. Seattle Seminary was established as a missionary training institution.
1891	North Michigan Conference urges purchase of Clarkesville Seminary.
1892	Greenville College campus purchased and Wilson T. Hogue elected president. Secondary school work offered the first year. College courses given in 1893.
1903	Los Angeles Free Methodist Seminary (Los Angeles Pacific College) founded by C. B. Ebey and the Southern California Conference. For many years it was the oldest private junior college in the state, now a liberal arts college.
1909	Campbell Free Methodist Seminary organized by the Texas Conference at Campbell, Texas.
1914	Central Academy and College located at McPherson, Kansas, by forty representatives of conferences in the patronizing territory.
1914	Lorne Park College, Port Credit, Ontario, Canada, established by representatives of the East and West Ontario conferences.
1927	Wesley-Roberts Deaconess School, Oklahoma City, Oklahoma.

1928	Oakdale Vocational School, Oakdale, Kentucky.
1930	Olive Branch Mission Training School, Chicago, Illinois.
1939	Nogales Bible School, Nogales, Arizona.
1940	Moose Jaw Bible School founded by the Free Methodists of Saskatchewan and other West Canada conferences.

Section 4—GENERAL EVANGELISTS

The 1882 General Conference seems to mark a shifting into second gear, a getting of the second wind, a setting the sail for the long pull, for the wider horizons, for the larger day. In addition to granting its approval for the founding of a "mission college" in Kansas to prepare "colored teachers" for the eventual evangelization of Africa and the reorganization of the Missionary Board with the tacit understanding that it was now time to go forward with overseas missionary work, a new office was created, namely that of General Evangelist. General evangelists were to be chosen, not by the General Conference, but by the General Superintendents. They were charged with opening new fields, organizing new societies, with authority to place temporary pastors in charge. They had oversight of the evangelists laboring with them. They received their support from the General Missionary Board on recommendation of the General Superintendents.[1] In 1886 provision was made for the election of these evangelists by the General Conference. The first to be so elected was W. B. M. Colt.

W. B. M. Colt, first general conference evangelist, elected in 1886

Extending the Work

"The Free Methodist Church is properly a missionary church, and as such it is not only her duty to support and take care of societies already organized, but to labor to create new societies and extend their work into 'regions beyond.' "[2] The preachers that gathered around Roberts and his associates were "devotedly pious, laborious young men capable of doing a great deal of service in the cause of Christ upon a very small salary. One of them walked sixteen hundred miles, visited and prayed with a thousand families. . . . Such men are not easily put down when engaged in spreading holiness with the Holy Ghost sent down from Heaven."[3]

The annual address of the Conference of the Methodist Church in Great Britain raises the question: "What is the church for?" It answers: "We are to spread scriptural holiness through the schools, the home, the office, the factory, and the councils of the nations."[4]

Recently there has been a wholesome emphasis on the church as "the people of God." It is the nature of the church, in this respect, to function as the "people of God" in the world of business, press, and radio, bringing the incarnate Word of God by work and deed into every human situation.[5]

Is this the church we know? A Michigan newspaper reports a recent church activity. There is a Sunday morning fire drill requiring two minutes to evacuate one hundred persons. The church bulletin announced: "Other safety measures have been and will be taken for the protection of those attending church." But the main concern of the church can never be its own safety.

Simeon Stylites' comment is that "There is always danger when the Holy Spirit gets loose in a church. . . . If a few people get on fire with the gospel, no board of underwriters can measure the results."[6] A Christmas message by one of America's best known pastors comments on sentimental Christmas songs. He thinks the one about "The little Lord Jesus asleep in the hay" is a perfect symbol of many churches. Just before my address to a Sunday-school workers' conference, the leader called for the song, "I am resting, sweetly resting, 'neath the shadow of His wings"! The great end of Christianity seems to be peace and comfort. Too much American religion today is off on the tangent of peace of mind and personal adjustment. There is "the tendency," says John C. Bennett, "to reduce Christianity to a gospel of happiness and success with no place for . . . the biblical warning against idolatry, judgment, repentance or the cross."[7]

In 1860 Roberts reported six thousand miles of travel with participation in "some four hundred religious meetings."[8] He preached to large congregations who came on dark nights over muddy roads to hear "the plain, searching truth of God's Word applied to their consciences." Thousands attended grove meetings. At St. Louis, Missouri, the meeting place for the "free church" seated only five hundred and was too small. The St. Louis theatre was rented. A few months later hundreds were turned away from the over-crowded Buffalo church. Free Methodism was a revival movement.

Missionary Board—General Evangelists

There is always danger in organizing and regularizing the movement of the Spirit. The election of a class of men to do the work of evangelism, open new fields, organize churches and appoint pastors may be an expression of concern for such work and a desire to intensify and increase such activity. It may also be a confession that there is a failure, a loss of the original love, a neglect of the first works. In any event, Free Methodists made provision for General Conference evangelists in 1882. Since that time, and until 1931, they labored under the direction of the Missionary Board, pioneering across the country and laying the foundations of the new church by the organiza-tion of all the conferences in Canada and the United States.*

The Missionary Board outlined the strategy that issued in the organiza-tion of both the home and overseas conferences. Each year these evangelists reported to the Missionary Board and submitted a financial statement of funds raised on the field for workers, church property, buildings and foreign missions. At Chillicothe, Missouri, the Missionary Secretary preached for ten days. He was followed by the General Evangelist, who held meetings for one month. A new church was organized. At Waterloo, Iowa, Evangelist Hanmer reported in the sixth week of his tent meeting that he is having suc-cess, plans to secure property and organize a new church to succeed the one disbanded some years before. At Milwaukee more than forty "experienced either saving or sanctifying grace." At the Browerville, Minnesota, camp meeting more than one hundred received definite help and thirty-five new members were received into the church. A new church was organized at Joplin, Missouri. Hanmer concludes: "We have labored in eight states dur-ing the year.... Over three hundred persons have found the great salvation."[9]

This was strenuous work. Hanmer's helper "could not stand the changes and inconveniences incident to the evangelistic work."[10] Hanmer had "part of a band of workers." He was "praying and planning to get out a full band of men, with strong voices, who can sing and shout the praises of God, as well as pray, believe and labor for the salvation of the lost."[11] He believed that "one of the greatest needs of the church and the age is a strong, radical, aggressive evangelistic movement."[12] At St. Cloud, Minnesota, "there was a great stir." In this city of twelve thousand "the meetings were powerful and fiery. Strong and pungent conviction took hold of hardened sinners, and they

*Excepting boundary changes.

40

were brought down crying for mercy." A new church of thirty-eight members was organized.[13] A tabernacle meeting on the inter-urban line, midway between Minneapolis and St. Paul, was one of "life, power, liberty and blessing. . . . The meetings were especially attractive . . . the singing . . . had a charm in it, and it was in the Spirit . . . at least one hundred fifty must have received definite help at the altar."[14] Hanmer rented a mission hall at Midway, a church in Minneapolis, and another in St. Paul. He organized the work and felt that another three months of "earnest evangelistic effort" were needed. The special services continued in St. Paul. Property was donated for a church with promise of substantial assistance on the building. Funds raised by Hanmer for workers, rent of buildings, travel and other expense totaled $931.27. In 1904 General Conference evangelist C. W. Stamp reported over three hundred saved or sanctified in his meetings. In 1905 he

C. W. Stamp, general conference evangelist, elected in 1903

had a band of workers and evangelists in the field, while 156 new members were added to the church. At Holland, Ohio, 106 were saved or sanctified. In Weedsport, New York, services were held in the town hall which was crowded, and many joined the church. At West Plains, Missouri, the entire town was stirred, while at Crawfordsville, Indiana, large crowds attended the tent meeting and a new society was organized. The Missionary Board requested Stamp to spend a part of each year in New England. By 1908 he was able to report the organization of seven churches and a New England District, with its own camp meeting.

Such was the work of the General Conference evangelists in the earlier days. They were successful. In 1907, Stamp reported 455 new members received into the church during the quadrennium.[15] The general evan-

41

gelists opened new fields, organized churches and received thousands into the fellowship of the church. They were asked to major on the new work rather than assist the established churches or camps.[16] Their "band" workers aided in the campaigns and were often appointed as temporary pastors of the newly established churches. A large share of the operating costs of the "bands," including the support of workers, rent of buildings, and travel expense, was raised in the meetings held. The general evangelists were supported by the Missionary Board. They served on much the same basis of sacrifice as the overseas missionaries. There was no time limit for a meeting. The schedule was flexible. Often the meetings continued a month or more until success crowned the effort. Much attention was given to securing the proper location, to visitation, to discovering interested groups without a church home, and to the organization of missionary societies in the new churches. The Missionary Board received the calls for their services, evaluated them on the basis of need and probability of success, and assigned the men to their fields of labor.

Less Emphasis on Outreach

But conditions changed. The newly established overseas program evoked an ever greater concern and sympathy. The complexity of the problems, the magnitude of the opportunities, and the outstanding success that attended the foreign enterprise resulted in an ever greater attention by the Board to this aspect of their responsibility. Likewise, the situation in Canada and the United States was different. The frontier had disappeared. Conferences had been established across the country. The work of outreach to new areas was more and more assumed by these conferences.

By 1912 Stamp reported that he was working more under the direction of the conference superintendents, doing less of the pioneer work than in former years. Gradually the General Board assumed less responsibility for directing the program. In 1915 the evangelists were assigned specific areas. Two years later they were instructed to choose their own fields of labor. The band work was discontinued and for all practical purposes the general evangelists were doing about the same work as other evangelists, holding meetings in the established churches and conducting camp meetings. Their missionary function as pioneer evangelists was practically ended. It was logical to transfer their work to a Commission on Evangelism when the new Board of Administration was organized in 1931.

Spiritual religion is ever tempted to become little more than orthodox theology. Referring to the Anglican Church in Britain, G. G. Atkins says: "The Evangelical party retained the theology and hallowed phrases which had fed the fire John Wesley kindled—and lost the fire. It takes something beside repetition to make a creed live. Nothing is so dead as words whose reality time and changing experience have dissolved."[17]

The Free Methodist creed became flesh and blood. The toil and sacrifice of the early circuit riders, the effective labors of the General Conference evangelists with their band workers, supported by the prayers and finances of the church, assisted in maintaining the fires of devotion and avoided for the moment the substitution of mere orthodoxy for aggressive soul winning and evangelistic outreach.

Temptation to Introversion

Nevertheless, another tendency appeared in the early church life that weakened its concern, deflected its energy and hindered the progress of the revival. It was an inclination to substitute reform for the preaching of the Good News of the gospel; a negative, critical attitude toward other denominations; a divisive trend within the fellowship. After 1875 this condition is specially indicated by the conference committee reports, the articles that appear in *The Free Methodist*, and *The Earnest Christian*, and by words of warning from denominational leaders. Negative criticism can become a disease. It is easier to diagnose ills than cure them. Conference reports in 1882 were anti-slavery, anti-Masonic, anti-liquor. Greasing buggies, blacking boots, riding in buggies, on street cars, or patronizing restaurants on Sunday were denounced. The David C. Cook Sunday-school literature was pronounced "trashy,"[18] and some of the advertisements in *The Free Methodist* were deplored.[19]

E. P. Hart, pioneer preacher, church builder, district chairman and later General Superintendent, was most effective in opening new work in Illinois and especially in Michigan. Some of Free Methodism's greatest camp meetings, revivals, and membership gains have been in Michigan. Explaining these early successes, Hart says: "Our services in those days were on the 'old line' of meekness and brotherly love, each esteeming others better than himself. There was an entire absence of the denunciatory, criticising spirit which in later years crept in. . . ."[20]

Return to First Principles

The essential nature of the movement is missionary. A providential chain of circumstances, and the wisdom of the denomination's leaders, inspired the movement to another frontier operation—the overseas missions enterprise. The church was thus saved from an ingrown, petty religiosity by the challenge to recover its original intention: "The gospel is for all; all must hear; every provision must be made to secure this object." In the 1880's Free

VENTURE!

Methodists discovered that this meant not only "free churches" in the cities of Canada and the United States, but also signified missionaries and mission stations in India and Africa.

Section 5—CHRONOLOGY

1848 September 16	B. T. Roberts joined Genesee Conference, Methodist Episcopal Church, Buffalo, N.Y.
1857 September	Charged by Genesee Conference with "unchristian and immoral conduct" for publishing article, "New School Methodism." Reproved by Bishop.
1858 October	Second trial. Roberts expelled from Genesee Conference. Perry, N. Y.
1860 January 1	First issue of *The Earnest Christian*, B. T. Roberts, editor and publisher.
1860 May 23	Dedication of Albion Congregational Free Methodist Church.
1860 May	General Conference denies Roberts' appeal.
1860 August 23	Free Methodist Church organized, Pekin, N. Y., by fifteen preachers and forty-five laymen.
1860 August 26	Organization of first Free Methodist church by B. T. Roberts at Pekin, N. Y.
1860 November 8	Organization of Eastern Convention (Genesee Conference) by B. T. Roberts.
1861 June	Organization of Western Convention (Illinois Conference) by B. T. Roberts.
1862 April 10	Susquehanna Convention (now Conference) organized by B. T. Roberts.
1862 October 8	General Conference at St. Charles, Illinois. First session.
1862 November 4	General Conference, adjourned sittings, Buffalo, N. Y.
1870 November 12	Organization of Kansas and Missouri Conference approved by General Conference, Aurora, Illinois.
1872 October 11	Minnesota and North Iowa Conference organized at "Stone Schoolhouse" near Plymouth, Iowa, by B. T. Roberts.
1874 September 2-4	Organization of New York Conference by B. T. Roberts at Brooklyn, N. Y.
1875 September 23	Iowa Conference organized at Birmingham, Iowa, E. P. Hart presiding.

1875 October 7	E. P. Hart organizes the Wisconsin Conference at Pierceville, Wisconsin.
1876 September 27	E. P. Hart organizes Michigan Conference at St. Johns, Mich.
1879 October 2	Work in Ohio organized as a separate conference by E. P. Hart at West Windsor, Ohio.
1879	Indiana and Central Illinois Conference organized.
1880 October 12	Canada Conference organized at Galt, Ontario, by B. T. Roberts.
1881 July 10	B. T. Roberts organized Texas Conference at Corsicana, Texas.
1883 September 19	Dakota Conference organized by B. T. Roberts at Providence, Dakota.
1883 October 18-21	First session of the Pittsburgh Conference, Oil City, Pennsylvania. E. P. Hart presided.
1883 Fall	West Kansas Conference to include Colorado. Organized from Kansas Conference territory.
1883 Fall	Missouri organized as conference separate from Kansas work.
1883 December 7	E. P. Hart organized the California Conference at San Jose, California.
1884 November 13	Louisiana separated from Texas work and organized as conference by B. T. Roberts at Welcome Home, Louisiana.
1885 June 10	Oregon and Washington Territory Conference organized at Beaverton, Oregon, near Portland, by E. P. Hart.
1885 October 21	Wabash Conference organized from territory of Central Illinois and Michigan Conferences, by E. P. Hart.
1886 November 5	George W. Coleman organized Colorado Conference at Fountain, Colorado.
1887 October 27	North Indiana Conference organized from territory of Michigan, Wabash, Illinois and Ohio Conferences. Knox, Indiana. B. T. Roberts presided.
1890 August 14	Nebraska Conference organized at Yutan, Nebraska, by George W. Coleman.
1891 May 21	Southern California Conference organized to include Arizona. B. T. Roberts presided and dedicated a new Free Methodist church building.
1895 September 4	Arkansas and Southern Missouri organized as separate conference at Fairplay, Missouri, by B. R. Jones.

1896 April 2-5	Columbia River Conference organized as separate from Oregon and Washington, by George W. Coleman, at Spokane, Washington.
1896 April 9-12	Washington Conference organized in chapel of Seattle Seminary by Superintendent Coleman.
1896 April 16-19	Oregon Conference organized at Gresham, Oregon, by Superintendent Coleman.
1896 September 2	West Ontario organized as a separate conference from East Ontario. B. R. Jones presided.
1896 October 29	Kentucky and Tennessee Conference organized from territory opened in Kentucky by Central Illinois Conference.
1899 October 21	Oklahoma Conference organized at Emporia, Kansas.
1906 July 5	Western Canada Conference organized by B. R. Jones at Moose Jaw, Saskatchewan.
1914 September 23-26	Saskatchewan Conference organized from Western Canada territory. Done at Weyburn, Saskatchewan, William Pearce presiding.
1914 September 30	Alberta area organized as separate conference by William Pearce at Edmonton, Alberta.

The General Missionary Board appropriated funds to assist the pioneers in opening up the work in these areas which ultimately became regularly constituted conferences of the Free Methodist Church.

Overseas Ventures,

1885-1910

Section 1—AFRICA

1885

The year 1885 is an important landmark of the nineteenth century. England has just provided universal suffrage for her citizens. Woodrow Wilson, David Lloyd-George and Georges Clemenceau, who are to have such a large part in shaping the future of the world in the 1914-1918 era, are young men with life and opportunity ahead. Ten years have passed since the death of David Livingstone, intrepid African explorer, emancipator of slaves, healer of wounds. More than any other, he brought the dark continent to the attention of the European nations, and so opened its need to the churches of Europe and North America that a stream of missionaries numbered in the thousands began a trek toward its shores. Africa was a largely unmapped, little understood, desperately needy continent of eight hundred languages, bloody tribal wars, revolting primitive practices and sub-human living conditions.

Moody and Sankey are at the height of their evangelistic successes in England and America. Stanley's African explorations have furnished a basis for the division of that continent among the European powers for purposes of pacification, civilization and development. Christian college students will meet the next year at Northfield, Massachusetts, to perfect their Student Volunteers organization. Their purpose is to direct students to foreign missionary service, provide fellowship, counsel, study and spiritual leadership until they are definitely connected with a foreign mission board.

The United States is now twenty years removed from its own Civil War. World affairs are pressing upon a young nation that sixty years before naively proclaimed a "Monroe Doctrine" no longer adequate for the new and changing world climate. Plans are already under way for the first Pan-American Congress. Just around the corner is the Spanish-American War that will result in the independence of Cuba, the ceding of Puerto Rico and the Philippines to the United States, and the annexation of Hawaii. America is on the first lowly round of the long ladder reaching up to world leadership.

Needed—A New Frontier

The Republicans lost the election of 1884. Slavery had brought the party into existence. Preservation of the Union and the slavery question, live issues in 1860, were both dead in 1884, and no new causes had yet crystallized.[1] Institutions exist for the sake of a "cause." They die when their work is done. The same is true of the church.

Living concerns gave rise to the movement called Free Methodism—free seats, simple living, the gospel for all, the unreached masses, total commitment to save the lost world, abolition of slavery, the Bible standard of Christianity, the message of holiness of heart and life. Any church must have live and relevant issues for which its constituency readily yields total loyalty. We have traced the trail of such devotedness. But the situation was changing. The movement was becoming more introverted, negative, and divisive. It is true that the first annual meeting of the Genesee Convention[2] (conference) registered its disapproval of "female preaching." But its major decisions were of an aggressive nature. They favored the establishment of a weekly paper, authorized the election of a Missionary Secretary, sanctioned a seminary or academy, and endorsed, as church papers, the *Northern Independent* and *The Earnest Christian*. Loren Stiles was elected Missionary Secretary. He was to travel throughout the conference, cooperating with the superintendent and district chairmen in extending the work. He was to assist especially the "younger preachers in protracted, grove, quarterly and sacramental meetings." Each church was to raise a fixed amount for his support and he was to collect "missionary" funds. There was a missionary committee which reported $115.10 cash on hand. For the Buffalo First Church debt, a missionary offering of $85.10 was received. Such were the aggressive plans of that early conference. Twenty years later attention was shifting from a deep concern for the salvation of a lost world to the perfection of a small church. Free Methodists were becoming reformers. In the same breath the New York Conference condemned "croquet" and disapproved the idea of a "missionary society."[3] Occasionally there was opposition to Sunday-school work. The moustache was considered "a worldly conforming practice."[14]

Women's dress was ever a prominent preaching topic in some areas. Neckties were practically a bar to membership in certain conferences. The causes that demanded total dedication in 1860 could no longer command the same loyalty. The slavery issue was dead. Free seats were being established in all the churches as they began to realize the logic of Roberts' attack on the "pew system." Free Methodists were ceasing to be a movement. Their work was static in particular areas, and growing only slowly in others. The most notable advances were being made by the western conferences where new churches were being established in what was left of the American frontier. Free Methodists lacked a really great cause to save themselves from themselves. They needed a new frontier, a really great enterprise eliciting supreme loyalty, a salvation from trifling negativisms and peripheral devotion. In spite of these considerations, twenty-three conferences had been organized. By 1885 there were over five hundred conference ministers and some seventeen thousand members.

Orland Campground, 1884

The Chicago district of the Illinois Conference held its 1884 camp meeting at a new location—the beautiful grove of Mr. T. Curry near Orland,* a small village of a dozen houses, twenty-three miles southwest of Chicago. The large tabernacle was sidetracked by the railroad and finally arrived three or four days late. Tents were pitched in the woods and open air grove meetings were not uncommon at that time. Unusually heavy and continued rains, however, did affect the meeting. After the tent arrived, the services increased in power and influence. Many of the friends who had accompanied the delegations from the churches were at the altar seeking salvation. The meeting was continued an extra week. After a few days, people from the community for whom such meetings were a novelty, presented themselves at the altar of prayer. A priest, working among the French Catholics of the area, was sanctified. A goodly number from the village and countryside were clearly converted. The meeting finally closed on August 3 amid scenes of great rejoicing.[5]

Foreign Missions Interest

Three weeks later, on Thursday, August 28, the Missionary Board met in the Curry Grove at Orland. Arnold and Travis were regularly printing letters in *The Free Methodist* from independent missionaries, besides the reports from the Ward family in India, even giving space to their financial reports

---

*Orland Park is on Highway Six midway between Hammond, Indiana, and Lockport, Illinois.

and appeals for support. There was a department of "Missions" in the paper where news of missionary activity around the world appeared. Abrams often reported for the mission school in Kansas, expressing the hope that this would be the Free Methodist steppingstone to mission work on the continent of Africa. The plan was rather vague. He conferred with B. T. Roberts, who favored the move. A retired missionary of forty-five years' experience in Africa, George Thompson, writing from Oberlin, Ohio, also requested Free Methodists to enter Africa's open door *now*. The August 27 issue was just off the press. Did Travis and Arnold bring copies with them to the Board meeting? Editor Travis published that week an exchange from the English *Presbyterian Record* on "The Idea of Foreign Missions." Since Christianity is a missionary religion, the article declares it is—

> "only by a wide extension that it can hope to reach the noblest and best life possible to it. . . . Our Lord surely knew best what His church was fitted for, and He said, 'Go into all the world'. . . . It can never simply be one among several religions; it must be either the one true religion for the whole world, or it is false."[6]

In the same issue some interesting mission statistics appear. There are 144 missionaries in India; less than 300 in China, with 15,000 communicants. The report concludes:

> ". . . The Sun of Righteousness has already touched the mountaintops of all heathen lands—breathe a prayer that the blessed light may soon girdle the globe."[7]

The Missionary Board

Three members were absent: the Missionary Secretary, C. B. Ebey; J. G. Terrill, able and eloquent; and W. W. Kelley, later appointed missionary to Africa. D. W. Abrams, layman of the Michigan Conference, was elected secretary pro-tem. The minutes begin in the usual manner, listing those present: J. Travis, T. B. Arnold, D. M. Sinclair, and D. W. Abrams. The last meeting's minutes are read and T. B. Arnold, treasurer, reports: "Amount received since last meeting, $133.52; amount disbursed, $137.15." Routine reports from home missionaries and evangelists are read. J. Cripps of the Texas Conference is given a three-month appropriation totaling sixty dollars. The officers were made a committee to prepare a code of by-laws to govern the Board and a special committee was elected to oversee the new work in Dakota.

Then, on this new campground, a bold resolution is adopted authorizing the sending of missionaries to Africa! This action revolutionized Free Methodism, and cast a shadow across the succession of events we call history.

Four men that 28th day of August, 1884, under the guidance of the Holy Spirit, set in motion influences that have reached to the ends of the earth. Multiplied thousands have been saved from the darkest night of heathendom. This unique venture helped the church recover its original sense of mission "to seek and to save the lost." In so doing, Free Methodism was spared the fate of becoming simply a reform movement devoted to the perfecting of itself, aloof from the world and impotent to meet its deepest need, while proclaiming its evils.

Who were these men? Travis was editor of *The Free Methodist*. He was an Englishman, small of stature, with a giant intellect. His preaching was masterful, as on the occasion of the dedication of the new Sherwood, Michigan, church, where he used the text: "The glory of this latter house shall be greater than the former" (Haggai 2:9). Arnold was publisher of Sunday-school literature. He and Travis were thus associated in the publication of *The Free Methodist*. It was a feeble operation, maintained by dint of the most ardent industry. "We could not afford," says Arnold, "the expense of an office boy; so I swept the office, built the fires, corrected the mailing list, kept the books, purchased supplies, paid the hands, wrote editorial and business notes, and ran the mailing machine. . . . My office hours were from six in the morning until ten at night."[8] With such economy the paper earned $150 in one year! This was the treasurer of the Missionary Board. He managed somehow to leave his publishing business and travel to Orland at his own expense.

Sinclair was from Wisconsin and within the year had transferred to another denomination. Abrams, more than is understood, was a prime mover in launching Free Methodism's overseas mission. In June he had said:

> ". . . much has been written about the mission of the Free Methodist Church, but none have dared assume that God has called us to evangelize the whole world. . . . Brother Roberts, who is in hearty accord, says we ought to take prompt and energetic action. . . ."[9]

King Tappa's Call

A year earlier, King Tappa, a petty chieftain in Liberia, had sent to the North American churches an eloquent and urgent plea for missionaries to bring the gospel to his people. His message fell into the hands of this Free Methodist farmer-local preacher named Abrams. This appeal was presented to the newly-organized Missionary Board, of which Abrams was a member. The Board had been so busy sending its "missionaries" to Philadelphia, St. Louis, Kansas, Texas and the Pacific Coast, that no time, money or personnel had yet been available for the "foreign" fields. There was one exception. One missionary family, from the Illinois Conference, had been in India a

51

few years on an independent basis. Their work was publicized in the denominational papers and gifts were solicited and forwarded through the church treasurer. King Tappa's call caught the imagination of the church. Although it was not adopted as an official church project, the Board allowed Abrams to appeal for funds and candidates in *The Free Methodist*. All were in favor of the project on this basis. Publishing Agent T. B. Arnold was, with the others, vitally interested in the venture.

Africa

Abrams is the secretary pro-tem. These are the men that approved the following resolution:

> "Whereas, God by unmistakable providential indications is moving the Free Methodist Church to enter the foreign missionary field in Africa: therefore, resolved that we, the Missionary Board of the General Conference of the Free Methodist Church, feel it our duty to inaugurate the work at once.
>
> "Resolved, that as a Missionary Board we proceed forthwith to adopt such measures as we judge will best answer the purpose to raise the necessary means to put missionaries into the field in Africa.
>
> "Resolved, that in our opinion it is not expedient to put into the field in Africa, at present, more than five missionaries.
>
> "Resolved, that the Missionary Board proceed to negotiate with those now ready to enter this missionary field to the intent of transporting them thereto as soon as monies are provided.
>
> "Resolved, that an appeal be made at once through the *Free Methodist* and other suitable medium to our people for the funds necessary to inaugurate and carry on this Africa mission.
>
> "Resolved, that our people be requested to take this mission work upon their hearts, and by their means and prayers to promote the same to the best of their ability."[10]

The First Appointed Missionary

A committee including Travis and Arnold was appointed to interview candidates. Louisa Ranf was appointed as the first Board missionary. She was to assist the independent workers, Rev. and Mrs. E. F. Ward, in India. Travel expenses of $4.80 for Abrams, and $2.13 to Sinclair were allowed.[11] The Board adjourned its historic sitting to "meet at the call of the chair."

How simple it seems! Raise the money; find the people; transport them to Africa "as soon as monies are provided." Where will they labor in Africa? What type of work will they carry forward? What will it cost to maintain five missionaries in Africa? How long should they remain on the field before a furlough? What are the living conditions? What are the health requirements for candidates? Of these problems the Board was unaware. Provision for adequate finance on a regular basis to carry forward the enterprise after the first burst of enthusiasm waned soon confronted the inexperienced overseas planners. How ill-prepared this Board was to meet the varied perplexities involved in the program they had approved.

With hearts aglow with a great desire to save a lost world, stumbling and falling many times in pursuit of wrong goals, often adopting and following ill-advised policies, the church has gone steadily forward in its main purpose, the salvation of men. In this she has been right. In the degree that Free Methodists have possessed this, their true sense of mission, they have prospered.

For all practical purposes, Arnold functioned as Missionary Secretary. He interviewed Harry Agnew and Rev. and Mrs. Robert Shemeld. The latter, an Englishman by birth, and his wife, were appointed to Africa. With Arnold's arranging, they spoke at conferences, churches, and district meetings, holding "Africa meetings," receiving offerings for the same which were sent to T. B. Arnold, treasurer. *The Free Methodist* suddenly comes alive with *missions*. Accounts of these missionary rallies are given full space. After a few weeks, itemized financial reports appear, giving names of churches or individuals, with the amounts contributed. In early 1885 the gifts average about $200 each week.

Self-Supporting Missions

Interesting information appears concerning the work of independent missionaries, the program of the China Inland Mission, and Bishop William Taylor's "self-supporting missions." Taylor had already established his "self-supporting" missions in both South America and India. That they were not successful in the "self-support" idea either had not yet become apparent, or was ignored. His plan for Africa, printed in detail, is held up as the ideal. Taylor was enlisting forty volunteers. Two parties of twenty each would enter Africa at about the same time, one from Luanda, on the west, the other from the east by way of the Zambezi, Lakes Nyassa and Tanganyika. For health reasons his parties planned to move quickly to the higher altitudes, establish a string of stations, then meet near the center of the continent as soon as possible. A fully consecrated "self-supporting" missionary couple is to be in charge of each station. The industrial equipment for one station is estimated at $1,500. This would include agricultural and other tools to be used in providing food for the missionaries, making them self-reliant and able to support themselves on the economy of the country. Taylor, offering a scant subsistence now, and full pay in the Eternal City, declared that the only missionaries adequate for the task were those who volunteered on this basis. Such hardy souls had the spirit that would guarantee success.

Roberts urges a quick response to the call for travel and outgoing expenses of Free Methodist missionaries who will be "largely self-supporting." Abrams lauds Taylor as an example to the Free Methodist Church, urging the immediate giving of the amount needed to transport five missionaries to Africa. The Missionary Secretary thinks that "a strong pull, a short pull, and all pull together will do it." How mistaken Taylor and the Board were they little knew at the time. To save his work from disaster, the Methodist Church took over and financed the Taylor missions. With few exceptions, Free Methodist missionaries were not and could not be "self-supporting."

First Africa Party

The recording secretary of the Board, W. W. Kelley, felt called to Africa. He had been in charge of a Negro company during the Civil War and had taught these men to read. He longed to do something for Africa. Roberts felt that Kelley should head the party. The location of a "self-supporting" mission station was most important. Roberts would trust Kelley on that. He and his wife were appointed. Together with Harry Agnew, a St. Paul businessman, who felt "called," the party of five was complete. Another thousand dollars was needed to equip and transport the band to Africa where they

W. W. Kelley, Missionary Secretary, 1890-1893

G. Harry Agnew

C. B. Ebey, Missionary Secretary, 1882-1890

would plant crops, raise animals, and live off the economy of the country, just as they supposed was being done on the Bishop Taylor mission stations.

There were no definite rules established. It was a sort of gentlemen's agreement. There were no stipulated salaries; no furlough policy. All were to trust the Lord, missionaries and Missionary Board alike.

Money for Missions

About $4,000 was raised in the few months after the Orland board meeting. The 1884 Conference Minutes shows that churches in Illinois and Indiana gave $475 for Africa. Only $29.00 came from other conferences, but the news had not really reached them. Abrams complains that "twenty years of church history without a foreign mission . . . is a strange feature of our work." He prays: "May God stir up every member to immediate duty."[12] Missionary Secretary Ebey urges all district chairmen to hold an Africa mission meeting at the next general quarterly meeting.[13] A glorious revival service that was spoiled when a missionary offering was taken, is condemned,[14] with the hope that "those who desire the extension of the

Redeemer's Kingdom add to their prayers the further grace of giving their substance. . . ." A large chart portraying the extent of the non-Christian world is printed and available as a banner for church display, enlarged to four and one-half by seven feet.[15] Attention is called to the fact that nine-tenths of foreign missions money is given by one-tenth of the members. It is suggested that church members give five cents each week for missions. Churches spending 98 per cent of their budget for home work while only 2 per cent goes to foreign missions hardly are giving the right proportion.[16] Kelley reports his missionary rallies: "Attica, Indiana, $15; Sugar Grove, Illinois, $25; Chili Sunday school, $7.70; Paxton, Illinois, $100; Praise the Lord."[17] A missionary candidate contributes his property to the Missionary Board.[18] By mid-April $2,695.69 has been received for the Africa mission, while in the same paper, receipts for General Missions (church extension) total less than $150, for a three-month period! Actually, for the first time, the young church was learning to give generously and sacrificially for others. This venture in overseas generosity was to be reflected later in more adequate support of the home-base work.

A Forestville, New York, missionary offering is reported with the comment: "We hail this missionary wave with joy."[19] "A gift of one hundred thousand strawberry plants worth four and five dollars per thousand, is pledged by A. D. Noyes."[20] At the Genesee Conference missionary service where Arnold and Terrill report on India and Africa, a small girl gives the dollar she has earned raising chickens. "Soon one hundred dollars is raised, then another and another until $330.00 is received."[21] Such hilarious giving was apparently a new thing. The columns of the paper are still open to independent missionaries as well, and no effort is made to influence any from making gifts to them.

In 1885 nineteen conferences contributed $1,889 to the Africa fund.[22] The following year seventeen conferences responded with $1,369.[23] The next year it was less. The church had been greatly inspired to launch the overseas enterprise. It did not yet realize that even so-called "self-supporting" missions have regular expenses for current operations. The Central Illinois Conference voted to take the foreign missions offerings the second quarter,[24] while Wabash left this to the option of the pastor.[25] With shouting and singing, Central Illinois pledged over $500 for Africa.[26]

In the first year of its existence, the infant California Conference, itself a mission field, sent $15.00 for Africa. Harry Agnew wrote: "I am ready . . . My life is consecrated to God for service in this mission." He thought 15,000 Free Methodists giving fifteen cents each could supply the needs of the outgoing band.[27] Henrietta Muzzy denied herself a bouquet of roses, and earned money by day labor for the Africa fund. "We can cut off needless indulgences," she said. " . . . I have been greatly stirred." The list of contributors is printed at stated intervals. The gifts are small, the largest on one long list being twenty dollars! Many are less than one dollar.[28] Reading the reports today, this seems a very small and discouraging venture. Actually they surprised themselves in raising several thousand dollars on a free-will offering basis for the new cause. It gave their morale such a big boost that one layman proposed the organization of a missionary society on the General Conference level, with conference, local church and Sunday-school auxiliaries. He felt that a more intense, organized effort would "preserve us from the mildew and blight which threaten us, and set us on fire with a holy zeal for God."[29]

The Missionary Board arranged for Robert and Mrs. Shemeld to proceed to England for a few months of study in a training college there. He also was to interview various mission boards with a view to locating a suitable field of labor. Kelley continued to raise money for the outgoing expenses of the party. In February, Shemeld reported from London and Liverpool. He was enjoying the Salvation Army services, and had interviewed five different mission board officers.[30]

Frequent reports of Bishop Taylor's plans for Africa, appearing in *The Free Methodist*, indicate approval of both his method and his Africa location. His eastern string of missions is to run from Lake Tanganyika westward. A new route has been established up the Zambezi, and by way of Lakes Nyassa and Tanganyika, reducing land travel to 280 miles, "the route our missionaries" will take![31] So Free Methodists plan for a Central Africa Mission. While waiting for Kelley and Agnew, Shemeld, still in England, preached on the common and in several churches.

Natal—Portuguese East Africa

The Kelleys finally sailed from New York on April 25. They were limited for time in London, but succeeded in securing their necessary supplies. Kelley, after a long interview in London with H. Grattan Guinness, an editorial correspondent of the *Missionary Review of the World*, became convinced that Central Africa was not the best place to open the new mission. On the other hand, he had no definite leading to another field. From Port Elizabeth, Kelley wrote, advising that he had no permanent address, that no decision had yet been made regarding the field of labor. At Durban, Shemeld decided to leave the party. He went inland one hundred twenty miles to Estcourt, establishing a school and mission station. This was at an altitude of five thousand feet and many times served the needs of malaria-laden missionaries who needed a healthful place of rest. As for Kelley, he providentially made contact with a Portuguese East Africa American Board Missionary, E. H. Richards, who was a congenial spirit. K. S. Latourette says:

"In 1885, through contact with American Board missionaries from Inhambane, Free Methodists from the United States established a center across the bay from that town. Activities were extended into the surrounding countryside. . . ."[32]

Writing on the boat from Natal to Inhambane, Kelley declares that: "Our hearts are already knit to Brother and Sister Richards, two American (Board) missionaries at Inhambane. We shall land at the same port, hoping to see more of them in the years to come . . . and to help each other in the work of the Lord. . . . We purchased three donkeys . . . and have them on board. Harry and I will do exploring, leaving Mrs. K. with Brother and Sister Richards to pray for us."[33]

Inhambane

The American Board missionaries assisted Agnew and Kelley to prepare for a four-week exploration. With four carriers they went fifty miles inland, traveling in a southwesterly direction toward the north side of the Limpopo River. However, the population was dense everywhere. It was expensive to transport supplies from the port. Remembering Roberts' advice to seek a healthful elevation near the coast, they decided to locate fifty miles southwest of Inhambane on Lake Njela,[34] a salt water body ten miles long. They established camp at an altitude of seven hundred fifty feet above sea level, three hundred fifty feet above the lake. There was a good breeze here, and they were surrounded by many large villages. The soil was fertile, and cattle, goats, swine, horses and donkeys thrived. The chief "sold" the mission forty acres of land in exchange for eighty yards of cloth and a flannel shirt, worth above five dollars.[35] No papers to sign. It all seemed very strange. Kelley explained that the location was near the coast in a healthful place surrounded by a large population. He added: "We have some money. . . . Do not forget the first pilgrim rest."[36]

They lived temporarily in tents and native huts, but a log house eighteen feet square with an iron roof was under construction. Crops planted after the first rain included beans, lettuce, peas, onions, peanuts, corn, and sweet potatoes. They also started seven orange and three lime trees, and eight banana plants.[37] Such was the life of a pioneer.

Malaria

From the first Kelley suffered most with the "fever." His wife wrote: "Mr. Kelley has fever most of the time. . . . Brother Agnew had one light attack. He keeps well and blest and is a necessity to the mission."[38] But fever is no disgrace. It was seven years before medical research established any connection between the mosquito and malaria. In India, Mr. Ward took the workers on long walks early in the morning to prevent fever. Many blamed the dampness and fog. It was a good policy to locate on a hill where the breezes blew above the miasma fogs. Good advice. Probably fewer mosquitoes on the hill; less malaria. A two-story house was recommended. Kelley said:

"I am inclined to accept Miss Sharp's theory, as reasonable as any I have heard. She says, 'The rapid growth of vegetation absorbs the oxygen; the rapidly decaying weeds with such thick stems and leaves that they seem made for food, throw off nitrogen, leaving a small amount of oxygen in the air and only strong lungs can get enough to keep the blood pure; hence, sickness results.' Our little party have all had fever and we do not relish it very much."[39]

One missionary reported that in those days nobody had any idea that malaria was related to mosquitoes. "They roosted on us like flies. It is a wonder that anyone lived."[40] When Kelley was able to write, there was nothing but faith, courage and cheerfulness. "We keep hearing of trials and hardships," he said, "but they are like the . . . will-o'-the-wisp. . . . We have joy and peace in the Holy Ghost."[41]

First Steps

Kelley had taught his Civil War company of Negro soldiers to read. He had studied the phonetic system, taking with him phonetic primers and New Testaments. Apparently he intended to teach the natives to read English and open up to them, as he said, the vast store of Christian literature. Once, on trek in search of a mission site, Kelley admitted: "We must learn their language." This they began to do immediately. The crops were "growing nicely" and "some very intelligent looking young men" visited them. Agnew thought they would "make good preachers." They were digging a well. "We are very happy here," he said. "This writing leaves us all able to be up and surround the table at meal time."[42]

On Sunday morning the natives gathered at eight for service, which consisted of singing in Tonga, "There is a fountain filled with blood," and "Come to Jesus." Mrs. Kelley read all the Tonga she had translated, sixteen verses from the first chapter of Genesis. Some of the natives repeated these verses afterwards. During the prayer, all was very quiet. This still happens in primitive areas. The author has seen hundreds of Africans hearing the Christian gospel for the first time. They cannot sing the songs, but when the missionary says, "Now, we are going to pray to God," all is quiet, while every head is bowed to the ground. One knows that even before the missionary arrived, God by His Holy Spirit has already been there; that some of the

59

New station, Massinga, Portuguese East Africa

"Light that lighteth every man" has come to these people. Their ideas of God may be very crude and unworthy, but they have eternity in their hearts, they are overbuilt for this world, they reach out toward spiritual reality. As Mrs. Kelley reads *Pilgrim's Progress*, those watching her say, "Umfundise ku lagana" [The missionaries are happy].[43]

Climate—Disease

Tom, their interpreter, was indispensable. He traveled with Agnew to the villages where preaching services were held. Tom taught school at the chief's village.[44] Already "some of our boys are commencing to pray," wrote Kelley,[45] who always seemed encouraged. They had translated the songs, "Come to Jesus," and "Sweet Bye and Bye," which they sang in the village services.

But Kelley continued to suffer with the fever. His strength was failing. He was "ready to work for Africa if not in Africa," and was not sure how long he would be able to remain.[46] One month later he felt that he must return to America. He had visited missions and missionaries on several fields. His crops were good. They had built three houses, but he felt that "the Lord . . . is leading me to return and lay plans before the next General Conference and its Missionary Board, that I may thus assist them in adopting a permanent foreign policy."[47]

By August, Kelley had reached America and was living in Utica, New York. He explained that—

"Since the latter part of November, 1885, I have had a very bad cough. My pulse has been near 100 per minute all that time and much of the time from 110 to 120.

"I knew enough about lung diseases to know that this would end in consumption in that climate. I waited six months, using the best remedies at hand, not forgetting a single day to lay the matter before the Lord.

"In forming my decision to return, there was not the least fear of suffering or death, nor the least unwillingness to die there, if that was the Lord's will.

"I had but little strength, but I had courage and ambition enough to do the work of a whole conference.

"My mind is too practical to admire mere sentimental heroism, therefore when it came to what I thought was a choice between an early grave in Africa or a few years of labor for God in America, common sense and Christian courage said, 'Return home, live, and go into the conflict again.' So here I am, glory be to God! Living or dying, I am the Lord's."[48]

Native War

The work continued. Agnew was very busy. He had "killed a wild cat," was planting two acres of peanuts, farina, and corn. He was anxious to make this a self-supporting mission and asked for seeds—tomatoes, onions, turnips, cabbage and lettuce.[49] Two months later he had a severe attack of the fever and for a time lost consciousness. The ever-helpful Richards gave valuable assistance. Meanwhile, tributary clans of the Umzilia tribe, angered by a new tax regulation, were marching in strength on the army of Portuguese natives at Inhambane. American Board missionaries were forced to evacuate. Agnew took this opportunity to visit Shemeld at Estcourt in South Africa where he profited greatly from the climate and enjoyed the Christian fellowship. He plunged into village evangelism with Shemeld. Meanwhile at Inhambane, a great slaughter took place. Thousands were reported killed, the Portuguese natives were defeated, and an estimated five thousand guns

61

First home of J. J. Haviland and family, Portuguese East Africa, 1892-1897

seized by the rebellious tribes. But Agnew would not leave Africa. While waiting for missionary helpers, Agnew said, "I intend going from kraal to kraal doing missionary work. . . . Pray for me, your brother in Africa."[50]

After Fifty Years

The work in the Inhambane area was temporarily suspended. Meanwhile, the Shemelds were at work in Estcourt. They did not feel clear about the Inhambane plan proposed by Richards. The five missionaries had traveled together as far as Durban. Apparently Shemeld favored the Central Africa proposal. He had contacted the Royal Geographical Society in London and arranged for Kelley to visit the office. When the decision was made not to go forward with the Central Africa plans, Free Methodists opened two fields rather than one. Considering the meager resources of the party and the expense of such extended travel inland, it is probably wise that no effort was made at that time to reach the Lake Tanganyika area. Fifty years later, in 1935, that missionary pioneer and statesman, J. W. Haley, did reach the Lake Tanganyika area and established what is now one of Free Methodism's largest and fastest growing fields.

Estcourt

Shemeld was a rough and ready, hard-hitting Englishman. He had lived in the States for several years. His father was a grocer in Kelvedan, England. While in Britain waiting for the party, the Shemelds visited the former home. The local paper reported their visit, saying:

"Mr. Shemeld . . . will shortly start . . . accompanied by his wife and a Mr. Agnew . . . on a mission to the natives of Central Africa."

Reference is made to the religious services held by Shemeld and his "rugged and direct style of eloquence" which was very effective. The article continued:

"Mr. Shemeld during his long stay in America has developed a stalwart frame, a vigorous and determined mind, which will stand him in good stead in fighting against the pestilential climate in some parts of Africa, in defending himself against the wild animals, and in dealing with the natives."

The article goes forward to indicate the policy under which these first missionaries operated by remarking that:

"As a proof of the earnestness and sincerity of the missionaries . . . they are entirely unpaid. Every cent given to them has to be strictly accounted for, and used only in respect of bare necessities."[51]

Shemeld was already beginning to question the practicability of the "self-support" policy. He had visited missionary offices in London with their secretarial staffs, and adequate budgets. He contrasted these with the Free Methodist program. Nobody at the headquarters office could give full time to the interests of the missionary program. Ebey was a district chairman. Travis and Arnold were overworked at the Publishing House, and Abrams must work full time to support himself. In view of this, Shemeld comments: "We see under what disadvantage they labor in this pioneer work and need help from on high just in proportion as they fail to get it on earth."[52]

At Estcourt Shemeld pitched his tent and started a night school for men. A Christian Indian used the school tent three nights, the Africans had it three nights, while on Sundays the missionary preached with an interpreter. Without his knowledge, a petition was circulated requesting land for his school. The Magistrate assured Shemeld that it would be forthcoming. He found a native teacher for a second school that was urgently requested. The building would cost $100. He proposed to build it near the Bushman River, promising the Missionary Board: "I will not go in debt. . . . If means are not forthcoming, I shall stop." Mrs. Shemeld taught sewing. There were new experiences, worms in the water, and "some of the boys are literally covered

Meal time at Fairview station, South Africa, about 1900

with vermin, while the fleas are so numerous that one jumped in a cup at the table." But the young missionaries are full of faith. After expressing regret that the party had divided to work in separate fields in Africa, Shemeld declared: "I may never see it, but I believe the time will come when our missionaries will be scattered in every colony, state, and territory on this continent."[53]

Shemeld left his wife in charge of a large congregation at the tent while he went to the market and preached to whites and Arabs. "South Africa," he said, "needs camp meetings. . . . No people are more attentive than the Zulus."[54] Six months later Shemeld referred to the difficulties of the Mission Board. They are unable to supply "the necessities of life." He reminds his American friends that "we have no home. . . . We gladly wander up and down in our ox-cart, jolting over rough roads. Camping once for three days in good range of nine dead horses . . . drinking all kinds of water, infested with fleas and ticks. . . ."[55]

Land could be purchased for $1.25 and $2.50 per acre. Shemeld hoped that the friends of Africa missions would help him secure a mission location. In the States some were considering migrating to Estcourt with the view of establishing a Free Methodist colony. The publisher of *The Free Methodist*, T. B. Arnold, was encouraging the idea.[56] Several conversions were reported at this time, and in September a special blessing attended the labors of the Estcourt Mission workers. An American colonist asked Shemeld to work for him. Poor as he was, this "self-supporting" missionary refused. He was working for God. The man was impressed and invited the new missionary to his home. He gave Shemeld £500 for developing the mission work. The church was challenged to match this gift to provide land and buildings for the mission. Ebey made a strong appeal for such assistance, and concluded with the exhortation:

"We should settle down to a regular, systematic, sensible, matter-of-fact business in our mission."[57]

Mr. E. Oates donated fifteen acres of land. Bethany Mission at Estcourt was established.[58] Three months later bricks were being made and stones laid for the house of worship.

Liberia

But King Tappa's call which stimulated concern for Africa had come from Liberia. However, the first Board-appointed missionaries had started their work in southeast Africa. Meanwhile, Abrams was in correspondence with several candidates who were ready to sail to Liberia, trusting the Lord and the church for their support.

65

Daisy Frederick and high school girls, Fairview, South Africa

The applications of these candidates came to the attention of the Board. Since some who favored sending the missionaries were opposed to the Liberia proposal, there is no record of any official action concerning their appointment. They did go with the tacit approval of the Board and by the generosity of the Free Methodist people who responded to the financial appeal. The Publishing Agent accompanied the party of three, Mr. and Mrs. A. D. Noyes and Miss Mary E. Carpenter, to New York, assisting them in procuring their outfits and their passage to Africa. "I assisted Miss Carpenter," Arnold writes, "as I did Brother and Sister Noyes, and as near as possible gave each an equal portion of money for outfit, for passage and for use after reaching the field. . . ." To Miss Carpenter the Publishing Agent said, "The Board had no instructions to give her relative to her course after arriving in Africa. She would . . . decide upon that when she knew what the conditions were by personal observation."[59]

And so the second Africa party of Free Methodist-sponsored, but this time independent, missionaries sailed. Their relation to the church missionary program was not clear either to themselves or to some of the members of the Board. The Publishing Agent, after twenty years, recalls this history-making event in the larger life of the church. He writes:

"The permission given Brother Abrams to collect funds and send missionaries to Monrovia (Liberia) was little thought of while the work was going on. What he did . . . was more as an assistant to the rest of us than as a leader in the movement. . . . He gave no instructions to the missionaries. . . . I spoke to Mary Carpenter as I did in answer to her request for instructions. It was impromptu. The Board did not authorize it; Brother Abrams did not authorize it. I expressed what I believed to be the feeling among those who had been active in the movement. . . . I did not recognize any difference in her status and that of Brother and Sister Noyes. Some time after . . . Brother Abrams . . . asked what I understood to be the status of Sister Carpenter as related to the Missionary Board. I replied that I had not thought much about it. He replied that he had not thought much about it either. . . . A day or two later he said, 'The Board gave me permission to raise funds and secure missionaries for Monrovia.' That the Board had (tacitly) given him that probably was correct, but I said, 'I think she understands that she is a Board missionary and it will be a great disappointment to her to be informed to the contrary.' Mr. Abrams advised Miss Carpenter of her status as 'independent missionary' and she was much surprised and grieved that she was not recognized as a Board missionary. Before there was an opportunity for the matter to be brought before the Board for a decision in regard to her status, she died."[60]

Such was the confusion that surrounded this sailing. The Missionary Secretary, C. B. Ebey, is probably technically correct in summarizing the situation: "While the General Mission Board of the Free Methodist Church . . . was in fellowship with the . . . independent faith mission and missionaries . . . it is nevertheless our opinion that Miss Carpenter (of precious memory) was not at the time of her death in any proper sense of the word a Free Methodist Board missionary."[61]

Evangelists in Portuguese East Africa

The "Monrovia," with its pioneer missionary party bound for Liberia, sailed on September 12, 1885. At their previous May meeting the Board had already taken notice of the project as follows:

> "Resolved, that the independent faith mission at Monrovia, Africa, is entitled to whatever moneys shall be directly subscribed therefor, and to whatever further consideration the Executive Committee of the Mission Board may from time to time see advisable to grant."[62]

Important Year

At a later date, Mr. and Mrs. Noyes received regular Board appointment in South Africa, and on October 13, 1905, twenty years later, the Missionary Board in session at its office in Chicago took the following action:

> "In view of the formative conditions and the irregular action of the General Missionary Board in sending out missionaries at the early date of 1885, it is the mind of this committee that Miss Mary E. Carpenter should be classed as a Board missionary. Signed: E. P. Hart, Thomas Sully, Mary Coleman."[63]

The report was adopted, and T. B. Arnold's trip to New York and services rendered these so-called independent missionaries were for regular Board missionaries after all. His concern was that of sending the great message of redemption to as many as possible, as soon as possible. In this he was right— and successful! So 1885 was a significant year for the world and for the Free Methodist Church, and especially so for Mr. Arnold.

India Too

Three months later, the Publishing Agent was in New York again. He had completed a short tour of the western New York area with newly-appointed India missionaries Julia Zimmerman and Louisa Ranf. Missionary rallies were held at Free Methodist churches in Albion, Rochester, Syracuse and Utica. There was an enthusiastic farewell at Chili Seminary. Mr. Arnold assisted these young ladies in the purchase of transportation and outfits, and with others gave them a hearty farewell as they sailed on Thursday, December 17. This was the third sailing of Free Methodist missionaries. The year was 1885.

Why should seventeen thousand members of a struggling young church not yet established on a very firm basis in North America take such an interest in Africa and India?

Section 2—INDIA

Pioneers

From the beginning, Free Methodists have been people of the frontier. By this we mean not only the geographical frontier but the frontier of ideas and methods. Free seats in the churches and lay representation in all official bodies were pioneer ideas in 1860. The methods worked best on the western frontier of Canada and the United States. It is dangerous to date turning points in history. However, it is no doubt correct that in many important respects, the western frontier ceased to exist about 1890. By this we mean not merely a frontier as a geographical location but as a state of mind. It was still possible to pick up land in the South or West, but after 1890 this was little more than moving from one living place to another. The average citizen that thus transfers residence does not, somehow, share in the great adventure of building a new community or state. "By 1890 the settlement had proceeded so far that the frontier was declared to have ceased to exist as an important part of the nation's life."[1] Commenting on this situation, an able historian says: "We might try to estimate what effects would flow from the ending of the frontier experience and from the closing of that avenue for the outpouring of the surplus energies of our restless and energetic population . . . and might say, somewhat cynically, that having lost our hunting ground for adventure, and now having seized and peopled all the continental land we could get, we should probably, like other nations, find some excuse for an imperialistic adventure overseas."[2]

India Calls

This is exactly what happened in the Free Methodist Church. The frontier was gone. The church was doing less of the pioneer work and already settling down to organize its gains, cultivate its constituency, and become an ecclesiastical organization. The Spirit of God has strange ways of breaking into history.

James M. Thoburn, long-time Methodist missionary in India, was at the height of his success. Under the influence of Bishop William Taylor, he felt it his duty to renounce his salary, depending only on God for his support. He was a powerful preacher and a great Christian. He said, "When I go down the gangplank and my feet touch the shores of dark India, I feel the Presence by my side." This was no figure of speech. Those who heard Thoburn knew that he was in touch with the Divine. He had the unique capacity

69

for making God and the world of the spirit real. Tears were on his cheeks and the glory shone forth from his face as he declared the unsearchable riches of Christ. From 1870 to 1880 India missionaries inaugurated extensive relief programs. During these years there was great increase in church membership. Central India experienced a large Telegu mass movement. Around 1880 the Oxford Mission sent workers to Calcutta dedicated to living the simple life in close contact with the Indian church. Their goal was to lift the level of the moral life of professing Christians. About this time, two Wesleyan Methodist missionaries began work among the lower castes in Hyderabad in central India adjacent to the field which was later taken over by the Free Methodists. The Salvation Army had missionaries in India in the early 1880's living simply on the Indian diet like the holy men of the country.[3] Most of the missions were experiencing a rapid growth at this time due in large measure to their works of mercy during the famine.

Ernest and Phebe Ward

In 1880 Ernest Ward, aware of the India situation and feeling that the Lord was calling him to be a self-supporting missionary, asked the Illinois Conference to appoint him to that country. This the Conference did in a resolution commending Rev. and Mrs. E. F. Ward, and assuring them of their prayers since they are "going forth with their lives in their hands and paying their own expenses."[4] The minutes of the Illinois Conference that

Pioneer missionaries E. F. and Mrs. Ward at beginning of service in India, 1880

year state that these are "our first foreign missionaries." The report of the action taken by the Illinois Conference was received with mild enthusiasm. Reports indicate that both the Illinois and Genesee Conferences contributed small amounts toward the establishment of the new mission in India. Their project was well reported in the columns of *The Free Methodist*, and in the years that follow, E. F. Ward was one of the most consistent and prolific reporters to that periodical. According to rules adopted later, no member of the faith mission was to ask for money. However, Ward usually included some such statement as, "Your check for $100 arrived. It came just in time." Mrs. Ward was a schoolteacher and had saved $500. It was used to purchase transportation from the States to India.

They arrived in Bombay on January 16, 1881. They proceeded to Ellichpur where they were guests of the Alliance Mission. Here they studied Hindustani, learning the language rapidly. After one year of language study, they established residence at Burhanpur, Nimar District, A Sunday school was started in the home and continued as long as the Wards were in India. Only two cents was in the treasury at the time of the first Christmas. However, a remittance from America arrived just in time to help make the holiday season a happy one. With no regular support from the home church, gifts were sent to Mr. Ward just as they were received. It was five years before additional missionaries came to assist in the work.

In 1882, six churches of the Genesee Conference reported contributions for India. That same year the Ohio Conference ordered offerings taken for India on each of the circuits. The Illinois Conference received E. F. Ward in full connection, he having answered the disciplinary questions by mail. He appealed for other workers. The next year the Conference received an offering amounting to $23.00 for support of the India mission. We have already noticed that the years 1884 and 1885 were marked by strong promotion for the Africa mission. Doubtless, this affected contributions for India. Susquehanna reported only $11.40 raised for India during that year, while Genesee reported $330.00. The Illinois Conference held an India missionary service at the time of the conference, and an offering was taken. The Conference annually took recognition of Mr. Ward's work and expressed its confidence in him.

The Missionary Board ordered coin boxes sent to the churches for their India missionary offerings.[5] These amounted to $440 for Ward's first year on the field, and more than double that amount the next year. The new bungalow must be completed. The missionaries needed both food and clothing, so Mrs. M. C. Baker urges: "Let us be careful to give of our prayers and of our means committed to our hands."[6] The church treasurer reported the following amounts transmitted to India in 1883: January 24, $300; April 6, $200; May 1, $100; June 11, $100. Missionary boxes were packed and sent to the India missionaries. Toward the close of 1883, E. F. Ward reports a total of $1,670 received since arriving in 1881. This covered not only living expenses but the cost of property and building operations. T. B. Arnold, publisher, offered to send without charge collection boxes for the Sunday-school offering for India. Ward, in acknowledging receipt of funds from Arnold, writes, "Your check for $100 found us as usual just about out, though the barrel of meal and the cruse of oil have not failed. . . . It is the longest test of faith in the money line since we have been in Burhanpur." After decision was made to open a mission in Africa, the Board decided that the Sunday-school offerings would be for all overseas missions, not exclusively for India.[7]

Ranf and Zimmerman

While E. F. Ward was an independent "faith" missionary, his work in India was promoted by the denominational paper. In 1885 he requested the Missionary Board, which had been organized after he had left America, to serve as an advisory board in sending missionary appointees. Louisa Ranf was ready to sail, but T. B. Arnold appealed for "another sister who is ready to start out on short notice and join this company before they start."[8] Julia Zimmerman of Attica, Indiana, applied for an appointment. She joined the Free Methodist Church November 21, having received word of her appointment to India the day before. December 17, less than one month later, she and Miss Ranf sailed from New York.[9] Miss Zimmerman's pastor recommended her by saying: "She understands music to some extent, can play the organ, piano, and fiddle."[10]

Arnold was in New York to assist the young ladies secure passage, purchase outfits, and see them safely on board. Missionary meetings had been held with Miss Ranf within the bounds of the Genesee Conference. The total amount raised on the trip was $174.07. Passage was secured to Liverpool for $30.00. Free Methodist ministers Arnold, W. Gould and N. Greene were at the boat. They "watched the vessel until all that could be seen of the missionaries were the waving handkerchiefs and then only the vessel."[11] Kind friends greatly assisted the young missionary women in Liverpool and were at the boat to bid them farewell. As the boat was leaving the dock, one of them called out, "Mizpeh, we shall meet beyond the river. . . . We'll meet in the morning when the mists have cleared away. The Lord bless the ship. Farewell."[12]

This Was India

Not certain of the time of their arrival, Ward had arranged with Methodist missionaries attending their conference in session at Bombay to meet the boat and care for the young women. First impressions of new missionaries reaching the mission field are always interesting. Miss Ranf wrote: "As we entered the city, everything looked strange enough. The streets were very narrow, and it seemed to me the natives were like grasshoppers for multitude. . . . People were buying and selling and doing all sorts of business. We would never have imagined that it was God's holy Sabbath day."[13] After Sunday school, the young women attended the preaching service and "felt the Lord was there." Miss Ranf added, "I must be one of the happiest persons on earth." The young missionaries met Ward on Wednesday. "There seemed to be so much of the Master in his appearance and his very presence seemed sacred."[14] All attended the holiness convention until Friday.

Burhanpur was mission headquarters. Here they traveled in a two-wheeled oxcart "without any springs." A large "Welcome to India" sign greeted them at the mission compound. Lovely bouquets of flowers decorated the house. "Brother and Sister Ward were so delighted that they hardly knew what to do for joy, and we were none the less happy to be with them."[15] The young missionaries delivered a message from America. Mr. Ward is not to work so hard this year. Ward replied, "I am going to do more for God and souls this year than I have ever done." Miss Ranf's comment was, "I think he is rightly named Ernest."[16] The new missionaries were amazed at the conditions of darkness and heathenism, but felt that it was "a blessed privilege" to be in India. They had new and startling experiences. Pilgrims en route to the sacred Ganges not only travel on foot, but measure the distance face downward on the ground, making "a mark in the sand with the tongue, then get up and place their toes even with the mark and lie down again, and so on until they have completed the journey. How dreadful, and all because they don't know our blessed Jesus."[17] So this is one young woman's reaction to the India of 1886.

The young missionaries sent home a list of items needed for a missionary outfit: "One pair of high shoes, aside from the pair the person wears on the journey: it is too warm here to wear them; plenty of light dresses, not many worsted ones; a good supply of collars and cuffs . . . collars for the week are cooler than lace. Cuffs, which I considered needless at home, are very useful here, as the sleeves of our dresses get so soiled about the wrists. . . . Two or three pairs of woolen stockings . . . American hats are of no use here. . . ."[18]

Indian idolatry included worship of snakes, account books, and tools. On New Year's Day Hindus gathered together all their money, trimmed it with flowers, and prayed to it. Idols were in every direction. A total eclipse of the moon in 1888 was explained as the serpent god, Rockshus, swallowing the moon. Everywhere people were giving alms, tearing their clothing, howling and screaming.[19] The Burhanpur bungalow was later sold to Bishop Taylor's Mission and the little group returned to Ellichpur where another bungalow was purchased for mission headquarters.

Within a few months, Miss Zimmerman left for Bombay where she engaged in more intensive language study and in the Zenana work. By mid-year, it was necessary for her to return home for health reasons. Due to their financial difficulties, Ward asked the church treasurer to remit at least "once a month provided you have $25 in hand." A bit later he says, "We should be happy to have the Board continue to act as our advisory committee."[20] Another check was received at an opportune time and in acknowledging it Ward says, "Sister Ranf did not have one pice* and she is so averse to taking any money from us after her share is gone. She usually gives us a good portion from her share, and her teacher is to be paid tomorrow." He reminds the treasurer to remit with "drafts on London" as the exchange is better. Articles of agreement were signed by the missionaries cooperating with E. F. Ward. No one was to receive a set salary or make an appeal for money. All donations were to be shared equally. Each missionary was to subscribe to the principles of the India Holiness Association. The superintendent was to oversee the work and make appointments which must be approved unanimously by the mission group.

Life Was Hard

The climate was difficult. Ward suffered a severe attack of pleurisy and "the Hyderabad climate pulled me down some, but the meetings for the promotion of holiness blessed me up much."[21] Ward urged the sending of more reinforcements, advising that new missionaries "can commence preaching at once through us as interpreters."

Health is ever a problem on a pioneer mission field. This has been especially the case in India. Ward emphasized divine healing, and we have the report that "this was the day for Brother Ward to have fever, but the Lord answered our prayers. . . . Brother Ward has felt better than any day since he came home." Did Louisa Ranf, who was so soon to finish her own earthly career, have some presentiment of it when she wrote, "One missionary died very suddenly with fever. He would take no medicine until it was too late. The doctor takes medicine and gives it to others. Brother and Sister Moore . . . all take it. I have not taken a bit since I left America and long before, and I don't intend to unless I see clearly God could have me do so. . . . I sometimes question whether it is not wiser to take medicine than die. We know of no one in India who feels just as we do. . . . Brother Scott did, but he died." One's sympathies go out to these sincere and devoted people who, on conviction, were not availing themselves of what medical aid was present. In the case of an Indian baby, Ward refused to anoint it for healing but took it to the doctor. The baby died later. The young missionary's comment was, "I should much rather have taken the Bible way than to have gone to a

---

*Small Indian coin.

physician."[22] Ward wrote, "Sister Ranf has been suffering much with prickly heat. Neither she nor any of us feels led to use medicine in any form for sickness. Our 'materia medica' is wrapped up in the promises." Large numbers of Indians were coming every day to hear the teaching of Christ and His gospel.

Language Study

The agreement with the Missionary Board was that candidates for India must be approved by the Board before any of the special funds received for Ward's faith mission could be appropriated. He asked the Board to make up anything that is lacking. He also expressed great interest in the Liberia Mission. Mrs. Ward instructed her brother, Frank Cox, to pay the balance of her money to defray the traveling expenses of another missionary to India. There was real motivation in the difficult language study. "I am digging away at Marathi, and earnestly praying that I may acquire it soon—only for Jesus' sake . . . so that I can talk to these people soon. . . . My heart is all taken up with the idea of fathering these precious souls, for whom Christ died." In India only one year, Miss Ranf was able to speak Marathi to a man engaged in idol worship. She commented, "He understood all I said."

Meager Finance

A bit later Ward was touring among the Korkoos. These were primitive people for whom he was preparing a written language. While working among these people his food was mostly the native chapatties. Without a stipulated allowance, the missionaries had a precarious existence. Meat was scarce and expensive. Miss Ranf received $28.43 from the Mary E. Carpenter Missionary Society at Chili and a good letter from Principal B. H. Roberts. Friends from Syracuse send $20.13. In mid-January "two boxes from the dear seminary filled with things carefully folded and placed in them by hands I love so much was received." Then she added this prophetic note: "A shade of sadness comes over me when I think of the precious saints in the household of faith. . . . In all probability I shall never see them again in this life." She never did.

The India property was deeded to E. F. Ward, but he made a will turning it over to the Missionary Board.[23] In sending in a small order for supplies, Ward made this comment, "I make bold to ask for these things because I see by report in F. M. just received that you have a balance to our credit." A box of curios was sent to the States to be sold and the money credited to the India mission. Also, an India report was printed and was to be sold at fifteen cents for the same purpose. In expressing thanks for a missionary box recently received, Mrs. Ward mentions especially the dolls. Ethel had wanted one, but she requested T. B. Arnold not to publish her letter as "some might take it for an appeal for funds."[24] Mrs. Ward reminded the publisher of *The Free Methodist* that "we do not forget your appeal in the Sunday schools on our behalf on first starting toward India."

No missionary sent longer reports, and they were printed regularly in *The Free Methodist*. In 1889 Ward was busy preparing a memorial against the opium traffic in China to be sent to the emperor. He said this situation had a bad influence in India. He also planned to print a tract on alcohol. He suggested that missionary boxes be sent with outgoing missionaries since ocean freight was so high.

Policies

Board policy was in the first stages of its development. There were no fixed terms of service. In those days "if his health was good and there were no special reasons for his return at the end of seven years, we would expect him to remain an indefinite length of time." The missionaries had the pioneering experiences of rain, mud, snakes, mad dogs, cholera, scorpions, bears and tigers. Inadequate health measures, poor food, unfavorable climate, and insufficient funds for a vacation in the hot season had their effect upon Louisa Ranf. However, her death was caused by burns received from an overturned lamp. Mrs. Ward felt that the church in America was weak in missionary outlook, but that the death of Louisa Ranf would be an eloquent appeal for overseas missions.

V. G. McMurry and Celia Ferries Mc-Murry. Miss Ferries was the first Board-appointed superintendent in India

Mrs. W. B. Olmstead, left, and Miss Elizabeth Moreland, right, visit grave of Grace Barnes

Pentecost Band missionaries arrived in India at about this time. The independent mission movement was strong in the Midwest. The Iowa, West Iowa, Missouri, Illinois, New York, Pittsburgh, Canada, and North Indiana Conferences took special action either disapproving, forbidding, or advising against the giving of Free Methodist missionary money to other than the regularly appointed missionaries of the church.[25] The Illinois Conference sent a letter to E. F. Ward strongly advising him not to join the Pentecost Bands. Celia Ferries, a Free Methodist already in India, wrote to the Missionary Board commending them for their stand against independent missions and placed herself at the disposal of the Board for missionary service in India.[26] Ward was happy to see the church establish a mission field in Africa, but also wanted to stress the great need of India. When, after twelve years, E. F. Ward and family finally returned to America for furlough, they sold their bungalow in Ellichpur to secure funds for their transportation.

Famine Relief

In the decade 1890-1900, missionary activity majored on famine relief and the establishment of orphanages. Thousands of dollars were sent to India where hundreds of orphans were saved from starvation. Many of them continued under the instruction of the church and from this group have come some of the strong leaders of the church in India today. It is a heroic tale. A small number of people overwhelmed by the immensity of their task, in poor health, suffering from malnutrition, a bad climate, and malaria, do the best they can. God honors their sacrifice and the church is established. Neither

Famine relief. Before . . . and after, 1902

cobras nor scorpions, famine nor summer heat, that sometimes is above 120°, stopped them. The author has visited the cemetery in India and has seen the burial places of our missionaries. They all died in the faith. Miss Grace Barnes' dying testimony was: "I would enjoy Heaven, but Oh to tell India about Jesus." And Miss Mary E. Chynoweth's parting message was: "I've only one life to live and I give that most gladly. Had I other lives to give, I would spread them over needy India."[27]

Sometimes there was no money for postage. On one occasion Ward headed for the mountains with "five annas in my pocket and a Bible with thirty thousand promises." Again he wrote: ". . . Often we come to the bottom of the meal chest."

The Indian famine aroused great sympathy in America. Funds came increasingly from friends in Canada and the United States. The *Christian Herald* sent money for famine relief. The missionaries were concerned about a permanent industrial program—a farm or some plan to help the orphans become self-supporting. They were much interested at first in an industrial farm, but this was rejected in favor of an industrial school. During the cholera epidemic of 1897 fifty of the orphans died. The missionaries wrote: "Could

78

the donors have seen the hundreds of hungry, starving ones to whom their gifts brought satisfaction and joy, this would have afforded them special pleasure. . . ." In connection with their relief work, some very desirable improvements have been made on the compounds and orphanages. But it is impossible to hurry the East. "Carpenters are snailing along as usual." Strong hopes were entertained that "the famine would prove to be a chastisement resulting in turning many from idols unto the living God."[28]

Pioneers Venture

In spite of pests, rats and scorpions, the missionaries continued to come. By 1906 there were nine Board-appointed missionaries in India, including the J. T. Taylors, the M. C. Clarkes, the Wards, Misses Rose Cox, Effie Southworth, and Mary Chynoweth. All of them except the Wards were at the new Yeotmal station which was secured for the mission by Miss Ferries, the first Board-appointed superintendent. A wonderful revival broke out in the Yeotmal area and fifty were received into the membership of the church.

In 1910 Benjamin Winget, the Missionary Secretary, speaking in retrospect of the life and labors of Mrs. Phebe E. Ward, who had been called from active labor to her reward, said: "For many years she labored as a pioneer. She has left behind for her co-laborers and the church an example of unselfish devotion, of patience and perseverance, which is a light set on a hill, which cannot be hid." Thirty years after volunteering with her husband for this pioneer venture in far-off India, Mrs. Phebe E. Ward was translated to higher service in the eternal kingdom. E. F. Ward gave forty-six years to the service of Christ in India. He attended the 1927 General Conference at Rochester, New York. At the morning service, a special offering was being received, and he pledged fifty dollars. In the afternoon a missionary offering was being taken. The response was not very generous. Ward stepped out on the platform saying, "This morning I gave fifty dollars in the offering. A friend came to me afterwards and gave me fifty dollars, saying that I was not able to give that much money. That is not true. I have fifty dollars to pay that pledge this morning, so I'm giving the fifty dollars that my friend gave me to the offering this afternoon." Needless to say, there was a hilarious missionary offering from that moment on!

Industrial School

At the beginning of the worst famine years, the first Free Methodist pulpit in India was set up at the Yeotmal church. During the famine years as additional funds were received, the Missionary Board periodically approved caring for additional starving children. Sometimes the reception of one hundred was approved at a single meeting. Toward the end of the famine period, the balance of the famine fund was used by Board consent to erect dormitories and establish an industrial school.

In 1900 H. L. Crockett reported the building operations to his home board. He had bargained for two hundred thousand bricks. They were of poor quality and he had been able to secure delivery on only eighty thousand. Lumber was scarce and "It has taken a great deal for boards on which to bury the children. We have lost about fifty children and they are still

Work program for famine sufferers, Yeotmal, India, 1900

dying."[29] Famine sufferers were employed to carry wood from the forest. Missionaries would burn the brick on the job. This would give employment to a large number. The missionaries were gathering those who fell by the wayside. Many were at the point of death. As soon as they were fed and had enough strength, they were put to work on the building program. A wall was being built around the orphans' school, making provision for the famined orphans and giving work to the needy. Other repair work, including the construction of roads, deepening the well, and clearing rocks from a poor farmer's field were included in the work. From three hundred to five hundred refugees were being cared for regularly. One missionary became so depressed with the situation that it was finally imperative for her to return to the States.

In 1911 the plague broke out again. Some of the missionaries left Yeotmal for the smaller towns of the district. Here there was an epidemic of rats. They were dying in and around the buildings and on the beds of the missionaries. Sick missionaries who should be home undergoing medical treatment continued to carry on their work since no one was available to take their places. S. D. Casberg wrote, "We need more men very badly."

A serious blow struck the mission in 1914. The London Bank and its branch in Bombay, where more than $3,000 mission funds were on deposit, failed.[30] Much of the money was intended for the industrial school. However, the missionaries were authorized to go forward with ordering needed

Girls' orphanage, India, 1924

machinery and equipment. Ultimately a fine school was in operation. V. G. McMurray was suffering with a fever of 105°. However, he was becoming stronger every day. McMurray also reported receiving £500 from the sale of a carload of corn and an additional $500 in cash, besides 250 blankets and another remittance of 190 rupees. These were all from the "*Christian Herald* Fund." McMurray established a "cheap grain shop." He had on hand a carload of rice and one of grain which he was selling, below cost. He thought that 400 rupees would recover his loss on this transaction.[31] McMurray was hopeful for the future. He said, "A discouraged missionary is no good anywhere."

Meeting Real Needs

The missionaries in India ministering to the famine sufferers from 1890 to 1900 are a striking example of the church implementing the gospel of

81

Christ in terms of current human needs and making that gospel relevant in the lives of men. Because the need was so apparent, the task, perhaps, was simpler in India than it is in North America today.

A recent article entitled "Storefront Religion: A Challenge," says: "Any church that refuses to serve the low-income people of its immediate neighborhood and ministers only to the elite who drive in from the suburbs has no right to exist."[32] The rapid rise of "storefront churches" in the big cities of America indicates that the mainline churches are failing to meet the real needs of people. Unless the churches take seriously their responsibility to low-income city dwellers, "storefront religion will probably expand."[33]

What is needed is clearer insight and a deeper understanding of the real needs of people. The church must find ways to bring the eternal message of Christ to the deepest needs of men in this modern day.

Section 3—LATIN LANDS

Change the World

American Protestantism is essentially activist. While no theologian of first rank appeared in American church life during the nineteenth century,[1] the so-called "social gospel" had its beginnings. At the mid-century, Henry James, a Presbyterian, urged the union of Christianity and socialism. A quarter of a century later Henry George wrote his epic, *Progress and Poverty*, and later Edward Bellamy pictured in *Looking Backward* a Christian utopia which he contrasted with the anti-Christian commercial, social and industrial order. Denominational rivalry and competition were increasing during the latter part of the century, punctuated by occasional efforts at cooperation and alliance. In 1894 an interdenominational organization known as "Open Door Institutional League" was established for the purpose of "saving all men, by all means, abolishing so far as possible the distinction between the religious and the secular and sanctifying all ways, by all means, to the great end of saving the world for Christ."[2] D. L. Moody was at the height of his power. His meetings went beyond denominational lines. Moody himself was not an ordained minister. In 1886, *The Free Methodist* noted that "D. L. Moody will hold revival meetings in Ithaca, New York, next month." The Oregon and Washington Conferences were taking steps to purchase a "sloop," the *Messenger*, for river mission work on the Columbia. It was in this atmosphere that Samuel Mills of Ashtabula, Ohio, felt led to move from his Ohio home, not to the Western frontier, but south into the West Indies.

Esther D. Clark

The Dominican Republic

The Dominican Republic occupies the eastern two-thirds of the island of Hispaniola, which is located midway between Cuba on the west and Puerto Rico on the east. It is approximately four hours flying time from Miami, Florida. The western one-third of the island is occupied by the Republic of Haiti. Ciudad Trujillo, the capital, is one of the oldest cities in the Western Hemisphere and the University of San Domingo, chartered in 1531, claims to be the oldest in the New World.

Just as on the earlier fields Free Methodist missionaries had attempted to establish work in areas not being served by other missions, so here Mills made a wise choice. Perhaps no place in the Caribbean area had fewer missionaries than San Domingo (Dominican Republic). He left the south side of the island, the capital city of Santo Domingo, now Ciudad Trujillo, and made his way north, locating first at Montecristi and later in Santiago. Great emphasis was placed upon the distribution of Scripture portions and home visitation. He sowed the seed and gathered together the nucleus of what later became the Dominican Free Methodist Church.

The "Mills Mission"

Work in the Dominican Republic was organized differently from that on any other field. The Ward family went to India as independent missionaries but with the approval of the church and with funds raised by the church.

83

They were in constant communication with the church. Their work was publicized in the columns of *The Free Methodist* and through the years thousands of dollars were raised for their support. In the case of Samuel Mills the situation was different. He, as a member of the Free Methodist Church, went with his family to the Dominican Republic in 1889 to establish himself in business and to labor as a self-supporting missionary. He continued in full sympathy with the beliefs and practices of Free Methodists, although he believed that church organization was a hindrance to the spread of the gospel. He requested the Board to send Esther D. Clark to assist him in the work. The Board did this, appropriating money for her transportation, and for many years gave her partial support. She began her work in 1893. Success attended her labors. Eventually several hundred persons considered themselves members of the "Mills Mission."

In 1907, on order of the director and in harmony with a request from Esther D. Clark, Missionary Secretary Winget went to the Dominican Republic to secure information regarding the country, the "Mills Mission," and to discover whether or not some cooperative program could be worked out. Winget was impressed with the needs of the country. He found the population composed of a mixture of the aboriginal Indians, Negroes, and Spanish. What little missionary work was being done was mostly concentrated on the south side of the island in and near the city of Santo Domingo (Ciudad Trujillo). The largest mission was working primarily with English-speaking peoples, leaving the great Spanish-speaking population without the gospel. The Missionary Secretary found that approximately one hundred fifty people had been baptized by Mills and he himself baptized sixteen during the trip.

Winget found that Mr. Mills was favorable to Free Methodist missionaries coming to the south side of the island. The Secretary felt that there was an opening for Free Methodist work and favored sending a few missionaries into the south side of the island in the hope that "the barriers of ignorance, superstition, and idolatry may be swept away, and the flood tide of blessing may come upon the people of that republic."[3] Winget held a workers' conference, probably the first of its kind on the island.

The missionary methods employed by Samuel Mills were good. He and his workers emphasized home visitation and Bible distribution. Mills was in full sympathy with the coming of the Free Methodist missionaries. Miss Clark promised to give her house and several acres of land and join in the work if the Free Methodists opened this new field.

Winget Decision

There were solid reasons for opening work in the Dominican Republic.

It was near to the United States; travel costs were low. There were opportunities for employment. Other missionaries were already engaged part-time in teaching the English language. There were few boards working in the Republic. The Free Methodist influence was on the island in the person and work of Esther Clark and Samuel Mills. Money and candidates were available. Winget took immediate action. In harmony with authority given him by the Board, he appointed J. W. Winans of the West Ontario Conference and W. C. Willing, M.D., self-supporting missionaries. He had agreed to pay fifty dollars toward the travel of Mr. Winans and also to assist Willing. Further than this the Board had no obligation.

Survey

The opening of work on the south side of the island was approved by the Directors.[4] At the same meeting Rev. and Mrs. Roy C. Nichols were appointed to be sent when in the judgment of the Missionary Secretary funds were available. In August, 1908, Dr. Willing reported that he was receiving enough from his medical practice to care for his own support and that the Missionary Board need not send him any further allowance. He was encouraged with the outlook. The new missionaries, with Mr. Mills, made a thorough survey of the south side. Winans reported the trip. It was a time of drought. Little food was available for the ponies they were riding. Included in the party were Mills, Willing and Winans. "Traveling in the mountains is not difficult, though the scene is bleak and parched. At times the trail is scarcely wide enough for our ponies to pass, while down for hundreds of feet the rocky bank is almost perpendicular. . . . We almost hold our breath. At one place the banks were not so perpendicular, but were of a crumbly nature. Thanks be to God, we all passed over without any mishaps."[5] Once they were caught in a terrible rainstorm and the ponies refused to go further. All were thoroughly drenched in the heavy downpour. Services were held in some of the villages which they passed through. "On a mountain under a scrub tree we spent the night. It rained twice during the night. The next day we pressed on toward San Juan."[6] Finally food was secured for the horses, "the first food they had had for two days." Several services were held on Sunday, accompanied by the distribution of tracts and other Christian literature. The country here was barren, with few inhabitants. Winans had "a good stout pony, good for cargo purposes as well as traveling." Rent was from two to four dollars per month for native houses. When a service was announced, fifty or sixty people gathered to hear the gospel. There was no disturbance.

Returning north, the missionaries visited La Vega, a city of twenty-five thousand inhabitants. A house with dirt floor could be rented for six dollars

First chapel, Dominican Republic

a month; with floor, eight to twelve dollars per month. Here pasture was secured for "twenty-five cents gold a day." It was the best agricultural area in the country. Miss Clark agreed that the mission should be established in the north where the converts were located and from where the work could naturally develop.

Macoris—North Side

Winans recommended La Vega for mission headquarters because it was on the railroad and in the center of a wide and fertile valley. A month later he wrote, "My horse got his foot cut badly on a barbed wire fence" so he had been unable to do much traveling. He made occasional trips with Mr. Mills and was well received by the people wherever he went. A decision had not yet been made regarding the location of the mission. Winans felt that it would be a mistake to work on the south side of the island. Population was sparse, the climate was hot and dry, and a larger number of missionaries were already at work in that area. The north side of the island was practically untouched. The decision was finally made to establish a school and mission headquarters at San Francisco de Macoris. Several new missionaries soon came to work in this new field. The first Protestant church and school on the north side of the island were built here. Later these were moved to Santiago, the second city of the country.

Both Winans and Miss Nellie Whiffen had attacks of malarial fever. Others had it regularly. Winans, feeling that too many missionaries were concentrated at Macoris, decided to locate elsewhere. He established his residence at Jarabacoa, a mountain town of two hundred houses where he

86

Miss Nellie Whiffen on tour with portable organ

was well received. He rented a native house for four dollars a month. On March 15, 1909, Winans reported, "Have preached once in Spanish. Have distributed sixty-seven Gospels."

Then, regarding his appropriations for the coming year, he said, "I wish $150.00 for the coming year, the same as I asked for last year. Received the past year from the Board and from other sources, including teaching, $242.00." His disbursements for the year were $274.00. His comment was, "The financial problem is the greatest difficulty I have to face."[7]

Self-Support

Dr. Willing, self-supporting missionary, planned to locate at La Vega. He seemed pleased with the prospects. His customs fees had been forty dollars, and freight charges approximately thirty dollars. In addition to this, there were other minor charges, so he said, "I think that the one hundred dollars allotted for establishment will about cover the needs now. . . . Please make a substantial remittance as soon as possible. I hope soon to be in a self-supporting position. I am encouraged with the outlook and greatly pleased with the people."[8]

The Missionary Secretary was happy with the prospect of Dr. Willing and others being partially or even entirely self-supporting, pointing to Samuel Mills as a splendid example of one who had been able to support himself without aid from the church. The Secretary explains that "the policy of our board has been to not make as large appropriations to work and workers in countries which are considered partly or wholly civilized."

Samuel Mills continued in fellowship with the Free Methodist workers, although he did not fully agree with them in matters of church organization. He never requested aid for himself from the Missionary Board. His faithful work in the Dominican Republic cannot be overestimated. He labored seven years before there was even one convert. Many of the early converts were persecuted. Some were put in jail, and at least one was killed. One of the charter members became a prominent citizen on the island. Some of his family have held high position in the government. This man regularly devoted a portion of each year to traveling through the country distributing gospel portions, preaching the gospel and otherwise giving his testimony. He himself had been converted as a young man long before the missionaries arrived, simply by reading the New Testament, with the consequent application of the truth to his heart by the Holy Spirit.

For health and other reasons, Dr. and Mrs. Willing did not continue long in the Dominican Republic and were released from Board appointment. Miss Esther Clark should be remembered as one of the real pioneers of the Free Methodist work in the Dominican Republic. In 1904, after serving eleven years in that country, she was recognized as a Free Methodist missionary, and given an allowance of one hundred dollars per year. She was partially self-supporting, teaching English classes as many others did. In 1905 she reported "teaching a small school."

In the beginning, very few appropriations were made by the Board. It was assumed that the missionaries were able to support themselves. In 1911 the Missionary Secretary was authorized to raise two thousand dollars for the establishment of a mission station, and the appointment of three new missionaries was approved. In 1914 work was opened in Santiago. Two hundred dollars was appropriated for rent, and two hundred for evangelism "if political conditions permit."

In 1915 the missionaries reported that they were using their surplus earn-

Mission residence, Santiago

Rev. and Mrs. George Mills, 1911

Ordained ministers, Dominican Republic

Students of Lincoln School for Girls, Macoris

ings from nursing and teaching to provide education for needy children on the island.⁹ Secretary Winget made his last visit to this field in 1915. At that time the Board approved an arrangement whereby the missionaries would receive a small salary in addition to their earnings on the field.

The Instituto

Because freedom of religion is fully guaranteed by the constitution, missionary work in the Dominican Republic has reaped the benefits. Fanatical opposition to the Evangelicals is not greatly apparent. The Instituto Evangelico at Santiago is a union of the Lincoln School for Girls at Macoris and the Santiago Boys School. It is the only coeducational boarding school in the country. It has served the children from some of the finest homes. Graduates of this institution now hold positions of influence throughout the island. Some of them may never become members of the Dominican church, but it will be hard for them to tolerate the throwing of rocks or the jailing of "convertidos." The newspaper editorials are different, the moral and intellectual climate is being transformed by the leaven of the "Instituto."

The Bible school is located on the same campus. Most of the pastors and their wives have been trained here. An aggressive program of evangelism utilizes the youth of the church, especially those in training at the Bible school, and is chiefly responsible for the large membership gains of recent years. The climate is difficult, the people are poor, and unreasoned opposition in isolated areas still exists. The Mills' venture of 1889 laid the foundation of what today is a thriving Christian church.

Section 4—JAPAN

The Nineteenth Century Closes

The westward movement of our frontier is one of the most significant features of American history. The settlement of the West was practically complete by 1890. America was seeking, perhaps unconsciously, another frontier. The short war with Spain, concluding with the Treaty of Paris, in 1893, gave the Philippines to the United States for twenty million dollars. Immediately interest developed in the Pacific and those countries bounding it. This also became the new frontier. This concern was felt in the church. The editor of *The Free Methodist* promised a series of factual reports on the Philippines, our "new possessions." He hoped to "pave the way for our Philippine mission that we believe is to be in the not far-off future."[1] During the decade 1890-1900 approximately one thousand Japanese entered the United States annually. In 1900 the number jumped to ten thousand, while two years later twenty thousand were admitted.

The year 1896 was a time of world-wide tension. The editor of the *Missionary Review of the World*, in his summary of the situation, said: "The first thing that strikes us in the outlook is the almost unprecedented *unrest in the nations*."[2]

Speaking more directly concerning the conditions in Japan, Dr. Arthur T. Pierson said:

"In Japan there is a net loss in membership of Protestant churches of over five hundred, in fact, a general decline in baptisms and Sunday-school attendance.... The gifts of native converts fall $10,000 below 1895. And the worst of it is that these statistics do not misrepresent the real state of things. It is quite too obvious that in spiritual state there has been a very noticeable lowering of the level of piety, of which the defection of the Doshisha—the institution founded by the lamented Neesima—is one conspicuous sign. And yet the more devoted missionaries, instead of losing heart and hope, believe that all this is only one of the inevitable reactions which come in spiritual work, and which are followed by an even more marked advance, as in the case of the sea tides."[3]

Overseas Students

Of the approximately one thousand Japanese admitted to this country in the early 1880's, two found their way to the A. M. Chesbrough Seminary (Chili), Mr. U. Uetta and Mr. Moku S. Matsumoto. The latter transferred to Greenville College. He visited Secretary Terrill at the Chicago office and later wrote regarding the translation of the Book of Discipline, the hymn book and *The Free Methodist*. He doubtless attended the General Conference in October of that year at Greenville. He expressed a strong desire to return to Japan as a missionary. He wrote:

"A few weeks ago I found that Mrs. C. L. Engstrom has been in my country for more than four years laboring under another denomination. I was glad to hear she was there, but sorry that she is not working under our denomination. . . . If God calls me to go out to work I am ready to go any time. . . . My desire is for four years only of help to the Japanese missionary by the Missionary Board . . . after that we will support ourselves. . . . I wish to organize the Japanese conference, and we will live under the direct guidance of the Discipline . . . also to start a training home or school."[4]

This young student on the campus of the newly founded Greenville College in the second year of its existence, had already caught the authentic note of New Testament religion and the spirit of Free Methodism. His sense of mission and willingness to venture in Japan to extend the witness of the church and on a sacrificial basis was likewise the spirit that dominated yet another Greenville student.

Paul Kakihara

In 1885 Mr. Paul Kakihara, an earnest young convert of a Congregational missionary, also came to America. He was in a storm and shipwreck where he lost all hope of being rescued. Clinging to pieces of wreckage and praying earnestly, he experienced heart cleansing. His life was spared. On reaching America, he lived for some time in Arizona with Rev. F. D. Christie who suggested changing his name to Paul in view of the similar shipwreck experiences. Friends urged him to attend Greenville College. In his eagerness to

Rev. and Mrs. Paul Kakihara. He was co-founder of Japan mission

J. G. Terrill, Missionary Secretary 1893-95

do so, he walked six hundred miles of the journey from Arizona! In broken English, he would report the providential experiences of his life. Large audiences were invariably moved to tears on such occasions. Mr. Kakihara felt a strong call to evangelize his own people. The Missionary Board, recognizing this call, accepted him as a missionary to Japan. The president of the college, W. T. Hogue, with F. H. Ashcraft, collected the needed $300 for outfit and transportation, and in 1895, Paul Kakihara sailed for Japan. He began the work of Free Methodist missions on the island of Awaji, a few miles off-shore from Kobe in Osaka Bay.[5] He started his evangelistic labors on the west side of the island where he met Mr. T. Kawabe from California, who was already engaged in gospel work in Awaji. These two brethren became associated in their endeavors, and on Kakihara's recommendation, T. Kawabe was also appointed as a missionary by the Board.[6]

The American churches' contributions to missions slackened during the depression years. The American Board (Congregational) secretary declared that there seemed to be "the backward setting of the missionary current in the churches. . . . Mission boards move in these days with timidity and apprehension, having little confidence in the solid backing of their so-called constituency."[7]

As for the Free Methodists, they were still a relatively small group. Their newly organized western conferences were loudly calling for "missionary" funds to assist in establishing new churches. The Woman's Missionary Society, in the process of being organized, was not yet a very strong force. Until 1891 there was no full-time secretary to promote the interests of the overseas missions. W. W. Kelley, elected in 1891, was forced to resign because of ill health. J. G. Terrill was elected in 1893 to fill his place. Two years later, en route to New York with a party of outgoing missionaries, he was stricken with pneumonia and died. B. Winget was then elected to the position in 1895. As late as 1898-99 the total missionary budget was only $12,702! That year Paul Kakihara returned to attend the General Conference in Chicago. No doubt impressed by the financial weakness of the Board, Kakihara returned to Japan and entered the coal business with a view to making the work self-sustaining. However, in this he was unsuccessful. His venture failed, he found himself heavily in debt, and in discouragement resigned from the Mission. However, his great contribution to the work of Free Methodism in Japan lies in his discovery of T. Kawabe. After Kakihara's resignation, Kawabe became superintendent. Fearful lest the entire operation collapse after Kakihara's departure, the Board advised Kawabe and his workers to join another mission.

Missionary Secretary Winget visits Japan

VENTURE!

The St. Paul of Japan

They did not know Kawabe. He was a Free Methodist and would continue as such. If necessary, he would engage in menial labor to support himself. He did sell some of his books, and disposed of household articles, to provide food for his family until the Board, after the visit of the Missionary Secretary in 1889, renewed the appropriation. Did ever so little accomplish so much? Continuing as leader of a small band of workers, Kawabe laid the foundation of a great church. Missionaries from America did not arrive until 1903. Kawabe knew how to help young inexperienced workers, ignorant of the Orient and its customs, and without the language. He was a great soul, the author of approximately fifty books, a successful evangelist and pastor. He founded Osaka First Church (Nippon Bashi) which at one time was Free Methodism's largest congregation. Today it is one of Japan's most aggressive churches. In many circles he was known in the days of his preaching power as the St. Paul of Japan. His visit to America with his wife was a great inspiration and encouragement to the church. These honored workers were the featured speakers at missionary rallies and conventions throughout the denomination and helped unite the churches of Japan and America in a friendship that even war could not destroy.

Osaka

The first American missionaries were the Rev. and Mrs. A. Youngren and the Rev. and Mrs. W. F. Matthewson. Youngren took up residence on the island of Awaji, assisting Kawabe in the opening and development of the new work. Matthewson was stationed at Osaka and served as Superintendent of the Mission. Kawabe, abundant in labors on the island of Awaji, had larger plans for the church. He felt led to that great commercial center, Osaka. During the International Exposition of 1903 he rented a small building near the Exposition grounds and began preaching services. This was the beginning of First Church and of the other Osaka churches to be established later. That same year Kawabe started Bible study classes at his church. This developed into the Osaka Bible School, with A. Youngren as the first principal. "Later, Dr. T. Tsuchiyama became principal, and in 1922 the new administration building, the boys' dormitory, the girls' dormitory, and the mission residence were built."[8] The following year a regular conference was organized.

Awaji

The new missionaries had many strange and interesting experiences. Their main purpose was still seeking and saving the lost. On the island of Awaji,

94

Rev. and Mrs. T. Kawabe, 1898

Students of Osaka Bible School. Standing at left, T. Tsuchiyama, president

Matthewson was favorably impressed with the opportunities. At Anaga there were only three believers, but the congregation of earnest listeners was polite, friendly, clean and intelligent. The policeman promised to seek Christ. At Sumoto Matthewson organized a society of twenty-two members. During the tour of the island he slept on the floor with a cold wind blowing on his head, walked nine miles one day, and was in a terrible storm in which the sailboat almost carried the passengers to a watery grave. He returned home feeling well, reporting, "This work is growing."[9]

Meanwhile, Youngren started Bible classes at Sumoto. His students included doctors and merchants. Nine accepted Christ.[10] The Russo-Japanese war was in progress. Angry Japanese threw rocks through the windows of a Swedish missionary's home. The police posted a sign, "This man is not Russian," and the stone throwing ceased. Many Japanese were greatly concerned, feeling that the war would determine the destiny of Japan. Indifference to the gospel seemed to increase during the hostilities.

Compassion Gifts

The summer rainy season with mold, mildew, mosquitoes and fleas had its trials. Mrs. Matthewson reported that her house was simple, with the fewest of things, but she was satisfied. The Missionary Secretary was reminded of the hot weather. It was dangerous for Matthewson to remain in the city during the summer months. Fifty dollars was requested to rent either one large house or two smaller ones in the mountains where all the missionaries might escape the heat.

Serious famine prevailed in many parts of Japan. There was a generous response from the Awaji churches where the crops were plentiful. Youngren reported: "Have forwarded yen 84.63 to the Famine Relief Fund . . . also sent to the famine district 325 bags of rice, valued at yen 45.00. In these bags we also put some tracts or Gospels, in the hope that some by reading these might find the bread of eternal life."[11] Genuine concern was also felt in the Africa church for the Japan famine sufferers. The Japan missionaries were "greatly affected" to receive eleven pounds ($55.00 in 1906) from W. S. Woods of the Fairview farm, South Africa, remembering "how these poor people in Africa are suffering."[12] Here is an early demonstration of world-wide Free Methodist cooperative action.

Evangelistic Success

Apparently the Missionary Secretary approved the summer vacation plans, for Youngren explained that it was arranged for the Matthewson family to go to Arima for the hot season. Youngren also planned to be there for the hottest weather. Arima was "a little town, situated in the midst of beautiful mountain scenery, with a high altitude."[13]

In April, Bishop Sellew's visit to Japan was enjoyed by the church and missionaries alike, and two months later Matthewson reported one hundred fifty new believers.[14] Four missionaries had not yet passed the first language examination, but the Missionary Secretary was asked to make an exception and receive them into full membership. In 1910 the training (Bible) school was "doing better work than ever before." There was a student from Korea who excelled both in his studies and in the evangelistic work. The students were busy with the evangelistic work which "we require of them besides attending the classes of the school."[15]

The work was in an encouraging condition. Twenty-nine had joined the church at Akashi. More inquirers were registered at Miki. At Akashi, located in a rich farming section, it was real pioneer work. A policeman was numbered among recent converts, and more workers were needed.

In 1910 a widespread cholera epidemic took its heavy toll. In Sumoto, thirty-seven of the forty-seven stricken died! The number of new cases increased daily. At Fukura the church was closed by sickness. A new location on a prominent street in the center of Sumoto was secured for the church.

To save expenses, missionaries traveled by third class coach even for an overnight trip. Japanese church leaders Kawabe and Tsuchiyama attended the mission meetings. Sometimes they continued all day considering only the appointment of one or two missionaries! Perhaps the Board would make the appointments?

The Bible school became increasingly important in the ongoing life of the conference. It was a center of evangelism. The students were busy in off-campus evangelistic activities, while there seemed to be a constant spirit

Osaka Bible School—old campus

Missionaries to Brazil, 1938

of revival on the campus. "The school is on fire these days and the way the students take advantage of their opportunities and witness for God is most heartening. . . . Chapel lasted from nine until twelve last Thursday. . . . If the future of Free Methodism here lies with our school, the future certainly looks bright."[16]

The course of study for preachers as recommended by the missionaries contained several Japanese titles. Approval was given by the Board with the understanding that there was "no taint of higher criticism."[17]

The Japan church stands among the first in aggressive evangelistic outreach. More than any other field, this church has reached the population centers. A long range program is now envisaged to expand both in the urban and rural areas. Missionaries from Japan have established Free Methodist churches in China, Korea, Manchuria and Brazil. In turn, the Brazil church is sending a missionary to Paraguay to work with island population groups of Japanese colonists now settling in that country. So the shadow of Greenville College and Paul Kakihara is today moving in South America. When President Hogue raised $300 to send one of his students to Japan, little did he realize the stream of holy influence being started that would one day reach to the interior of Paraguay where today large numbers of Japanese colonists are going to develop hitherto waste areas, rich in agricultural possibilities.

The Japanese have a resourceful, energetic, self-reliant church, in full fellowship with the Free Methodist churches of the world, but eager to carry its own load and not depend unnecessarily on outside assistance. Generous aid given at the close of World War II will never be forgotten. Churches and school buildings have been replaced and new congregations established. An ambitious program of church building jointly financed by the local congregations, the conference laymen, and the Mission Board, is now nearing completion.

The home church will always remember the message that came from Japan in the midst of an unparalleled economic depression in 1932. Rev. H. H. Wagner wrote: "The Free Methodist churches in Japan . . . have thrown off all support from the Commission on Missions. This wonderful event happened on December 2, 1932, at 10:30 p.m."[18]

The Japan church requested that funds normally sent to them be appropriated for the churches in China, India, and Africa. This generous act was heartening to a Missionary Board struggling with a heavy debt. Budgets already cut to the bone were revised so that the work on the fields less fully developed was able to go forward. Japan has a large investment in the world outreach of Free Methodism.

Rev. and Mrs. Harry F. Johnson visit Japan. Mr. Johnson was Missionary Secretary 1932-1942.

Section 5—CHINA

A New Century

China's defeat at the hands of Japan and the ending of the war in 1897 awakened this vast Asiatic mainland to the existence of a modern world. Shortly, Li Hung Chang, leader of the Progressive Party, visited Europe. He expected that military railroads would be built across his country. A great religious awakening was reported in China where churches were filled, with large additions to the membership. The question was being asked, "Is this a genuine revival or are the Chinese only trying to learn the foreigner's secrets?"[1] Already Free Methodists had become sufficiently interested in this part of the world to send Paul Kakihara, a Greenville College student, to Japan as a missionary. Twenty years earlier India and Africa held the spotlight. Now the focus of interest shifts to the Far East. The Japan crisis, the war in China with its massacres and revolution, the great areas still

Miss Clara Leffingwell, left, and fellow missionary

hardly touched by the missionary and the Christian gospel, called for a new crusade.

Clara Leffingwell

In 1896 Clara Leffingwell responded to that call, enlisting for service under the auspices of the China Inland Mission. Bishop Sellew, knowing of her conviction, strongly urged her to accept appointment to Japan under the Free Methodist Board. While she preferred service with her own church board, China's call was so strong that she was unable to escape its demands. While she was serving under the C.I.M., the Bishop and Missionary Secretary kept in touch with Miss Leffingwell, securing valuable suggestions on missionary policy from the long and rich experience of that board. Miss Leffingwell recommended the appointment of both single women and single men, a policy favored by the Training Home in Toronto where she had studied previous to her first term. In the event Free Methodist missionaries were sent to China, she thought they might come as associates of the C.I.M. "Rev. Hudson Taylor was so unselfishly anxious to get workers to China that this course used to be pursued."[2] Subsequent correspondence with her indicated that if her own denomination would open work in China she would much prefer serving in that relation. Accordingly, Miss Leffingwell was appointed superintendent of the new China field and deputized to travel throughout the borders of the church promoting interest in the enterprise. The directors requested her to raise $7,000 to establish the mission. Bitter experiences in India and Africa had convinced the Board that larger sums of money were required, not only to procure property and to build the needed residences and institutional structures, but also to care for current operations. Miss Leffingwell followed a heavy speaking schedule across the church, promoting interest in China and raising the needed funds. She worked far beyond her strength. As interest increased, calls for her services multiplied and before the time of sailing, Miss Leffingwell's health began to fail. "I am not sick," she said, "but I am not strong. Sometimes I cannot sit up for a half day. Then again there comes an uplift and I am up and busy all day. I am in God's hands. What health and strength I have is God-given."[3]

Completely exhausted upon her arrival in Seattle, March 23, 1905, she canceled all speaking engagements but one. She was "so ill three days before sailing that it seemed impossible for her to go." President and Mrs. Alexander Beers of Seattle Seminary "secured a skilful physician and a trained nurse. She was greatly helped, and although still very weak, sailed with Miss Graves and Miss Meyers at 5:30 Saturday morning, April 8."[4] Mission policy today would not approve such procedures. Missionaries must have adequate rest, physical examinations and release from regular deputation service for approximately one month before sailing. But in 1905 there was no rule to cover this situation. The sailing date had already been postponed several times and the two single men of the band had gone ahead. It was the wrong season of the year to enter the country but it seemed that a longer delay could not well be explained. Her going to China at this time was undoubtedly premature. She needed several months of rest and recuperation before plunging into such strenuous activity. As superintendent she was given power of attorney and with the Missionary Secretary, authority to select a location for the new mission.

Province of Honan

It was decided to establish work in the province of Honan, making the cities of Chengchow and Kaifeng the centers from which to operate. A few weeks later Miss Leffingwell and her young women companions were in Chengchow. She reported her trip to the Secretary, making no reference to the serious illness in Seattle, simply saying: "We went on board at Seattle April 7 and sailed the following morning."[5] They went by way of Yokohama and Shanghai. From Shanghai it required three weeks to reach the Chengchow destination which "we hope is the end of our journey."[6] She reminded the Secretary of the China budget:

> 8 missionaries @ $250 (travel) $2,000
> Salaries of 8 missionaries the
>   first year @ $250 each $2,000
> For two mission homes $3,000

Housing was needed as renting was difficult, unsatisfactory and expensive. A rented house would need flooring "lest the sisters get rheumatism and malaria."[7] Apparently the recent discoveries concerning malaria were not yet well known. In any event, they were living in a Chinese inn, which was not desirable. She asked: "Could not $1500 be sent at once. It might save much sickness."[8] Already she had procured, probably in Shanghai, an appropriate letterhead for the mission:

FREE METHODIST CHINA MISSION

Our Confidence—"God is nigh . . . in all things we call upon him for."
Our Command and Promise—"Seek ye the kingdom of God and all these things shall be added unto you."
Our Prayer—"Lord, it is nothing for thee to help whether with many or with them that have no power, help us, O Lord, for we rest on thee and in thy name we go."

Our Confidence—"God is nigh * * * in all things we call upon him for."

Our Command and Promise—"Seek ye the kingdom of God and all these things shall be added unto you."

Our Prayer—"Lord it is nothing for thee to help whether with many or with them that have no power, help us, O Lord for we rest on thee and in thy name we go."

Miss Clara Leffingwell, Supt.,

Shaftsbury House,

Seaward Road, China.

rent- but- would have spend so
much putting in floors be
the sisters get rheumatism and
malaria, that- it- seemed ~wrong~ to wa
so much money on a tempora
home and it- is so hard f
the sisters to live in one row
in an inn, I want- to get-
it- all cleaned before the Ho
come.

could not- $1500 be sent- at-
once, it- might- save much sic
ness, for we are only in an
inn

Usually it- takes so long to fi
property for sale but- God seems t
have gone before and prepared a p
for us to pitch our tent-
We are going now to look all th

How Long in China?

The weather was extremely hot as Miss Leffingwell searched early and late for a suitable residence. At last she found an available property adequate for the Noah S. Honn family and the single women. There was a porch that could easily be remodeled for a chapel. Workmen were hired to rush the project to completion. Miss Leffingwell was everywhere present, directing the cleaning, giving instructions to the carpenters, and talking, talking, talking all day long to the crowd of eager women who hung on her loving words concerning the way of salvation. "When asked why she did not rest she replied, 'I don't know how long Jesus will let me stay in China, and I want to do all I can while I stay.' "[9] Everyone was happy when the chapel was open for services. It was crowded the first day. "During the long, hot, weary Sunday of July the second, she stood in the chapel preaching to the people who began to gather even before we were through our breakfast. . . . Weary and worn, she would start a hymn and sit down a few moments, then she would begin as earnestly as before. . . . About four o'clock in the afternoon, so worn out she could no longer speak, she rested her head upon her hand and told them she was very tired. . . . Little did we realize that this was to be her last opportunity of preaching Christ to the Chinese whom she loved so well."[10]

The best nursing and medical aid available was secured. At times she appeared to gain strength, but it was only temporary. With a high fever and severe dysentery she grew weaker. Early Sunday morning, July 16, Miss Leffingwell, realizing her situation, called her companions to the bedside and expressed the hope that the mission work of the Free Methodist Church in China would go forward even though she herself was unable to share in the enterprise. That afternoon this great pioneer of prayer and faith who ventured out on the promises of God and claimed every province of China for the church, went home to her eternal reward. Paralyzed and stunned, the young missionaries, assisted by neighboring missionaries, quickly arranged a Chinese funeral for their beloved leader.

The Missionary Secretary, in reporting this seeming tragedy, said, "The sudden and unexpected death of our new superintendent in China has been deeply and extensively felt, both on the home and foreign field. Although we cannot trace the ways of God, we in living faith can trust the word of promise that all things work together for good to them that love God, and in the exercise of such faith hope's vision brightens and our courage is inspired."[11]

Two of the new appointees were young men, Mr. C. Floyd Appleton and Mr. George Scofield.[12] They were engaged in language study in the mountains. The Board requested Appleton to become superintendent. He and Scofield made the fifteen-hundred-mile journey from the mountains to the

Rev. and Mrs. C. F. Appleton

blistering plains of Honan. Rushing to Chengchow, on foot part of the way, carried by natives some of the way, and by rowboat and steamer the remainder of the journey, they joined the group to plan for the next steps. The matter of purchase of property was still being studied. Money was available from generous gifts of interested friends. Mr. N. B. Peterson made an initial gift of $4,000 toward the purchase of property. A year later he added another $1,000 and sent his own daughter Lily to China. Within two years she too finished her missionary career, but her sister Mattie also volunteered, giving her life to the cause of Free Methodist missions in China.

The Fellowship

Possibly too many missionaries were appointed and sent to China before any one of them had mastered the language and understood the country well enough to be recognized as leader of the group.

In spite of prayer and good intentions, a spirit of division crept into the group. The directors at this time gave some helpful advice to the young workers, reminding them that "there is a certain and infallible cure for this state of things, namely, confess your faults one to another and pray one for another that ye may be healed. And further, brethren, if a man be overtaken in a fault, ye which are spiritual restore such an one in the spirit of meekness, considering thyself lest thou also be tempted. Wherefore, resolved that we direct the superintendent of our mission in China to call a meeting of all the missionaries and appoint a special day of fasting and prayer immediately preceding the meeting, and that in the meantime each missionary prayerfully consider the teaching of our Lord as found in Matthew 18:15-17 and Luke 3:3-4, and faithfully and believingly carry out the same in order that the general meeting may be what it should be—a time of melting and unifying power, as well as a renewal of Pentecost, whereby confidence shall be restored and the spirit of division so utterly routed that it will come again no more."[13] This is sound advice at any time.

The China missionaries have been beset by famine, drought, war, poverty, political unrest, banditry, and bad weather, sickness and death. Almost every sort of affliction has been visited upon them. In these trying experiences they have learned to pray, and through the years marvelous answers have been received to their united and faithful prayer and labor together. As indicated before, Lily Peterson was on the field only a few months when she was returned home because of serious illness. She passed this life at Seattle, Washington, on March 16, 1908. Some had already heard the gospel and were converted as a result of her short ministry. The cook in her own home became an evangelist in Honan. Even before going to China, while Miss Peterson was working in a Chinese mission in the city of Seattle a young Chinese was converted under her labors. He returned to China to preach the gospel. Near the end of her earthly career she seemed to forget the English language and spoke in Chinese, exhorting those nearby to be true to the Lord.

Referring to Miss Peterson and Clara Leffingwell, the Missionary Secretary in his report of June 4, 1908, said, "We mourn with her parents . . . who have contributed so generously for the founding of our work in China. . . . The influence of her life, as also that of Sister Clara Leffingwell, will plead eloquently for others to take up the work where they, in God's providence, were compelled to lay it down."[14]

Famine

A severe famine was sweeping the country in 1907. The Board approved the opening of an orphanage. Generous gifts were received from the churches of America. In addition to this, the *Christian Herald* contributed liberally to the orphanage program. This work, including erection of buildings, purchase of property, and the daily operation of the institution, engaged much of the attention and time of the young missionaries. At first the orphanage was located at Tsing Kaing Pu. Because of its distance from the main work of the mission, the orphanage was later released to the supervision of another mission. At Kaifeng a Bible school was established and at Kihsien the hospital was placed in operation. An orphanage was maintained here also in connection with the Boys' School. Good relations were maintained with other mission groups. In 1910 Bishop White of the Canadian Church of England was requested to ordain missionaries Frank R. Millican, George

106

Kaifeng Bible School students, 1925

Scofield and George Schlosser. At one time it was planned to open a work in Shanghai, but limited finance and personnel led the missionaries to concentrate their operations in Honan, where a large and influential church and conference developed. Some of the best known names in Free Methodist missions have been connected with the work in China. In 1910 Bishop Sellew visited China to investigate all aspects of the work and ordain eligible candidates. The balance in famine relief funds was used to complete the orphanage buildings.

The Woman's Foreign Missionary Society exhibited a special interest in the China field. In 1910, at the request of the Missionary Board, they made a special appropriation of $1,000 from their contingent fund to expand the program. In 1912 the Missionary Secretary, Benjamin Winget, visited this field and upon his return raised the question whether or not the field should be continued—the income of the Missionary Board was so limited, the demands so great, the China beginnings beset with so many difficulties, and the accomplishments so meager. Apparently some preliminary negotiations to that end had already taken place. His successor, J. S. MacGeary, also visited the field and took somewhat the same attitude. He proceeded to sell a portion of the property at Chengchow. However, the Board decided to continue with the work. Subsequently this field proved to be one of the most fruitful in evangelistic results. A strong, self-supporting and self-governing church has developed.

In 1919 James Hudson Taylor of the China Inland Mission was received

107

as a missionary on the field. He and his wife Alice have given a lifetime of service, both on the mainland of China and now in the rapidly growing and expanding Formosa field where Mr. Taylor is the superintendent.

Medical Work

Almost from the first, the missionaries urged upon the Board the necessity of a hospital program. In compliance with the request, A. L. Grinnell, M.D., was appointed. The W.F.M.S. assisted in the expense of his medical education. In beginning his work, Dr. Grinnell was invited into an association with the China Inland Mission Hospital at Kaifeng. Here he engaged in language study and at the same time received valuable mission hospital experience. In 1915 the Woman's Foreign Missionary Society of the Southern California Conference asked permission to raise funds for the China hospital. The General Board of the woman's society appropriated $500 of their contingent fund for the same purpose. Twelve hundred dollars for equipment, $1,800 for buildings and land, were approved. The Southern California women were granted the privilege of raising these funds as "specials." In October, 1916, the treasurer reported $2,634.74 on hand for the hospital; a total of $3,000 was needed, and a request for payment of pledges was made. Building operations were to begin soon.

One hundred dollars was appropriated in 1919 to assist in a public health campaign. The same year the hospital was completed and open for service. Dr. Grinnell's furlough was due and there was no one to take his place. The call went out for the appointment of a second doctor. In 1920 the Missionary Board urged the China missionaries to cooperate with the China Medical Missionary Association of Peking in every possible way.

On November 14, 1934, Grinnell Memorial Hospital was reopened under the direction of John D. Green, M.D. Closed for several years but intermittently occupied and looted by wandering bands of soldiers, the buildings were at last made usable. They were fundamentally sound except, as Dr. Green explained, "there are leaky roofs which should be repaired. One of the large arches . . . should be rebuilt. Most of the hardware and window glass must be replaced. Sagging floors must be supported. . . . Cupboards and furniture, including heavy hospital equipment . . . operating room table and sterilizer, have been lost. . . . Even the trees have been destroyed by soldiers' horses chewing on the bark."[15] Opening the hospital involved procurement of lumber cut by farmers. The price must be "talked," the "material measured, lumber stored until dry, or fired; a time-consuming process. . . . Bricks vary in size and quality. . . . Lime is brought by wheelbarrow over thirty-five miles of rutty, dusty roads. . . . Constant supervision of every detail . . . reckoning of accounts is a most tedious but necessary part of the work . . . constant interruptions . . . new bricks have come. They are half an inch shorter . . . the masons are out of hemp and haven't mentioned it until it is needed."[16]

At last everything is "clean and orderly." The opening was not "advertised." There was a secret hope that patients would be few in number until the workers were better trained and all the carpentry complete. "Twenty-three patients passed through that day." An evangelistic team was organized to regularly follow each patient back to his village where preaching services and Bible study groups were arranged. The results were very gratifying. This same year John Schlosser, now superintendent of the Philippines field, was unable to return to America for college work. "He is a 'jack-of-all-trades' around the hospital compound and a great help in the drug room."[17] Funds were severely restricted for the hospital work during the depression years. Dr. Green tells the Secretary that "we have stayed within our budget for this year. However, we haven't purchased even five dollars' worth of the many instruments which we have been so urgently in need of. . . . It would seem impossible . . . for us to consider opening again this fall until sufficient funds are on hand . . . to continue for a few weeks."[18] What work! What doctors!

The Board approved the printing of a Chinese Book of Discipline. Extensive repairs and improvements for the girls' dormitory and the Bible school, a contagious ward, and residences for workers were authorized. The directors were requested to proceed with these improvements as soon as possible.

Even Unto Death

Generous gifts from Dr. W. E. Blackstone made possible the purchase of a tabernacle which was used successfully in great evangelistic services. The Bible Training School was also established and maintained largely through his generosity. The influenza struck the mission field in a serious way. At one time eight missionaries and children were very sick. Mrs. Grinnell had the diphtheria, Miss Bernice Wood was near the point of death with smallpox, and Tom Beare, a newly arrived missionary of excellent attainment and strong physique, was stricken and dying. These were dark days for the China mission. Perhaps no other field has suffered so much.

The author was a student at Los Angeles Seminary in the days of that great movement of the Spirit in 1917 which came to be called "the Olmstead Revival." Many were led into full-time Christian work both at home and on the mission field as a direct result of these meetings which reached not only the school and the Hermon Church, but the entire conference. Here Tom Beare received his call to missionary work and Profe sor and Mrs.

Rev. James H. Taylor, left, and
Rev. I. S. W. Ryding, right,
"off for the great Northwest,"
May, 1940

Bishop and Mrs. G. W. Griffith
visit China

Miss Bessie Reid (Mrs. Luther Kresge), left, and Miss Geneva Sayre

Rev. and Mrs. Harold Winslow. He served as Missionary Secretary from 1942 to 1944.

Miss Maud W. Edwards with Bible woman and helpers

E. P. Ashcraft were led to dedicate themselves to the needs of China. Tom was a popular student on the campus, a superior athlete with remarkable physique, a radiant Christian in whom everyone had confidence. In China, he gave himself without reserve, not taking the usual precautions of carrying his own food and water. In evangelizing the villages he slept on their floors, ate their food, loved them and won them. But even Tom Beare could not stand such a life. After a few months he too sickened and died, leaving his broken-hearted wife alone. This youthful critic, ardent admirer of Tom Beare, suggested to Missionary Ashcraft that it would have been the part of wisdom for the enthusiastic young missionary to be more conservative, take more care of himself, carry his own food and camping equipment. "Perhaps

111

so," replied Ashcraft, "but since Tom has lived in their villages, slept on their floors, eaten their food, loved them and prayed for them and died for them, it has been easier for us to tell them about Jesus! They have seen Jesus living again in the dedicated life and sacrificial death of Tom Beare." And this is "venture on the highest level"! There has been practically no mission-church problem on this field. The church in China has, from our point of view, too regularly attended the funerals of our missionary martyrs. But these losses with the suffering involved have revealed an outpouring of love for China that was unmistakable to the Chinese.

When missionary nurse Grace Stewart contracted typhoid fever while laboring at Grinnell Hospital, and after a brief illness was released from service there, the grief-stricken Chinese prepared a revealing tribute for her. She, too, had been in China only two years. The Chinese themselves said: "Her love was great, she came to China to preach for us and now she has died for us." No more fitting eulogy could be spoken than the ode given by the Chinese and translated literally by Dr. Grinnell:

"This ode is in remembrance of our teacher who left her relatives, father and mother, and home, in the far western country, traversing mountains and sea, prepared to endure hardships and arriving at Ki Hsien to search out the lost sheep. In her labors for the Lord in city and country, her influence was without bounds, opening for us a fold. Her two years with us, from beginning to end, were in no way idle, but to the contrary she showed extraordinary zeal. Christians and inquirers all greatly rejoiced in her, but heaven does not console, for a great misfortune has come upon us. She was suddenly taken ill and suddenly taken away. Men are not iron or stone, how can we but grieve? Our tears drop as the rain, our hearts are breaking, but the Lord has taken her away. She has left this dark world for one of brightness. Her body is committed to the ground, but her soul ascends to heaven and from now on she is with the Lord. For us is grief, for her is eternal happiness. These words are but a few of what might be said."[19]

"Service Temporarily Discontinued"

Today there is no possibility of receiving direct reports from the China Free Methodist Church. One of the airline maps shows a dotted line from Tokyo to Shanghai indicating "service temporarily discontinued." This is the faith we have with reference to our church in China. Normal contacts for fellowship, planning and mutual encouragement are no longer possible; they are "temporarily discontinued." It is our fervent prayer that soon normal relations will be re-established so that some of the "old China hands" may return to the mainland to share once more in the work of the kingdom of God in that great country.

III

Women Venture

in World Missions,

1890

Near Failure of First Missionary Ventures

We have now concluded the first phase of the overseas venture. Acting in harmony with its own true nature, and obedient to the main teachings of the New Testament, nevertheless, the infant church, without money or a sound missionary policy, almost failed! The Missionary Secretary reported at the 1890 General Conference, five years after sending the first accredited workers to Africa and India, that "much looks like defeat."[1] Several missionaries had died; the faint-hearted returned home. There had been misunderstandings. Missionaries could not develop "self-supporting" missions as soon as expected, nor as completely as intended. Several of them had accepted temporary employment with other missions, as the Board was not prepared to send regular allowances for living expenses and current operations. Superintendent Roberts had repeatedly said: "I want the most healthy location that can be selected without bringing us into competition with other denominations."[2]

But either through ignorance, or because such situations were not available, the first missionaries established themselves in Liberia and in Portuguese East Africa. Even today these climates are not favorable to European colonization, much less seventy-five years ago before anyone suspected that malaria and mosquito bite were related. At Bethany, Natal, where the climate was delightful, there were few natives, the land was poor, the station which could not become self-supporting was discontinued and sold. The Fairview, Natal, station alone became self-supporting, but only after the appointment of a full-time farm manager and considerable capital investment. Several thousand dollars from the income of this 2300-acre farm was used in the construction and equipping of the Ebenezer Hospital. But even here there was misunderstanding with the founding missionary, who sometimes went beyond his instructions, who misunderstood the Board and who was misunderstood.

History has vindicated the sound judgment of A. D. Noyes who ventured at Fairview, using his own personal money—some of it saved while employed by the American Board until his own church was financially prepared to regularly support a "band" of workers in South Africa. He purchased this strategically located 2300-acre farm in July, 1891. This has been mission headquarters of the Natal field for many years.

In spite of inadequate finance, ill-advised policy, the death of pioneer missionaries Mary Carpenter, Eunice Knapp, A. Y. and Abby Lincoln, the zealous and successful promotion of independent missionary work by sincere members of the church which "worked a great injury to our mission work, and seriously retarded our efforts in the foreign field,"[3] the genius of Free Methodism—its faith in God and the power of the gospel—shines forth in an otherwise dark hour. Secretary Ebey declared that "while we have met with much to discourage and dishearten us in our efforts, and have been at times cast down, still we have not lost heart nor faith in the ultimate triumph of the pure gospel as proclaimed by our missionaries in Africa."[4] This tremendous affirmation of faith was made by the Secretary, knowing full well that besides the terrific obstacles to the work at home and abroad, he had a paltry $779.14 cash balance in the Mission Board treasury! Let it never be forgotten that this is the background for the 1890 General Conference action to the effect

". . . that the Missionary Board be authorized to organize a Woman's Missionary Society, auxiliary to the Board."

First Woman's Societies

Reporting on the organizing of woman's societies during the quadrennium, the Missionary Secretary said:

"This has been done by the Board, and the institution is a part of the church organization; and those engaged in the work are doing what the General Conference has authorized them to do. They are doing good work and are worthy of honor for so doing. . . .

"The (Missionary) Secretary desires that the secretaries or presidents of all our Woman's Missionary Societies report immediately . . . the number of organizations and the number of members, active and honorary. Please attend to this immediately."[5]

Even before the 1890 General Conference, there had been sentiment for some missionary society on a denominational basis. Prior to the previous General Conference, a friend and financial benefactor of Roberts and the Chili Seminary exhorted:

"Let us . . . organize ourselves into a foreign missionary society . . . each annual conference a branch . . . every society an auxiliary . . . Sabbath school (a) juvenile auxiliary . . . (with) collectors appointed by every society. . . . Let the missionary fires be lit up in every part of our work. . . . It will preserve us from mildew and blight which threaten us, and set us on fire with *a holy zeal for God.*"[6]

Here is a layman, close to Roberts, aware of the dangers and pitfalls of too much negativism, of placing reforms above soul saving, calling the church back to its original intention, the salvation of the world. He wants a missionary society to promote interest in such a crusade and collect needed funds for its successful prosecution. The 1886 General Conference took no action!

The position of women outside the influence of Christianity is not good. That women should be interested in missions is a natural. By the middle of the 19th century they were organizing to promote missionary concern. The Congregational Woman's Foreign Missionary Society was established in 1868. The following year the Woman's Foreign Missionary Society of the Methodist Episcopal Church came into being. The Presbyterian and Baptist women soon followed with their own organizations. At the same time *The Free Methodist* reported the successes of the gospel in Spain, with an account of the Spanish Revolution and its effects on Protestant evangelism.[7] The churches and shrines of Russia, the revival in Madagascar,[8] together with an intriguing study of "Traces of Ancient Sabbath in Chinese Rites and Language"[9] all found a place in the denominational paper, together with the declaration that "Christianity has done more for woman than it has for man, and she responds with purer devotion and a more vital attachment."[10] This was in connection with a tribute to the wives of missionaries, especially Mrs. Adoniram Judson.

Mrs. J. S. MacGeary

The General Conference neglected its opportunity to establish a missionary society, but the women of the church did not remain inactive. They were alert to what was happening in other communions. Roberts had long cherished the hope for such an organization, and his wife, as already indicated, was closely connected with the missionary work of the Methodists through her uncle George Lane, treasurer of the Methodist Missionary Society for twelve years. The superintendent's wife living at Verona, Pennsylvania, Mrs. J. S. MacGeary, was greatly concerned. Almost by accident, this first society came into existence. At Verona, Pennsylvania, a Mrs. Sarah Mays, formerly a Methodist, joined the new church. She had been an active worker in the W.F.M.S. in her former church, and was amazed to discover that the Free Methodist women had no such society.

Mrs. MacGeary directed a letter to the general treasurer under date of December 3, 1889:

"Dear Brother:
"We want to organize an auxiliary missionary society on this circuit, and if it is within your province to do so, and will not take too much of your time, I wish you would give me a plan . . . how to organize and what to do afterward to make the meetings interesting and successful. Shall we call it 'The Woman's Missionary Society' as they do in the M. E. Church? Any suggestions you can make will be thankfully received."[11]

The Assistant Missionary Secretary, T. B. Arnold, replied that the church had no such organization and proposed that Mrs. MacGeary prepare a constitution for one.[12] The official historical survey of the society credits Mrs. MacGeary with founding the very first such society at Verona. This is no doubt correct. But four years earlier a missionary society with thirty members was organized at Chili, New York, to continue interest in Louisa Ranf, former student there, appointed to India. There was an annual membership fee of one dollar.[13] The next year, following the untimely and unexpected death of Mary Carpenter in Liberia, the Chili society took the name, "Mary E. Carpenter Missionary Society." They reported fifty-five members and $71.00 raised.

The Role of Women

Women have played an important role in the Free Methodist venture around the world. Mrs. E. F. Ward had saved five hundred dollars from school teaching. This she gave for the outgoing expenses of her husband and herself, first Free Methodist missionaries to India. The first reference to "foreign missions" in the records of the General Missionary Board relates to Mrs. Anna Romack, donor of $75.00. Inadvertently the money was used for evangelism. With no money in the treasury and a deficit due the treasurer, the Board voted to return to the president this amount of money for forwarding to the foreign field.[14] India was the only Free Methodist field at that time, and by coincidence, three of the five men present were members of the Illinois Conference where Ward also held his membership. It is easy to believe that this seventy-five dollars found its way to India, the donation of a *woman!* The first officially appointed missionary was a woman, Louisa Ranf, a martyr to missions.[15] She rendered noble service, enduring privation and hardship with joy. Women soon proved to be valuable agents for the collection of missions funds. The General Conference assessment of "ten cents per member" for conference missions (evangelism) was not being sent promptly to the treasurer. The alert Missionary Board took action, urging the collection of the disciplinary amount from each member "and that whenever practicable a *female* member of our church" be the collector.[16]

Penny-A-Day—1891

With the official approval of the General Conference to organize Woman's Missionary Societies, the Secretary encouraged such activity. Emma Freeland while a student at Wellesley College came under the influence of the Student Volunteer Movement. She wrote Missionary Secretary Kelley on June 23, 1891, referring to "the subject of which I wrote you." Miss Freeland agreed with the Secretary concerning "organized missionary giving." She suggested that the Sunday schools can "do a great deal," adding "If fifty persons were to give a cent a day, it would support a missionary with nearly the salary allowed by the American Board. By taking pledges of those who would give a cent a day, two cents, etc., and providing them with boxes for their savings, the missionary impulse would be continued."[17] Even though she had borrowed money to attend college, Miss Freeland was ready to travel for the Board, organizing Woman's Missionary Societies and raising funds for missions. In this work she was to be successful for many, many years. Miss Freeland explained to the Secretary:

> "I should wish to be duly authorized by the Board. I have no sympathy with independent movements that take away interest and means from the legitimate channels. The local W.M.S. would be auxiliary to the General Board and the secretaries confer with you as you suggested."[18]

Roberts and Kelley furnished her with a document authorizing her to establish such societies.[19]

Across the church, women were busily engaged organizing the missionary societies. Long and sharp debate at the General Conferences only resulted in a refusal to ordain women preachers. But foreign missions offered them an avenue of service and they had the official blessing of the General Conference in doing it.

Getting Started

Missionary Secretary Kelley retired for health reasons in 1893, and J. G. Terrill succeeded in the office. He aggressively promoted the organization of the woman's societies. At some places there was opposition. Terrill thought this was strange since "these societies have the approval of the General Mission Board of the church and of the Executive Committee."[20] He might have added that the General Conference had authorized their organization. A Woman's Foreign Missionary Society was reported at Brantford, Ontario, with twenty-one members and twelve honorary, organized in May, 1892.[21] Miss Emma Freeland addressed a letter to "Dear sister workers," reminding them that long ago B. T. Roberts wanted a Woman's Missionary Society, and exhorted: "Let us unite our forces." She suggested a missionary prayer meeting each month.[22] Newcastle, Pennsylvania, started with seven members. Soon there were thirty. They reported a Sunday evening missionary meeting, an offering of $7.56, and eight missionary volunteers.[23] Exhorted Mrs. MacGeary: "My sisters, let us put on courage, keep this matter before the people on all suitable occasions, and we shall succeed in our part of this effort. . . . Jesus will help if you try."[24]

"Wanted!" wrote the assistant secretary, "An application from every Free Methodist circuit which has not yet organized a Woman's Foreign Missionary Society, for copies of our printed constitution for such societies."[25] At Seattle there was a society of twenty-two members that raised $75.00.[26] Ransom, Michigan, had ten members. Meetings were held in the homes, collection envelopes were used to "Do without for Jesus' sake" as "advised by Sister Freeland."[27] The local societies in some instances effected conference organizations. In 1892 one such was established in Dakota with five societies and sixty-six members. The next year Mrs. Grace Webb reported the annual meeting of the Wisconsin W.F.M.S.[28]

The second annual meeting of the Pittsburgh Conference society was held in 1893.[29] Missionary Secretary Terrill was present with "information and encouragement." An offering of $350 was received. At Linden, there were sixteen members, opposition was decreasing, interest increasing, with seven dollars in contributions.[30] At Topeka, Kansas, there were fifteen members.[31] But it was not enough to organize missionary societies. There must be a program. Mrs. MacGeary gave some suggestions:

> "The secretary of one of our Woman's Missionary Societies writes for suggestions of topics for monthly missionary meetings. Most any book of travels in Africa and India will furnish material for a large number of topics. Descriptions of the country—its relative size, its topography, its peoples, history of exploration, etc., etc., will be of interest and instructive. There are various histories of missions, biographies of missionaries, gleanings from which would add interest to missionary meetings. These various topics might be assigned to different individuals to prepare papers on them. The young people may be enlisted in this with profit to them and the cause. Added to the foregoing might be the consideration of ways and means of helping the missionaries."[32]

She also suggested a meeting of missionary society members to be held at the General Conference:

"There ought to be a meeting at Greenville during the General Conference of members of the Woman's Missionary Societies to consider what improvements can be made in the constitution and bylaws of the societies, and to perfect the organization. The Missionary Secretary suggests that each conference organization authorize some of their members who may attend, to act as delegates."[33]

The General Society

During the quadrennium a "greatly increased interest" in "both the general and foreign missions work" was evidenced by increased contributions.[34] J. G. Terrill, the Missionary Secretary, was made editor of the *General Conference Daily*. On Monday, October 15, he inserted the following notice:

"All interested in the Woman's Foreign Missionary Society should be on the watch for an announcement for a meeting of representatives of these societies, to be held this week."

Tuesday the conference voted down the ordination of women. Four days later on Saturday the *Conference Daily* announced that—

"This afternoon at two o'clock there will be a meeting of the members of the Woman's Foreign Missionary Societies held in the college chapel. . . . Our object is to form a central organization so as to unify the entire work and give it all the effective force possible."[35]

On Monday following, the *Daily* reported on this Saturday afternoon meeting:

"The Missionary Secretary was requested to preside at the meeting. Mrs. M. L. Coleman was elected secretary. The Missionary Secretary stated the object of the meeting.

"A committee on nominations of permanent officers for a general society was appointed, consisting of Mesdames Hart, Barnhart, Beers. Also a committee on constitution, consisting of Chesbro, Arnold, Sage.

"Another meeting was ordered for today (Monday) at 1:30 p.m., the place to be announced."[36]

On Monday the necessary business was cared for. On Tuesday the *Daily* reported:

"The Woman's Foreign Missionary Society has perfected its organization, elected its officers, completed a constitution and by-laws, and will report to the General Conference through the committee on missions."[37]

The Missionary Secretary, temporary editor of the *Daily*, commended the missionary women:

"They have done glorious work during the short time of their existence,

119

though many of the number were without experience in such work when they began. The Missionary Board has been quite dependent on them during the financial depression that has been upon us. God bless them."[38]

General Conference Approval

This General Conference officially recognized the missionary society work by placing Mrs. Mary L. Coleman, the president of the Wisconsin Conference W.F.M.S., on the committee on missions. She was appointed by that committee to prepare the report on the woman's organizations. She was likewise requested to read that portion of the report to the General Conference, and it was adopted without a single dissenting vote.

"Thus the organization becomes a part of the church organization. . . . Now, therefore, let everybody, preachers and members, take hold and work with the women who are doing so nobly for the cause. None can say that it is not an institution of the church, nor a part of the church, for it is; and those who are at work in these societies are doing the work the church wants them to do. God bless them."[39]

Mrs. B. T. Roberts was elected the first president of the general society, Mrs. E. P. Hart was first vice-president, and Mrs. Ella MacGeary corresponding secretary. The public missionary meeting featured addresses by Ida Heffner, Grace Allen, and Harry Agnew. An offering of $150 was requested to provide Miss Allen and her helper, Martha Isaacs, each a horse, saddle and bridle. "When the money was counted we had $164 and one saddle and one bridle."[40] This service was "one of the most enthusiastic of the whole General Conference."[41]

Grace Allen,
"circuit rider"

Foreign Missions Strengthens the Church

The proper emphasis on foreign missions always brings rewards to the church that obeys our Lord's command. The Christian paradox of losing life and finding it is demonstrated in the depression years of the quadrennium 1890-1894 when, largely through the activities of the newly organized missionary societies, contributions for foreign missions were doubled. However, for the same period, the collections for home evangelism tripled![42] The promotion of foreign missions strengthened the home church.

The W.F.M.S. was immediately harnessed to tasks near at hand. In South Dakota many church members were without adequate food and clothing for the winter. Some were unable to attend church. Second-hand clothing, including "boots and shoes especially for children," was needed most. The Missionary Secretary turns this first project over to the newly organized Woman's Missionary Society with the suggestion that—

"Doubtless many outside the church would help. Merchants will give remnants of cloth, shoes shelf-worn and out of date. . . . Some of our societies might make up garments . . . for the wives and mothers in the northwest."[43]

As every pastor will testify, some of the most effective community service, home visitation and church outreach is through an efficient woman's missionary organization. If the societies will keep to their main business, they will succeed. The General Conference action approving their constitution should "certainly disarm all fear of an independent organization. . . . Strive not so much to entertain," advises Ella MacGeary, "as to instruct and convict the young people. Leave plenty of room in your program for the Holy Ghost."[44]

Success

From the beginning the work of this society has been blessed in a remarkable degree. The year following the approval of a general organization something over $2,000 was raised. This amount was doubled in each succeeding year, making a total of $18,497.54 for the quadrennium. The General Missionary Board was frank to admit that the accomplishments were "beyond our most sanguine expectation."[45] Even at the close of the first year the Missionary Board voted to "extend to these intelligent and energetic toilers the assurance of our high appreciation," trusting that "the formation of these societies be rapidly extended throughout all our borders."[46] Contributions to Free Methodist missions, largely through the work of the W.F.M.S., almost tripled during the next quadrennium, and rapidly increased each succeeding quadrennium until 1923-1926. During the depression years contri-

WMS Executive Committee, 1938. Seated, left to right: Mrs. Emma S. Hogue, Mrs. Carrie T. Burritt, Mrs. Emma Freeland Shay. Standing, left to right: Mrs. Jenne H. Howland, Miss Alice E. Walls, Mrs. Mabel J. Moyer, Mrs. Ella Maze Daniels, Mrs. Evaline D. Green, Miss Helen I. Root, Mrs. Edna McCarty.

butions dropped to half of their former level. Since the 1943-1946 period when there was a half-million dollar gain over the previous quadrennium, there has been a net gain of from $200,000 to $300,000 reported each quadrennial period. Currently 65 per cent of the missionary budget comes through the channels of the Woman's Missionary Society. Since 1894 they have raised more than eight and one-half million dollars for Free Methodist missions! As important and necessary as is finance, other activities must be mentioned.

Study and Service

The necessity of a missionary magazine was considered by the Missionary Board in 1894 and referred to the Executive Committee. At first a missionary supplement was proposed for *The Free Methodist*. Later the Board urged the W.F.M.S. to elect an editor for *The Missionary Tidings*, who was to be approved by a special committee of the Board. The first issue was published in January, 1898. Today the subscription list exceeds 27,000. The mission study program has resulted in an informed corps of missionary workers throughout the denomination. In a recent year 95,000 books were read! The stewardship department organizes food and clothing shipments to charitable institutions and needed supplies are sent to mission dispensaries and hospitals. Several thousand such shipments are processed annually. The Young People's Missionary Society was sponsored by the Woman's Society until 1931, when it was transferred to the Commission on Christian Education. The Junior Missionary Society was first organized on a local basis in 1895. There are now

122

approximately 25,000 members in 885 societies. The aims of the Junior organization are:

1. To win boys and girls to Christ.
2. To instruct them about our church and its program of missions.
3. To guide them in giving their lives in service to others both at home and abroad.

This remarkable group contributes annually approximately $70,000 to missions.

The production of missionary literature is most important. Information is basic in continuing and extending the denomination's overseas witness. More than fifty books have been published under the sponsorship of the Woman's Missionary Society and the Free Methodist Publishing House. These are books written either by the church's missionaries or about their work.

Prayer for Missions

Other important services include the organization of hundreds of prayer groups, home visitation, sewing for the needy, and the development of a systematic program of support for the overseas work. "Prayer for Missions" is an organizational responsibility of the Stewardship Secretary. The plan functions as follows:

"Under the Stewardship Department there are two important plans: 1. *Prayer Partners* are those for whom we promise to earnestly pray by *name*. Our missionaries urge and appreciate this. When Prayer Partners were first reported in 1935, there were thirty-two. By 1959 the number had grown to 30,741. Active and honorary members, friends and neighbors, cooperate. To add interest, "pencil sketches" (pictures, brief accounts of location and work) are most valuable. Although it is not required, frequently birthday cards, Christmas cards and small gifts, are sent. Lengthy individual answers from the field are not encouraged, but form letters are most welcome, since they contain much of human interest and also up-to-date prayer requests.

"2. *Prayer Circles.* What is a prayer circle? A group of two, three, or more who meet weekly, if possible, or at least once a month to pray for missionary personnel, problems or situations. Some groups meet before the Sunday evening service. Many use one church prayer meeting a month. Some on larger circuits meet in various areas of the city. Sometimes there is a stated time when those who cannot meet with them join their prayer time at home. Shut-ins, those far from the church, and mothers of small children appreciate this opportunity.

"Many prayer circles were already functioning in 1931 when Mrs. Evaline D. Green took office as Home Missions Secretary. In 1932 the first prayer circles were reported, totaling 227. The number in 1959 was 1070. The goal set by Mrs. Lillian B. Griffith prior to 1931 remains the same today—'A prayer circle on every local.'

"A World Day of Prayer promoter is elected by the Executive Committee of the Woman's Missionary Society.

"In both plans it is well to know the many sources for subjects of prayer. We would mention the *Free Methodist, Missionary Tidings*, form and personal letters from missionaries, mission study books, the daily papers, other churches' periodicals, deputation addresses and, more recently, information from the growing number of enthusiastic missionary-minded pastors.

"The stirring, urgent appeal for a great increase in missionary prayer was expressed by James Gilmore of Mongolia who said, 'Unprayed for, I feel like a diver at the bottom of a river with no air to breathe, or like a fireman on a blazing building with an empty hose.' "[47]

The Woman's Missionary Society hold membership on the Missionary Board (Commission) and have proposed many significant policies which have been adopted. They took the initiative in bringing the Home Missions work to the attention of the Board and have been most active in the development of this aspect of the program. Their influence has made missions the central concern of the church. This is the pattern of the New Testament church as described in the Book of Acts.

United in a Great Cause

The missionary society is of great value to the women themselves. It is good for women to leave their kitchens, study the problems of the world, pray for world revival, unite in service and sacrifice for the deep needs of millions without the gospel. The psychological value of such activity is incalculable. It helps the women if not one conversion is ever reported. But it does have overseas value as well. Thousands of converts in the younger churches bear powerful witness to this fact.

The woman's organization has unified the women of the church by giving them a common purpose and aim. The objectives of the society are:

1. To promote missionary intelligence.
2. To deepen interest in world evangelism.
3. To secure systematic contributions for missions.

In 1890 the church was suffering from serious divisions. There were several journals published by Free Methodists, all claiming to be the "genuine," and advocating special causes. There were Bible school programs, city missions, and an independent missionary society. Amazingly enough, *The Free Methodist* opened its columns to answer criticisms. A running debate was carried on with the organ of the rival missionary society. The cause of Free

Methodist missions was almost defeated. Other factors enter in, but a church-wide missionary society with a single aim to which its members are fully committed has done more to unify the church than the death of certain rugged individualists or the pronouncements of General Conferences. The members of the women's societies are the wives of laymen, pastors, superintendents, general officers, and general superintendents (bishops). After reading hundreds of articles in the denominational paper, and contrasting the spirit of 1890 with even 1904 or 1910, the author is convinced that the twenty-six thousand members of the Woman's Missionary Society have been more effective than any other one influence in unifying the church and keeping its vision clear regarding the main business of the kingdom.

Miss Mabel Cook, Office Secretary, General Missionary Board, 1912

WOMEN IN MISSIONS

Books listed in *Lights in the World* bibliography of Free Methodist missions—69
Books by or about women—30 (43%)

PERCENTAGE OF WOMEN MISSIONARIES

	Men	Wives	Single Women	Total	Percentage of Women
1902	10	8	7	25	60%
1920	38	32	40	110	65%
1940	31	32	38	101	69%
1960	58	59	45	162	64%

SUMMARY

Of all appointments made 1885-1959:

Men	Wives	Single Women	Total	Percentage of Women
166	149	157	472	64.8%

NEW FIELDS

Where Women Were Either the First Superintendent,
or the First Appointed Missionary

1885—India ....Louisa Ranf, Julia Zimmerman, first Board appointees
1891—India ....Celia J. Ferries, first Board-appointed superintendent
1891—South Africa ....Grace Allen and A. D. Noyes, established field
1893—Dominican Republic ....Esther D. Clark, first Board appointee
1905—China................Clara Leffingwell, superintendent and founder
1913—Pacific Coast Japanese....Bertha Ahlmeyer
1914—Kentucky Mountains ....E. E. O'Connor, founder of first permanent work
1917—Mexican Missions........Nella True, superintendent and founder
1941—Tampa Spanish.........Ruth Landin with E. E. Shelhamer, founders
1946—Brazil ....Lucile Damon, first missionary

WOMEN WHO HAVE SERVED AS DIRECTORS OF INSTITUTIONS
(Past and Present)

AFRICA

CONGO
Nyankanda Leper Colony....Esther F. Kuhn, M.D.
Kibuye Hospital ....Esther F. Kuhn, M.D.
Kibuye Station School ......Elizabeth E. Cox, Evelyn Rupert
Teacher Training School ....Elizabeth E. Cox, Evelyn Rupert
Muyebe Central School......Estelle Orcutt, Eileen Moore
Usumbura Schools ....Elizabeth E. Cox
Kibogora Station School ....Ila Gunsolus
Kibogora Clinic ....Margaret Holton, R.N., Elizabeth Van Sickle, R.N., Myra Adamson, R.N.

126

PORTUGUESE EAST
Girls' Boarding School ...... Margaret Nickel, Mae Armstrong
Rudimentary School .... Mae Armstrong, Adelaide Latshaw,
           Verna Tite, Esther Clemens
Inhamachafo Clinic .... Florence Carter, R.N.,
           Georgia Slosser, R.N.
Massinga Clinic .... Kathryn R. Smith, R.N.,
           Marguerite Palmer, M.D.
SOUTH AFRICA
Fairview Girls' School ...... Grace Allen
Ebenezer Clinic .... Mary Current, R.N.
Edwaleni Technical College.. Gertrude Haight
SOUTHERN RHODESIA
Lundi Central School ...... Daisy Frederick, Ruth Smith
Lundi Clinic .... Nina Detwiler, R.N.
Chikombedzi Clinic .... Naomi Pettengill, M.D.

ASIA

INDIA
Yeotmal Station School...... Edna Puffer
Umri Boarding School ...... Loretta Root, Jessie Yardy
Girls' Orphanage .... Celia J. Ferries McMurry
Bible School .... Grace Barnes
Mobile Medical Unit ...... Helen Rose, R.N.
CHINA
Kaifeng Bible School .... Florence Murray
Grinnell Memorial Hospital.. Alta Sager-Green, M.D.
Refugee School .... Edith Frances Jones
Chengchow Middle School .. Geneva Sayre

LATIN AMERICA

DOMINICAN REPUBLIC
Lincoln School for Girls .... Nellie Whiffen
Mission Press .... Helen Abrams
School for Missionaries'
  Children .... Ruth Mills, Ruth Hessler
School Dispensary .... Rachel Smiley, R.N.
PARAGUAY
Asuncion Clinic .... Elizabeth Reynolds, R.N.
Orphanage .... Ruth Foy
School for Missionaries'
  Children .... Lucy Huston

HOME MISSIONS

Tampa Friendship School. . . . Ruth Landin, Helen Crawford
Oakdale Christian High
   School . . . . Myrtle Anderson, Jennie Greider
Mexican Day School. . . . . . . .Mildred Leatherman
San Antonio Day School . . . . Ruth Tarin

CONTRIBUTIONS THROUGH THE WOMAN'S MISSIONARY SOCIETY

Quadrennium
  Ending

1898. . . . .$	18,497.00
1902.	45,673.00
1906.	96,297.00
1910.	166,401.00
1914.	184,570.00
1918.	253,814.00
1922.	509,837.00
1926.	499,082.00
1930.	455,136.00
1934.	270,980.00
1938.	312,622.00
1942.	393,481.00
1946.	910,720.00
1950.	1,135,820.00
1954.	1,453,827.00
1958.	1,789,867.00

IV

Independent

Ventures

Overseas

While Bishop William Taylor was advocating and establishing "self-supporting" missions in South America, Africa and India, his work was closely followed and favorably reported in the denominational journal. However, in 1885, sensing possibly the peril of unrestrained and independent activity, the editor printed an illuminating appraisal of Taylor, who was a bishop of the Methodist Church. He had raised $25,000 in the States and $9,000 in Britain for his missions, diverting this money from the regular mission treasury of his denomination. He seemed to be in the Methodist Church, but not of it, a wheel within a wheel, a sort of ecclesiastical comet, a blazing nucleus that whirls near the sun, then darting off into infinite space bids "farewell, slow plodding planets" only to return a century later exclaiming, "You see, I belong to this solar system."[1] In spite of close-knit organization and sometimes overweight of supervision, Free Methodists too have displayed a genius for independent action. A movement has life. God speaks to men. When they obey, sometimes they are far along with the assignment before anybody thinks about official approval.

It is this free lance activity that needs our consideration. What are the meanings and implications of such enterprises? What do they tell us about the past? Are there lessons for the future?

E. F. Ward went to India before the church had officially adopted any plans for foreign work. Three years later, King Tappa's call from Liberia resulted in the establishment of work in that country, with the tacit consent but not official approval of the Missionary Board. V. A. Dake, founder of the Pentecost Bands Movement, shared with the Board his sense of call to

129

Vivian A. Dake

Africa. The church took no action to send him. Subsequently, he organized bands of earnest workers for the work of home evangelism. More than one hundred young people were working in his movement at the height of its influence, supplementing the regular activities of the pastors and district chairmen. He organized great summer camps on an interdenominational basis but with a large core of Free Methodism at the center. Eventually, frustrated by the slow-moving denominational program, he raised the necessary funds to send Missionary Bands to Norway, Liberia and India. He organized a Free Methodist Church at Durrenentzen, Germany, holding the first Free Methodist society meeting there on June 5, 1889.[2] This same year Samuel Mills went to the Dominican Republic as a self-supporting missionary, and Robert Shemeld was refusing to follow the instructions of his home board and even attempted to take his case to the people and procure financing for his mission in spite of the denomination's plans for him and his work.

The first officially sponsored missionaries went to Southern Africa. We have already noted the dissatisfaction of D. W. Abrams over this turn of events. Tappa's call had come from Liberia. Money had been raised on that appeal, but the missionaries had not gone to Tappa's land. Abrams again presented the cause of Liberia in *The Free Methodist* and raised enough money to send a small band there on an independent basis. Once in Liberia, the individualism of pioneer missionaries exhibited itself in their inability to agree on the best location for their field. The Board urged them to respond to Tappa's call even though necessary to divide the band. S. V. Ulness, who went to Norway under the Pentecost Bands, ultimately was received as a regular Board missionary. An appropriation was requested for work in England.[3] Proposals were received to initiate work in South America,[4] and to recognize the independent mission of A. P. Miller in Portuguese East Africa.[5] The latter was referred to the missionaries who recommended he continue on an independent basis, since distances would make it impractical to unite the two fields. The same year the Rev. and Mrs. Fred Fletcher went to China, where they opened an orphanage that was largely supported by the *Christian Herald*. Shortly thereafter they were accepted as regular Board missionaries and were among the most successful of that field.

Independent thinking and acting were not the activity of an irresponsible fringe of malcontents. An editor of *The Free Methodist* urged the sending of a delegate to the Methodist Ecumenical Conference to be held at City Road Chapel, London. The conference purpose was "to devise means to prosecute home and foreign work with economy and efficiency, to increase the moral and evangelical power of a common Methodism" and "to secure the most speedy conversion of the world."[6] Roberts also called attention to the same conference, but *The Free Methodist* editor independently went further by declaring that—

"For various reasons it would be to the advantage of the Free Methodist Church to be represented at this conference . . . form acquaintances with Wesleyan Methodists, Primitive Methodists . . ."

so that when any of these came to America, they might contact the Free Methodist Church. He adds:

"We have long felt that some representative man should visit Europe and open work there, and this conference seems to afford a favorable occasion for an introduction."

This was proposed by the editor five years before Board missionaries were sent to Africa or India, and even before Ward blazed the overseas trail to India! It was nine years later that Dake's organization of a Free Methodist Church in Germany occurred. Succeeding issues of the paper carried on a vigorous debate on this question, with generous space given to proponents of both sides of the controversy. To have a matter that involved delicate denominational policy and the opening of church work in Europe made a matter of church-wide discussion in the church paper before any official pronouncement is made seems strange indeed. Such was the faith in democracy

131

and the reverence for independent thought and action. It was both the weakness and strength of the new movement.

The Pentecost Bands

Ten years later such "independent thought and action" was getting out of hand. The autonomous "wheel within a wheel" activities were coming into conflict with the regular work of local societies and conferences. Competitive Pentecost Band camp meetings and revival efforts divided and weakened rather than contributed strength to the young church. The sending of Band missionaries overseas involved the raising of thousands of dollars from Free Methodist churches whose money was desperately needed to support the slowly developing foreign missions program of the denomination. Taking cognizance of this situation, the committee on missions at the 1890 General Conference reported that in view of the—

> "rapidly increasing interest in missions we recommend all our ministers carry out the provision of the Discipline on the subject of missions by holding meetings and organizing auxiliary societies in every circuit . . . to educate the people in giving and thus raise the desired amount (by voluntary contributions) for missionary support. . . . It would serve also to direct the liberality of our people into the regularly organized channels of the church. We greatly regret that it is not so concentrated. . . ."[7]

The committee further declared that there were "two different lines of missionary work among us, each having its special advocates. . . . They antagonize each other and cause schism."[8] The conference took the following action:

1. Disapprove so-called independent work which appeals for support and antagonizes Board work.
2. The general superintendents to appoint a committee of three to confer with V. A. Dake with a view to "harmonizing his missionary movement with that of the Missionary Board, and his Band work" into unison with the doctrines of the church and the Discipline.

The committee was to present a written report on the above matters to the next session of the Illinois Conference where Dake held membership.

Let it be said that Dake and his Band workers were all members in good standing in the church. Dake himself had served as district chairman and as pastor of some of the largest churches. He also had been a student at Chili Seminary. His sense of mission and concern for the salvation of the lost knew no bounds. He wrote:

> "Wanted! Ten thousand to labor in every land. Wanted! Those who will work without salary. Wanted! Those who will take the fare by the way

and shout, 'Glory to God!' Amen! They are coming. . . . There is a call from Jamaica, West Indies. Who will fill it? There are calls from Australia, Tasmania, and New Zealand. Who will go? Calls from Sweden and Germany wait for workers. . . . Let all the faint-hearted pack their satchels and leave quickly to make room for the Gideons, the Shamgars, the Daniels, the Davids and the Deborahs, the Marys, the Priscillas, and the Dorcases, who are coming. . . . With fingers in your ears, eyes on the mark, feet on the thorny path, hands filled with pitchers and lamps, hearts aflame, on to victory! Fellow-workers, I am with you on the battlefield and will be in the triumphal march."[9]

In organizing the Bands, Dake had the blessing of B. T. Roberts, who wrote him:

"My dear son in the gospel:
"Organize your Bands. Push out. Be as aggressive as the Salvation Army, but more holy, more serious, and have no nonsense about it. Let the Holy Spirit take the place of the tambourines to draw the people. . . . We must not let the Free Methodist Church become a feeble imitation of the M. E. Church."[10]

An Evangelizing Force

In 1890 Dake's bands were a powerful evangelizing agency at home, and a strong force abroad. As yet the denomination had no full-time secretary to promote foreign missions. To an outside observer, Dake might seem to be secretary of evangelism, missionary secretary and general superintendent, all in one package.

The General Conference, anxious to conserve the good features of the Band Movement; but at the same time guard against its doctrinal deviation that some suspected, and provide better coordination of the evangelistic activities under duly elected conference leaders, adopted the following rules:

1. Chairmen of districts, and evangelists appointed by the General or Annual Conference, may organize Bands for evangelistic work; but no person shall become a member of such a Band without the recommendation of the society to which he belongs.
2. The rules and regulations of such Bands shall be subject to the approval of the annual conference to which the leader belongs, or within the bounds of which he holds his membership.
3. No evangelist or Band shall appoint or hold meetings where they will interfere with the regular work of any preacher duly appointed to a circuit, or station, or district.
4. Those who labor successfully in a Band for one year may be licensed by the quarterly conference from year to year as Band workers.[11]

The Band workers were undoubtedly a dedicated group. Some probably held extreme views, but in the main they were a revival movement in a revival church. Under the leadership of Dake, they prospered and proved a blessing to the church. Some were not satisfied, however, with their independent program. Dake's own conference, the Illinois, petitioned the next General Conference[12] to consider this

> "movement that should be tenderly cared for, and which in our judgment can be utilized properly and with the greatest and best results by its being brought into closer relation with the church."[13]

The Conference was requested "to draft such general rules as in their judgment will best aid these brethren in promoting the work of God in the Free Methodist Church."[14]

However, the General Conference felt that the action taken four years earlier was adequate. It adopted the following statement concerning the Bands which to us would seem to cover the case in a spirit of Christian love.

> "It is with no small degree of satisfaction that we notice the disposition of and effort on the part of the Pentecost Bands to come into perfect harmony with the church in their operations. We look upon them as honest, earnest brethren, and most sincerely hope the differences which have agitated us as a church in the past may be completely destroyed. However, we do not believe that this (end) can be obtained by legislation. We see no way of adopting 'rules' which will more amply provide for their operations than those which we (now) have. It is our earnest request that all our brethren throughout the church, chairmen of districts, pastors and members, extend their arms of Christian fellowship to these earnest workers, and that the Bands observe the rules on 'Bands' in our book of Discipline. This being done, we are confident all differences will adjust themselves, and peace and harmony will be restored to the church."[15]

Separation

Mr. T. H. Nelson, leader of the Bands, following Dake's death in Africa in 1892, was neither the leader nor the theologian as was his predecessor. He was a man of considerable ability but impractical and visionary.[16] He was not satisfied with the action of the General Conference. On the conference floor he complained that district chairmen were continually calling in question his theology and that of his colleagues. He felt that the action expressing—

> "our earnest request that all our brethren throughout the church, chairmen of districts, pastors, and members, extend arms of Christian fellowship to these earnest workers . . ."

was inadequate. He wanted something more than a pious hope. Nothing less than a complete vindication would satisfy. Nelson accepted the role of a martyr, stated that the conference action was not satisfactory, and with other leaders in the movement, withdrew from the Free Methodist Church to continue the work as an organization free from any denominational supervision. This action was perhaps the only one that could be taken under the circumstances. Unfortunately, a vigorous B. T. Roberts was not alive in 1894 to encourage this spiritual life movement and conserve its work to the church.

Losing the "First Love"

The rate of church growth suffered a drastic moderation from this time. To the present day, Free Methodism does not have the early evangelistic drive, the sense of mission, the sacrificial concern for saving the lost world that characterized the founders of the movement and that was incarnate in Vivian Dake. In correcting errors and regulating the fiery zeal of youthful Band workers, the church itself seemed to somehow lose its "first love" for the lost world. It is possible to be theologically and organizationally correct and at the same time to lose the fires of Pentecost essential to effective witnessing "in Jerusalem and Judea" to say nothing about the "uttermost parts of the earth."[17]

Overseas Again

On the foreign field the church had better success. Shemeld either could not or would not work under Missionary Board regulations and finally after years of controversial correspondence, withdrew. On the other hand, E. F. Ward from the first considered the Board his advisory committee and welcomed its advice "as it commends itself to us in the Lord."[18] He finally applied for status as a regular Board missionary, and was received "on trial" together with his family in 1904.[19] Shortly thereafter they became missionaries in full relation. The Liberia work gradually waned and at length disappeared. The Pentecost Band Movement in India organized an independent Board which currently operates mission work in Eritrea and Egypt, securing support from interested individuals and non-denominational independent congregations. The shadow of Vivian Dake still lives, but in no appreciable degree interferes with the denominational overseas program of the church.

The foreign missions work seems to grow more vigorously than the home base program. Are there lessons to be learned from the rapidly expanding overseas program that are applicable to work in North America? We think so.

135

Publications

The Free Methodist was the official organ of the church. Roberts, however, continued throughout his life to publish *The Earnest Christian*, a journal of holiness and evangelism, in which he made no special effort to promote the interests of his own denomination. He was an excellent writer and his paper's influence reached far beyond the bounds of Free Methodism. Other journals, edited by members of the church and each with some special interest to serve, made their appearance. Included in that category was the *Fire-Brand* of Shenandoah, Iowa. There was a close connection between this publication and the Pentecost Bands Movement. A training school was also operated here. The letterhead indicates that the *Fire-Brand* was published by the Fire-Brand Publishing Association and Faith Work. The special issues advocated are explained:

> "The *Fire-Brand* is radical in holiness, and is strictly opposed to secret societies, intemperance, the use of tobacco, tea and coffee, the wearing of gold, pearls, and costly array; church sprees, suppers, theatricals, concerts, and choirs, renting of pews, wearing of corsets, bustles, bangs, feathers and lace, ruffles, tucks, extra ribbons, etc."[20]

A student of the Bible school, making application for missionary appointment, is quite subjective in giving the secretary information concerning her call to foreign work:

> "I asked the Lord to show me if he wanted me at the *Fire-Brand*, and while I was praying there came to me a shock all through me like electricity, with the impression that this was the place. . . . That evening . . . I asked the Lord to show me in some way in a dream if He wanted me to go to Africa, and that night I saw the Lord in a dream, and I said, 'Lord, do I really have to go to Africa?' He said, 'You do.' "[21]

Other independent publications were the *Law and Gospel, Orleans Advocate, Michigan Holiness Record*, the *Life Boat*, the *Vanguard*, and *Fire and Hammer*. The last two journals espoused the cause of Free Methodist missionaries working either independently of the Board or who were having difficulties with the Board. The *Fire and Hammer* was especially concerned over the supposedly unjust treatment of Robert Shemeld. Its editor questioned the motives and veracity of B. T. Roberts who had published an article setting forth the Missionary Board position. The *Vanguard* more especially promoted interest in the Liberia Mission and D. W. Harris, its chief worker. This paper was published by a prominent Free Methodist minister in Portland, Oregon. When Noyes or Shemeld had any criticism to offer the Missionary Board, the *Vanguard* seemed to hear about it even before the Missionary Secretary, and in publishing the reports, nothing was lost with the telling. Both Roberts and Chesbrough sought to set the record straight. Roberts explained the Board policy. He personally believed, he said, in "self-supporting" missions and in a Missionary Board accountable to the church for its financial operations. He urged loyalty to the church and its missionary work with the exhortation:

"Let us have an end of all such acts of insubordination."[22]

Three months later, Chesbrough, the church treasurer, who admitted a financial misunderstanding with Missionary A. D. Noyes, but which had already been adjusted, took sharp issue with the *Vanguard* for its divisive activities. He said:

"The time has come for the editor of the *Vanguard*, while professing to be one of us, and preaching in our pulpits as a Free Methodist, to cease his warfare against the honesty and integrity of purpose of members of the Missionary Board."[23]

In answer to the charges that the meetings of the Missionary Board were held in secret, Roberts assured the *Vanguard* that the meetings were open to all.[24] Apparently the *Vanguard's* editor wanted a change of Board policy and was nominating in his paper those whom he thought should be elected to Board membership. Ebey thought it was unusual for one man to name a Board whose election was provided for by the General Conference.

Such were the trials of the first five years of foreign missions experience. Undoubtedly the spirit of division, arguing over methods, policies and personalities, weakened the fervor of the church and tended to deflect its energies from the main concerns of the kingdom.

Home Missions

Free Methodism's mission is to save the lost, to preach the gospel to the poor. This concern has resulted in diverse individualistic enterprises entailing a great investment of personnel and finance. Some of these efforts have commended themselves to the church, earning official recognition and support. The extent of such activity is another index of Free Methodism's concern for human need and its loyalty to first principles.

Between 1860 and 1880 approximately five hundred thousand immigrants from eastern and southern Europe entered the United States. In the next twenty years the number admitted was eight million! In 1891 only one thousand Japanese entered the country but in 1903 twenty thousand came to our shores. Along with the increased immigration came a concern for home missions admittedly as valid a responsibility of the church as the foreign enterprise. The needs of the home field weighed heavily on the hearts of the church leaders. Only by searching minutes of individual conferences has it been possible to present even the following partial chronology of activities:

HOME MISSION VENTURES—A CHRONOLOGY

1865 New York City: "What a field for missionary effort." (B. T. Roberts)[25]

1865 "A vast field of missionary labor is being opened in the South. The thousands emerging from slavery to freedom need the gospel. They must have it."[26]

1868 Powhatan Freedman's Mission. Rev. John Green, superintendent.

1876 Bradley Mission, Chicago, opened in the basement of Morgan Street Free Methodist Church. An article entitled "The Poor of Chicago" by B. T. Roberts appealed for a more generous support. "The want and suffering of great cities is unbelievable," he says, and reminded them of the "Inasmuch" of Matthew 25:35-38.[27]

1880 Kansas Freedman Mission.

1882 Mission College for Kansas freedmen.

1885 German work started in New York City.

1886 Oregon "Sloop"—River Mission.

1888 Gerry, New York, Orphanage and Home.

1889 Chicago Industrial Home for Children.

1889 French Mission. Quebec, Canada. Conference action.

1889 Ohio River Boat—Floating Chapel, seats 700. Ministering to both Negro and white. (I. R. B. Arnold)

1890 Colored work in St. Louis.

1890 French Mission, Los Angeles.

1891 Swedish work, Chicago (J. D. Kelsey, A. F. Hall).

1894 Pentecost Training School, St. Louis (T. H. Nelson).

1895 Providence Mission and Rescue Home, Pittsburgh.

1899 $800 received for Swedish Mission.

1903 Rest Home, Woodstock, Illinois.

1904 St. Louis Mission, J. H. F. Flower, pastor and superintendent. Located in the worst part of the city. Large crowds attend. Many cannot find a seat.

1905 Indian work, southern California.

1906 Scandinavian Mission, Illinois.

1908 Renew local preacher's license of worker in Mexico (Texas Conference).

1910 Home Missions Secretary, Mrs. Adelaide Beers.

1910 First appropriation for Home Missions work—$10 per month, G. M. B. Equal amount by W. F. M. S. "if needed"(!).

1911 Mexican Boys' School approved, Los Angeles.

1911 Italian work near Albion, New York.
1911 $2,000 gift; Home Missions committee.
1912 Alaska, R. M. Whitcomb of Washington Conference in government service, with his wife, doing missionary work.
1912 Kentucky Mountains.
1912 Mexican Missions School, Los Angeles, impractical.
1913 Chinese Mission, Los Angeles, N. S. Honn.
1913 Japanese work, southern California.
1913 Mexican work. Financed jointly by G. M. B. and W. F. M. S. No personnel. Unwise to start now.
1914 Ellis Island. Grace Barnes, Brooklyn Church, in charge.
1914 Japanese, Seattle, W. F. Matthewson.
1915 Kentucky Mission reopened. E. E. O'Connor.
1916 Home Missions week observance.
1916 Mexican Missions, Los Angeles. Nella True. $20 per month, one-half by W. F. M. S.
1918 Japanese, Berkeley, California.
1919 Mexican Church, Chino, California. Sunday school in "Dogtown" section, Los Angeles.
1919 Japanese work, San Francisco.
1919 Scholarships for two Italians preparing to evangelize their own people.
1922 B. H. Pearson, superintendent of Mexican Missions.
1923 Hospital, Mexican Missions.
1925 Indians, Gallup, New Mexico, Carl Volgamore.
1931 Mexican Provisional Conference.
1932 Japanese Conference.
1939 Nogales Bible School, Mexican Missions.
1941 Florida Spanish Mission, Tampa, Florida.
1943 Northern Ontario, Canada.
1948 Texas Latin American, San Antonio, Texas.
1952 Saskatchewan Indians, Broadview.
1958 Province of Quebec.

Venture in Planning

The long list of home mission projects indicates the church's concern. It represents an outpouring of life and material resource on a large scale, considering the size of the denomination. What are the implications of this feature of the church activity for future denominational policy?

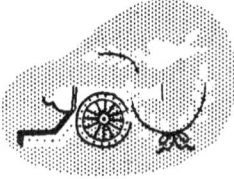

World War I —

The Larger Concern,

1918-1930

Causes of World War I

The alliances of pre-1914 Europe, the competition for world markets, the armaments race, national pride, and fear created the conditions that one assassination turned into a world war. Germany, Austria-Hungary and Italy, the Central Powers, were pledged to mutual aid, while Russia, France and Britain were allied in the Triple Entente, better known in America simply as the Allies. On June 28, 1914, Archduke Francis Ferdinand, heir to the throne of Austria, and his wife, visiting in Bosnia, were shot by a young Bosnian-Serb. Austria waited a month before taking action, meanwhile securing from Germany assurances of assistance. A forty-eight hour ultimatum was given Serbia to suppress all anti-Austrian propaganda and influence, and allow Austrian officials to sit in Serbian courts and try the guilty. Serbia agreed to every stipulation but the last, which she suggested be referred to the Hague Tribunal. Austria, bent on breaking Serbian power, refused the answer, declared war on Serbia, July 28.

Russia, friendly to Serbia, began to mobilize. Germany, interpreting this as an unfriendly act, declared war on Russia (August) and demanded a statement from France on her position. It was indecisive. So Germany promptly declared war on France, and in a hurry to strike first, occupied neutral Luxembourg. When Belgium refused to allow passage of German troops through her territory, the German army proceeded by force. Britain, pledged to aid France and Belgium, declared war on Germany on August 4. Japan declared war on Germany in November. Turkey joined the Central Powers. The war years 1914-1918 have been called "The Four Longest Years in History."

The United States' Decision

A high school boy's recollections of this period are most vivid. Europe hardly existed for us in pre-1914 times, except at Christmas when we became aware of Germany, the Santa Claus Toyland of the world. The main facts that finally influenced America's entrance into the war on the side of the Allies were: (1) that the Central Powers had taken the initiative in declaring war; (2) the freedom of the seas had been challenged; (3) our dubious trade with "neutrals" was menaced by the intensive German submarine warfare which at last was unrestricted; (4) and the leadership of Woodrow Wilson, to "make the world safe for democracy." Mr. Herbert Asquith, speaking in the House of Commons, referred to the American decision to aid the Allies in glowing terms. He said:

"I doubt whether even now the world realizes the full significance of the step America has taken. I do not use language of flattery or exaggeration when I say it is one of the most disinterested acts in history."

Whether or not it was, the people of this country felt that way about it. We gladly wore cast-off and patched clothing, used sugar sparingly or went without, denied ourselves what we think of as necessities, for the crusade— a world safe for democracy. In five Liberty Bond drives more than $21,500,-000,000 was loaned to the government. On July 4, 1918, one hundred ships were launched on that one day, so effective was the industrial participation in the war effort. By July, 1918, there were one million of our soldiers in France and in November that number was doubled. Our participation was for a relatively short time, and the losses small. In the Civil War there were 600,000 casualties as contrasted with 126,000 in this conflict. In relation to the combined armies of sixty million, with twenty-one million wounded and eight and one-half million dead, American participation was hardly more than a token. However, it was just enough to make the balance of power needed to bring the bloody holocaust to a speedy end.

Losing the Peace

If America won the war it is now clear that she lost the peace. Or perhaps nobody ever wins in any war. The world was not safe for democracy, as the subsequent rise of dictators revealed. Wilson's whole conception of a League of Nations, the 1920 equivalent of the United Nations, was too advanced for American acceptance. Unfortunately, foreign policy became a political football. Brokenhearted, Wilson was in some real sense killed by his political opponents who defeated the League of Nations idea. The powerful America of 1917 became a fearful mouse in 1921. Refusing the responsibilities and opportunities of world leadership, the Congress declared—

"The state of war declared to exist between the Imperial German Government and the United States of America by the joint resolutions of Congress, approved April 6, 1917, is hereby declared at an end."[1]

The war changed America from a debtor to a creditor nation to the extent of approximately ten billion dollars. There were high prices and general prosperity in 1918. National prohibition became the law of the land in 1919 when the States ratified the Eighteenth Amendment. The next year woman suffrage was likewise approved. The stock market went sky high as many of the sixty-five million Liberty Bond owners caught the fever of wild speculation. First, tired of idealism, we at last wearied of material prosperity, and in 1929 the long predicted depression struck. The "safe" realists, the hard-headed businessmen who had "killed" the Wilson idealism of a decade earlier now marched to their own funeral. The fruits of war are spiritual also. Noble ideals faded, the high vision was lost, the more mundane task of getting a living and as much more as possible took over. "Things in the Saddle"[2] describes the post-war decade. It was also called the "Decade of Liquidation." It was the mission of Harding to liquidate the war, Coolidge to do the same for the scandals of the Harding regime, while the unfortunate Hoover witnessed the disappearance of the Coolidge prosperity.

Post-War Missions

What was happening to the church during these eventful years? Christianity was becoming a social force in the life of the nation. Prohibition and woman suffrage were ideals advocated by church leaders for many years.

As for the Free Methodists—

1. *It was a period of marked advance for the overseas work.* The stark reality of the so-called Christian nations engaged in a world-wide struggle of incredible cruelty with widespread suffering beyond description, gave a new meaning and sense of mission to the whole overseas effort. It was more than the transplantation of a few churches to foreign soil. The regeneration of individual persons must issue in the transformed world. The church is beginning to understand that nations must "manifest the spirit of the kingdom of righteousness," and that instead of "strife and tumult throughout the world," the "paramount need everywhere is the gospel of righteousness and the enthronement of the Prince of Peace in men's hearts."[3] The world-wide proclamation of the gospel is as essential for our own salvation as it is for those to whom it is sent. In 1920 the Board meetings were in session on Armistice Day. The general officers of the W.F.M.S., facing east, engaged in earnest petition "to God for help for the nation and for the war sufferers."[4] The missionary task was being conceived of in relation to the future history of the world.

2. *There was a closer cooperation with other church agencies.* The very first establishment of Free Methodist missions in Portuguese East Africa was by invitation of and with assistance from American Board missionaries. The Board had elected B. T. Roberts and T. B. Arnold delegates to the 1888 World Missions Conference in London.[5] Roberts attended the conference and participated in the program, giving a short address on "The Place of Female Agency in Mission Work." Appropriations were made on several occasions to establish a New York office for the Foreign Missions Conference, and delegates were regularly sent to its annual meetings. In 1917 the W.F.M.S. cooperated in the interdenominational Winona Lake School of Missions, and two years later sent delegates to the Student Volunteers Convention. Both Winget and MacGeary served as denominational reporters for the *Missionary Review of the World*. A cooperative medical program was approved in Portuguese East Africa in 1917.

In 1916 Dr. Grinnell was associated with the C.I.M. Hospital at Kaifeng, China. General approval was given that same year for a united Bible school in Japan with the Christian and Missionary Alliance Mission.[6] In a response to Booker T. Washington's invitation, the Missionary Secretary was sent to the International Conference at Tuskegee Institute, called to consider the improvement of the Negro in the West Indies and Africa.[7] The China missionaries were urged to cooperate with the China Medical Missionary Association in "every possible way."[8] In 1926 W. B. Olmstead and B. H. Pearson were delegates to the El Paso Conference on the Welfare of Mexican and Spanish-speaking people, while L. G. Lewis served as Board delegate to the conference on missionary work in Africa which was held in Lezoute, Belgium.[9] Cooperation was not an end in itself. Free Methodists were eager to learn of unreached areas of need, successful methods that might be adopted, plans and procedures that would make them more effective in reaching a lost world with the gospel of redemption.

3. *There were no new overseas fields opened during the war and recovery years.* However, there was the increased interest in home missions as evidenced by the founding of the Kentucky Mountain mission, together with the opening of work on the Pacific Coast for both Japanese and Spanish-speaking peoples. This was a period to solidify gains already made, provide additional personnel on established fields, and expand the institutional work. This involved capital investments and greatly increased the annual budget.

4. *One of the most significant features of this period was the further development of Board policy to cover matters that heretofore had been subject to special action in individual cases.* Special committees were appointed by the Board to study the programs of each area. To these were referred problems for consideration and recommendations to the Board. A definite policy

on furlough salaries had been approved in 1909 whereby each missionary would receive the stated amount for one year "regardless of talents, health, or service for the Board."[10] Other policies had not yet matured.

Developing Policies a Long Process

As already indicated, the first missionaries were sent to Africa without instructions as to location, method of work, or any definite promise of salary or operating expense. It was then believed that mission stations could become self-supporting. Establishing a mission field in a foreign country was considered to be more or less equivalent to taking up government land on the Western frontier. The missionaries were the first to discover that this was impossible. Approximately four months was required for an exchange of letters. An inexperienced Board needed to ask questions. It takes time for a Board to change its mind; longer still for a church to do so, and still more time to raise money for a project not planned for. Meanwhile missionaries must live. In one way or another practically all of the first Africa Band accepted temporary employment with the American Board who needed their services, and for whom the opportunity was a very great blessing. Here the young venturers got an insight into missionary method, studied the language, received a salary which was later used in some instances to secure mission property or build residences when at long last the Free Methodist Board was willing to change its policy on "self support" and also financially able to do so.

On his furlough in 1889, Agnew explained to the Board that "much of our failure thus far in Africa is attributed to the want of system in properly caring for our missionaries after they reach their fields, and of rules to govern them in their lives and labors." He "represented the fields in Africa as white unto harvest, and expressed very strongly his determination to devote his life to the work of Christ in Africa."[11] The Board at that time prepared an agreement to be signed by all newly appointed missionaries:

It was decided that the following questions should be answered by every person offering himself to the Free Methodist Missionary Board for a foreign mission:

(1) When were you converted?
(2) Do you enjoy perfect love?
(3) Has your religious experience been uniform and satisfactory?
(4) Have you a steady faith in God and are you hopeful under difficulties, and not easily discouraged?
(5) What experience and what success have you had in laboring for souls?
(6) Do you feel called of God to the missions work?

145

(7) What is your age? Your height? Your weight?

(8) What is your constitution and the general state of your health?

(9) What have been your advantages for an education, and how have you improved them?

(10) Have you any trade? What pursuit in general demand can you follow to obtain a living?

(11) To what extent are you able and willing to help yourself in going to a mission field, and in supporting yourself after you get there?

(12) Are you willing to sign the enclosed agreement?

This agreement made this the_____ day of_____
18____ between_____ of_____
and the Missionary Board of the Free Methodist Church, witnesseth that the said_____ feeling called of God to undertake a Christian mission, does hereby agree that:

(1) He will set sail for _____ by the _____ day of 18____ or as soon thereafter as his outfit and means of transportation are furnished as hereinafter provided.

(2) That he will labor as a Christian missionary in harmony with and under direction of_____(If he is to have charge of a station, insert the name of the Board, if not, insert the name of the superintendent of the station.).

(3) That he will use all diligence to acquire a knowledge of the language of the people to whom he is sent; and will exert his influence to the utmost to persuade as many of these people as possible to become true Christians, as the terms are understood among us, and to build them up in that holiness without which no man can see the Lord.

(4) That he will, as the means are furnished and the way is opened, acquire as much real estate as may be needed for the wants of the mission, with a view to making it, as soon as possible, self-supporting. He will use due diligence to erect such buildings as may be needed, and after they are erected to keep them in good repair; to plant and properly care for fruit and shade trees adapted to the country, as may be needed and opportunity affords; to put and keep the land in a good state of cultivation; that he will procure and properly care for such domestic animals as may be needed and the condition of the country will permit; and will make all reasonable provisions to have the mission become self-supporting as fast as circumstances will allow.

(5) That he will take all proper pains to secure a good title to all such property, real or personal, as may be acquired, for the use of the mission, and have such title vested in the Free Methodist Church.

(6) That he will not only preach to the people and labor with them personally for their salvation, but as soon as Providence permits, open schools for their benefit, and teach them the elements of a Christian education. In return for such instruction he shall obtain from them such an

amount of manual labor, or native productions, as may be proper, and as may be agreed upon.

(7) That he will treat missionaries of other denominations with Christian courtesy and properly respect their rights, but form entangling alliances with none; in short, that he will keep on his own territory and attend to his own work.

(8) That he will remain upon his field of labor for at least five years, unless sooner released by the Board, except in case of war, pestilence, or such adverse providences as would in the minds of the Board and of our people generally, justify his return or his removal to another field of labor.

The said Board on its part agrees:

(1) To provide and pay over to the said _____ sum of _____ dollars, or in lieu thereof to furnish tickets of transportation to his field of labor.

(2) To furnish him with such an amount as may be agreed upon to purchase real estate, to erect and repair and furnish buildings, and to purchase domestic animals for the use of the mission.

(3) To furnish the sum of seventy-five dollars to provide clothing and personal outfit, and one hundred dollars to furnish the station and to assist him as far as is convenient in his purchases.

(4) To pay said _____ for his support the sum of _____ for the first year, the sum of _____ for the second year, and the sum of _____ for each of the three succeeding years; and such sum yearly thereafter as may be agreed upon by the contracting parties. Said payments shall be sent on the first of each quarter of the year, in drafts payable on London.

(5) The Board will cooperate with said missionary in every suitable manner to make his mission a success.[12]

It was now understood that "self-supporting" missions were not possible from the start, but the idea was not abandoned. According to the contract, the salary schedule was fixed at $400 for a couple and $250 for a single missionary, with the understanding that this would be reduced each year for a period of five years, giving time to develop a station farm to produce food and salable crops.[13] Previous to this, the support of missionaries had been by voluntary contributions,[14] which was an impossible arrangement. Additional regulations covering the work of missionaries were approved at this time.

They included directions to be followed in locating a station, the use of time, the establishment of schools and the election of superintendents. Their emphasis on conversion of the students before education has much to support it. Some of the worst enemies of the church are the mission school graduates who, as a result of their education, are simply clever pagans with

147

greater capacity for evil. On the other hand, many conversions have been registered in the schools. These first rules of 1889 have historical interest. Some were submitted by B. T. Roberts, president of the Board, others by T. B. Arnold who handled most of the business for the Board. This was just one year after Roberts' experiences at the World Missions Conference in London where he learned much regarding mission procedures. The minutes read:

> On motion, the rules read by the President and as many of those read by Brother Arnold as pertain to the missionaries were adopted.

RULES FOR MISSIONARIES

1. We hereby direct our missionaries in Africa in selecting new fields,
    (1) To go to regions where the gospel is not preached to a people wholly in heathenish darkness.
    (2) To select a field contiguous to some of our present stations not more than two or three days distant journey.
    (3) To select as healthy a location as is consistent with foregoing directions.
2. When settled on their field they shall,
    (1) Observe carefully the rules laid down in our Discipline for a preacher's conduct, especially those in sections g, 10 and 11 of Chapter III. While laboring for the conversion of heathen they shall take especial pains that they do not themselves backslide.
    (2) They must aim directly in their instructions of the heathen, and in their labors among them, at their conversion, and to seek to educate them afterward in the doctrines and principles of the gospel. They must avoid the mistake of seeking to give them a general education first, and to convert them afterwards.
    (3) They must establish Christian schools and give the people a Christian education as fast as circumstances will permit.
    (4) They shall give, whenever practicable, from one to three hours a day to manual labor, and set the natives an example of industry, and teach them so far as possible the more ordinary arts of civilized life.
    (5) In organizing societies, they shall see that the provisions of our Discipline, so far as they are adapted to the conditions of the people, shall be carried out.
    (6) They must be particular and not lower the standard of Christian morality, and, in particular, must give no countenance to polygamy.
    (7) The superintendent of a mission station is to have custody of the funds and the property of the station.
    (8) In case of the resignation, death, or removal of the superintendent, the funds and property of the station shall be left for the benefit of the remaining members of the band laboring at such station.
    (9) In case the superintendent of a mission station or stations removes,

resigns or dies, a successor should be elected by the remaining members of the mission band, who shall hold his office until the General Missionary Board shall appoint a superintendent.

(10) In case there is a tie in electing a superintendent, the superintendent of the nearest mission station shall be communicated with by each of the members of the band and asked to vote with the band, and a majority of the votes thus obtained shall constitute an election.[15]

Self Support Undesirable

It was later reluctantly discovered that missionaries cannot spend their time operating farms to provide their own support. It is not wise for them to enter the field as settlers and employers, bent on earning a living on the economy of the country. This takes time from missionary work. It also places the missionary in the position of employer and further widens the gulf that already exists between him and the very people he has come to serve. It was a bitter lesson, and one most difficult for the first missionaries who went to the field committed to such a policy. Attitudes of paternalism develop easily and are most difficult to eliminate, especially when it seems that those we love and serve need our direction and control.

At first all missionaries, under the regular support plan, received the same amount regardless of years served or position held. This is still true with the provision for extra cost-of-living allowances in cities or where inflation obtains. This was first recognized in 1917 when the allowance was $300 per missionary. In China the missionaries submitted price lists: Butter was $1.03 per pound, and cornflakes, thirty-five cents a package. The price of coffee at ninety-seven cents seems high even today. A cake of Ivory soap sold for eighteen cents, sugar was fifteen cents per pound.[16] The Board gave this field an extra hundred dollars living allowance, or a total of $400. Gradually the policy of additional assistance in the form of children's allowances, educational assistance, and travel paid for missionary children was established, but not without difficulty. In some instances no provision was made for the children's travel to the States. In 1910, children under eight received a yearly allowance of $25.00, over eight, the same, such allowances to cease at age sixteen for the boys, eighteen for the girls. If in the homeland, children received benefits until the age of fourteen.[17] The following year the allowance was increased to $50.00 and has been adjusted upward since. In 1913, the Board agreed to an educational allowance of $75.00 for children over eight years.[18] Missionaries receiving remuneration for their services, if the work is an aid to the mission, might continue with such employment, the receipts to be turned to the mission treasurer. Furlough allowances were first granted on an individual basis of need, health condition, and service to the Board during the

149

furlough period. In 1909, the furlough allowance was fixed at $350 for one year "regardless of talents, health, or service for the Board."[19] However, nine adjustments in allowances were made at this same meeting, modifying the policy in each instance. An outfit allowance of $50.00 was also approved. In the beginning, the Board furnished the mission residence but expected the missionary to keep it in good repair at his own expense. This later was accepted as a Board responsibility. Responsibility for certain house furnishings was accepted by the Board in 1919.[20]

Missionary boxes were encouraged from the first. For many years the gifts were collected and packed at the Publishing House by the Publishing Agent. This was later supervised by the Missionary Secretary. Finally donors were requested to secure lists of needed items from the Secretary, but arrange their own packing and shipping. Those sending such boxes were expected to pay the freight. Later, duty and freight made the sending of large boxes impractical and not so necessary, as stores with larger selections of merchandise were being established. Transportation for the first missionaries was arranged by Arnold, the Publishing Agent, who traveled to New York City and made the purchase himself. In 1912, the Board, on recommendation of the Secretary, established a flat rate allowance for travel, based on a study of fare schedules. If missionaries wanted better accommodations they would pay the difference. If they traveled in a lower class, the savings accrued to the missionary's benefit:

> Seattle or San Francisco to Kobe, $104; return, $110.
> Pacific Coast to Shanghai, $115; return, $125.
> New York to Bombay, $227.50; return, same.
> New York to Durban, $195; return, same.
> New York, Philadelphia to Dominican Republic, $52.65.

Children were to go the same class as parents. Incidentals including meals to destination were paid by the Board.[21] As yet were to be developed adequate medical and retiral policies, furlough rental and travel arrangements, with understandable and workable arrangements regarding special projects and their support.

Rules for Missionaries

Since the first "rules" were established, as we have seen, in 1889, there has been a continuous development in mission policy. This is normal. New conditions call for different methods. Sometimes more effective ways are discovered to handle old situations. Policy established by the Board grows out of experience. This is a living, vital process. We are under obligation to do the best that is possible for us in any given situation.

150

Dr. and Mrs. W. A. Backenstoe in Portuguese East Africa

The Board's changed attitude on terms of service and length of furlough is enlightening. At first there was no prescribed term. As late as 1914 the Secretary was requested to remind missionaries that they should plan to remain a minimum of ten years, and if their health was satisfactory, a longer period. The first term was one year less, whatever that meant. A 1935 Manual indicated that some missionaries might make the mission field their home, spending an indefinite number of years there without furlough. Today the concept of a furlough has changed. Health matters need attention, but there are other reasons for furloughs. The rapid increase in educational opportunity in most countries, with the raised educational level of national church leaders, together with new conditions calling for different types of missionary endeavor, make furloughs a first priority. Frequently missionaries must spend a portion of the furlough in special study to better prepare for these new responsibilities. Then, too, the sending church has a claim on its overseas representatives to return and give report. The missionary also needs the inspiration and fellowship of the sending churches.

Medical policy has been modified. In 1885 many of those who believed in healing by prayer and faith were opposed to using medicine or availing themselves of medical service. It was later seen that God's healing power often works through the skillful physician who has discovered some of God's laws of health. Almost from the first there were urgent calls for medical missionaries. As far as we can ascertain, the first report is from Dr. Backenstoe covering the period April 13 to July 30, 1904. He had cared for 137 patients, made 609 visits in treating thirty-five different kinds of disease. In commenting on this report, the Secretary in a rather noncommital manner says:

> "We judge that the service he has rendered to the bodies of the natives has lightened many of their sorrows and made them more receptive to the gospel."[22]

The early retirement of missionaries for health reasons and the too rapid increase in the number of missionary graves on the hillsides of far-off mission fields were eloquent arguments for the more careful screening of candidates healthwise and for the establishment of clinics, dispensaries, mission hospitals, and maternity centers. One year after the untimely death of Clara Leffingwell, who had sailed to the field when seriously ill, the Board ordered missionaries to take a rest period before their sailing. In the succeeding years approval is given for vacations in the hot summers, the same for study and health reasons. Tents were first used in India and Japan. Later, houses were rented. India and China were authorized to purchase summer cottages in 1912 and 1913. World War I with its testing program for millions of young men in the draft revealed great health deficiencies in the population. The Board became increasingly health conscious during those years, adopting a more adequate health blank for use in examining candidates. The years 1915-1917 were times of special Board interest in this matter.

Medical Missions

At this same time interest increased in the medical missionary work. We have noted Dr. Grinnell's work with the C.I.M. in 1913. A hospital for China

Grinnell Hospital, China. Inset, John D. Green, M.D., 1937

Ebenezer Hospital, South Africa

Umri Hospital, India

Missionary Secretary W. B. Olmstead and W. A. Backenstoe leaving Ebenezer Hospital, South Africa. Mr. Olmstead was Missionary Secretary 1919-1932.

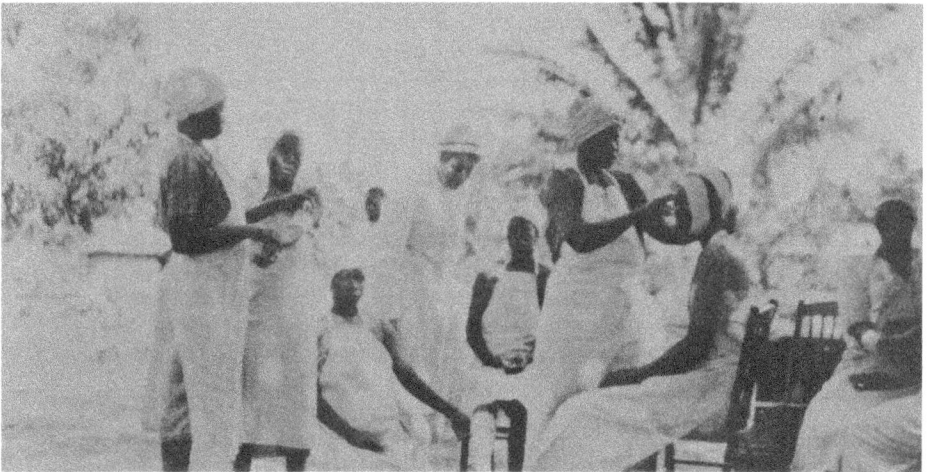
Nurses' Training, Portuguese E. Africa

was approved that same year although construction did not begin until 1917. The year 1919 is Free Methodism's high-water mark of medical expansion. That year hospitals were either under construction or being opened in South Africa, China, and India. In Portuguese East Africa a nurse began cooperative work with the Methodists, and chemical toilets were requested for India mission residences. It was declared, however, in 1921 that the medical work was only in its infancy.

In appointing personnel, there has been a marked shift in policy. In the early days great importance was attached to the sending of single men and single women. They could study the language without home distractions and become acclimated to a field before taking on household responsibilities. More recently the trend is primarily to appoint married couples. However, there are teaching and medical assignments still demanding the services of single women. On the other hand, it is almost an iron-clad policy of the Board not to appoint a single man missionary. Terms of service, length of furloughs, summer rest, have all been established by policy. Only an unusual emergency would interfere with the regular scheduling of furloughs. Missionaries are seldom sent to the field before the age of twenty-five or after thirty. This has been followed rather consistently since 1913.

Mission-Church Relations

A careful reading of Board minutes of seventy-five years ago as contrasted with the last fifteen years indicates that the home office now refers more decisions of a purely field nature to those in authority on the field. In turn, the missionaries are able to turn more responsibility over to the national churches. A board in America is hardly competent to judge the merits of "Lobolosa." The exchange of gifts at the time of marriage in Africa does much to stabilize the marriage. However, it is closely connected with bride purchasing. Experienced missionaries do not agree among themselves on the proper mission policy to follow in such cases. In 1908, the Missionary Board made a decision regarding this matter. It may have been the right one; it may have been wrong. The point is, such matters now would be studied together on the field by church leaders and missionaries.

Only in rare instances does the home office make the specific appointment of any missionary. This is done by the mission or the mission conference. Theoretically these and all other mission actions are subject to home board approval. It would be a very exceptional case in which the home authorities interfered. It has been discovered, however, that disciplinary cases can be handled best by the national church leaders. This was unheard of in 1908 when Bishop Sellew, speaking for the adoption of a Book of Discipline for South Africa, said:

"It is our opinion that it would be unwise and contrary to our polity in mission work in Africa to allow natives who may have violated any part of our Discipline to be tried by a committee composed of natives alone. Such committee should have at least enough missionaries on said committee to constitute a majority of one."[23]

Conditions have so changed that the Bishop, if he were here today, would take a different line. The church leaders know their own people better than anyone else. They can detect hypocrisy that the missionary would miss. Where the principle of self-support obtains, the church is careful not to pay its hard-earned money to any unworthy person. The Holy Spirit talks to the church there as here. They have the Bible. Their insights into moral and ethical situations are keen. They want the missionary to help them in these matters, but the missionary shares responsibility in such cases, not as a missionary representing a foreign church, but by virtue of his membership in the mission conference and on the same basis as all other members of the committee. This is progress!

In 1910, South Africa missionaries complained that the organization of a mission conference there had not given them more authority to proceed with their work independent of Board approval. This criticism reveals a misunderstanding of the distinction between the conference which is the church, and the mission which is a committee of missionaries functioning in their capacity as agents of the home board. In this last instance, they are appointed and supported by the home church. They work under certain rules mutually agreed upon which may be modified from time to time. They report to their home church, make recommendations to and requests of the home church and accept the decisions that are made. On the other hand, the missionary as a minister of the gospel holds membership in the mission conference. He accepts responsibility in the conference as it is delegated to him, under the rules approved for such conference. In the conference he is free to function as a conference member. The acts of the conference, unless it is a provisional one, are not subject to Board approval, but are under the authority of the General Conference. The Free Methodist churches around the world are as much the church of Jesus Christ as is the church in North America. The Holy Spirit is leading and guiding them as He does the home church. We rejoice in this fact.

Missionary Bishop

At the beginning of the Africa work when only a few congregations were organized, it was deemed necessary to have an ecclesiastical leader for the young church. Accordingly B. T. Roberts was made superintendent of the Africa work in its ecclesiastical relations. The missionaries and African preachers stood in the same relation to him as ministers in conference relation did in Canada and the United States. Superintendent Roberts died in 1893, but in 1911 J. S. MacGeary was elected Missionary Bishop. Here again

Rev. J. S. MacGeary, Missionary Secretary and Bishop, 1911-1919

the Board made a clear distinction in the function of the Bishop as church leader and the Missionary Secretary in his organizational relation to missionaries as missionaries. The office of Missionary Bishop has been vacant since 1915, the work having been jointly assumed by the Bishop who serves as chairman of the missionary department of the church, and the Missionary Secretary. The rapidly developing national churches with their strong leaders and their greatly increased membership call for some plan of ecclesiastical leadership consistent with the general church structure.

In many respects the minutes of a half century ago sound much the same as today. Bishop Hogue complained that the meetings were too long, suggesting that agendas be prepared in advance, and that committees be appointed to study and recommend action on personnel and budget. A committee was ordered to study the needs and opportunities of each field with a view to a better balancing of budget and personnel.[24]

The Missionary Secretary

The role of the Missionary Secretary has developed from that of keeper of minutes to a full-time executive with office staff and wide responsibility in the home church besides regular field visitation. In 1890 Secretary Kelley was to receive compensation for any special services rendered the Board on the basis of time spent. Terrill's salary was jointly supplied by the Board and the Publishing House, the latter having the benefit of his field services. Winget was the first full-time Secretary, elected in 1896 upon the death of Terrill. His annual reports, his recommendations on Board action and policy, his preaching and foreign field visitation, mark him as a great man. The work in the Dominican Republic as well as the home mission activities were placed under his direct supervision. His responsibilities were discharged with vigor and in the fear of God.

Promotion

The Missionary Secretary, under the direction of the Commission on Missions, and its president (a bishop), has "charge of the missionary interests of the church. . . . In a sudden emergency . . . he may be at liberty to act without waiting for orders . . . make general calls for special collections . . . travel at large throughout the church . . . visit the foreign fields . . . ordain all eligible candidates . . . make yearly . . . a full and detailed report to the Commission. . . . All money collected for foreign and home missions . . . to be drawn only upon the order of the secretary and the treasurer. . . . Answer all correspondence relating to the missionary work of the church. . . ."[25]

This is a polite way of saying that to the office of the Secretary falls the responsibility of collecting funds, locating and recommending for appointment missionaries to labor on twenty-three home and overseas fields. The number of such workers now exceeds two hundred and the annual budget approximates $800,000. As indicated earlier, this is far from adequate, considering the extent of the operation. Fortunately for the Secretary, the Commission and the church, the active and efficient Woman's Missionary Society now turns to the Commission on Missions sixty-five cents of each dollar in the missionary budget. Without this aid, the work would be well nigh impossible.

At first special missionary projects were presented to the churches such as—Africa fund, India fund, and China field. As the number of fields increased this method was wholly inadequate. A long process of education has

157

Rev. and Mrs. F. L. Baker. He was field secretary 1912-1956

resulted in most gifts being sent through the churches and missionary societies for the general fund. "Special projects" can create real problems unless they are items approved by the Commission and included in the budget. In 1904 and 1910 the Missionary Board (Commission since 1931) strongly protested the raising of such funds without authorization. Today it is simply a matter of policy that each missionary understands and there is no problem.

Field Secretary

To assist in the rapidly expanding program, a field secretary to solicit funds was elected in 1912. The choice was a happy one in the person of Rev. F. L. Baker. He gave a lifetime of effective and sacrificial service to the cause of Free Methodist missions. He visited Panama and the Dominican Republic, and carried heavy responsibilities in his great heart. His hours of prayer for the salvation of a lost world were doubtless of greater value than the hundreds of thousands of dollars which he raised during his term of service. This great and good man did much to "set the world in (the) heart"[26] of Free Methodism. His shadow reaches around the world.

Special Days—Organizations—Pastors

The observance of Men and Missions Sunday annually the second week in November by practically every Free Methodist church in the world is truly a remarkable occasion. Compassion Sunday is annually dedicated to concern for the church's works of mercy—medical service, agricultural uplift, direct relief, and vocational education. In a recent year 400,000 medical treatments were administered at Free Methodist hospitals and dispensaries. Self-denial week, Penny-a-day for missions, the second tithe for missions, are additional means employed in securing the desperately needed funds for the work of Free Methodist missionaries who today serve on the basis of sacrifice and with the same sense of mission their predecessors possessed. The Junior Missionary Society, the C.Y.C., the Light and Life Men's Fellowship, Free Methodist Youth, the Sunday schools, all unite in raising the missionary budget by free-will offerings. There is no general budget. All must be secured annually through the voluntary gifts of those who believe in the cause. Furloughing missionaries are in popular demand for conventions, camps and local church missionary rallies. For several years area secretaries were employed. They divided their time between field visitation and home base fund solicitation. At the present time the missionary department is depending on the leadership of 1,350 Free Methodist pastors with their churches and related organizations to supply the resources to carry forward the expanding program.

Just in Passing

The hymn, "Guide Me, O Thou Great Jehovah" was reported sung more frequently in the early Board meetings than any other. When Bishop Coleman was president, he used it three years in succession as the opening devotional hymn. Bishop Jones frequently made the motion to adjourn, while Hogue, who complained of the long sessions, was frequently excused from further attendance.

The first automobile was purchased for missionary use in 1916. It was a Ford roadster. In 1921 a group from the Pittsburgh Conference was discouraged from making a tour of the Africa field at their own expense on the ground that it would consume the time and money of the missionaries, that the American type of preaching would not be suitable for Africa, and that such a trip would establish a precedent.[27] An honor list was started in 1913 to include the names of all missionaries who had returned from the field. The Executive Committee of the W.F.M.S. since 1908 has recommended all women candidates for appointment.

Idealism

The war years, high-water mark of North America's world concern, were times of financial prosperity with large increases annually in the missionary receipts. The W.F.M.S. observed their twenty-fifth anniversary in 1919. The

159

year previous their receipts registered a $20,000 gain. The following year's gain was 40 per cent, or $33,532 above 1918! The following year the missionary budget totaled $115,000, almost double the appropriations of 1917 and the largest ever recorded to that time.

Along with this outpouring of material resource, more young people were applying for missionary service. There were thirty-seven appointments made between 1916 and 1919, almost double the number sent out in the preceding four years.

Isolationism

This remarkable outburst of generosity was followed by the decadent retreat of the twenties. Selfish isolationism kept America from exerting leadership in world affairs. Giving to missions decreased. There were fewer appointments made. No new fields were opened. We made our way to the financial crash of twenty-nine and the world-wide depression of the thirties. During our bankrupt, suffering thirties, Free Methodists established two new and important fields where thousands have been converted and brought into the fellowship of the church. In distress, the church cried unto the Lord and was heard.

The

Depression Years,

1930-1944

Section 1—THE 1885 PLAN

Economic Conditions

Ten years of prosperity followed the Great War. Almost the entire world was in need of repair. Vast reclamation projects were in progress in Europe. Factories and machinery were being built and obsolete equipment replaced. In America, plants were enlarged and production increased. The American industrial capacity was soon more than adequate for the domestic needs and the world market was unable to absorb the mounting surpluses. Production was curtailed with consequent unemployment. Meanwhile, an unprecedented wave of speculation in the stock market had resulted in raising security prices out of all relation to the earnings of their companies. The bubble burst in late 1929. Fear gripped businessmen, while investors frantically sold over-priced securities. Everybody stopped buying. Business was paralyzed for years. Enormous government-spending programs, liberal experiments in social legislation with a heavy income tax structure to support the same, together with changed world conditions including a second world war more destructive than the previous one, at last brought material prosperity. The price was very great.

Depressed economic conditions had their effect on every area of life. This was true in the work of the church and resulted in decreased contributions to missions. In 1924 the missionary receipts were $181,972. Ten years later they declined to $105,955. In addition, the Board was struggling with a $111,000 debt! Missionaries came home and transferred to other types of service. There were few appointments, while every effort was made to hold the line and pay off the crushing debt.

Venturing Back to the 1885 Plan

The first "Africa Band" sailed to Durban and divided, one part settling at Estcourt, Natal, and the other, headed by Kelley and Agnew, established a mission in Portuguese East Africa near Inhambane. This was not the original plan. When the party left America, the Lake Tanganyika area was their destination. In London, Kelley interviewed mission board secretaries enough to become convinced that the "Congo is not the place for us." We now think travel expense was involved in the decision, for Kelley wrote that passage to South Africa was $175 with an additional $200 to the Zambezi and Lake Nyassa. From here there was still a long inland journey to Lake Tanganyika and the boat passage to the head of the lake. In any event the Congo was not reached at that time. In 1919, another Africa party was equipped for Central Africa but it, too, was diverted and actually located at Pilgrims Rest in the Union of South Africa. In 1926 the Missionary Board took the following action:

> "In view of the fact that our responsibilities in South Africa are gradually passing into the hands of the native church, thereby relieving, in a measure, the home church, we deem the time has come when we should favorably consider opening a new field.
>
> "We recommend that the place, when opened, should be an unoccupied field, to find which we should probably have to go to the Belgian Congo, or Tanganyika Territory.
>
> "The Belgium mandate seems to offer an attractive opening, with dense population of a very good type of natives, and a country fairly healthful. The southern province of the mandate is reported to have one and a half million natives and no Protestant missionary.
>
> "We recommend that the Missionary Secretary take up with the Belgian government, through the Committee of Reference and Counsel and Dr. Anet in Brussels, the matter of securing permission to carry on mission work there, with a view to sending a representative of the Board to locate a suitable field when permission has been granted.
>
> "On separate motions, these recommendations were approved."[1]

Congo Survey

Meanwhile, the economic depression struck and J. W. Haley, who was serving in South Africa, heard little or nothing from the home Board about the Congo venture. He kept seeking the Lord's plan for him in this matter. In 1932 he said, "The way opened for me to make a preliminary trip to investigate." He traveled by car over impossible roads with a small party of friends. The journey was pleasant enough through Natal and the Rhodesias and "into the Congo eighty miles north of Elizabethville, traveling including the

162

return journey 5,140 miles by motor." He saw the 410-foot high Victoria Falls pouring 110,000,000 gallons of water per minute over its mile-wide rim. In big game country where lions and leopards roamed at will, he camped without benefit of fires for protection at night. But to Haley "these are only incidental to the trip." At Jadotville he came to the end of the journey—for the motor car. To ship the car forty miles by rail, ferry across a twelve-mile swamp for five days with native helpers, then be pulled by ropes over a steep mountain, and conclude the journey by lake steamer, seemed just too much. Haley's significant comment at this point was: "The car was reluctantly turned homeward *and I went on.*" The author's eyes filled with tears on this morning as for the first time he read this modern St. Paul's affirmation— another way of saying, "None of these things move me." (Acts 20:24) ". . . and I went on." This is venture at its best. The theme of our report and the essential spirit of Free Methodism in its world missions venture—". . . and I went on."

Providence surrounded him. The representative of the (Danish) Mission that Haley had learned of in Brussels was in Usumbura the very day of Haley's arrival and offered to take the stranger home to his mission and show him the country. But "before taking me into his confidence, he, not unnaturally, wanted to know just where I stood with reference to the inspiration of the Holy Scriptures. . . . Being assured that I accepted them in their entirety as the inspired Word of God, we were joined at once in the most cordial bond of fellowship."[2]

Haley visited the new station where "it is all so primitive." The school with three hundred pupils and the church congregation of similar size impressed him. The people were friendly and intelligent and densely crowded on this high plateau near the equator. The altitude made the climate almost ideal. He noted that "oranges, bananas, peaches, coffee, strawberries, potatoes, wheat, peas and beans thrive. Cattle of a small type with very large horns are seen everywhere, and these share huts with the people, together with calves, goats and sheep." The villages are usually not visible, being tucked away in the large banana plantations. In the evening, pillars of smoke ascend from the mountainsides everywhere, revealing the presence of the people and forming a mute appeal to heaven in their great need."[3]

The hospitable missionaries urged Haley to establish work in the country, saying that they "had been praying for years for missionaries," and believing that this Free Methodist mission superintendent's visit was the answer! One hundred thousand people could be reached from one station, Haley affirmed as he urged the Board to "pray that means may be supplied so that a beginning may be made in May, 1933."[4] In this he was to be disappointed. Depression-bound America was not opening new fields when those already

163

Rev. and Mrs. J. W. Haley

established could not be maintained. His own budget in South Africa had been cut from $27,000 to $5,000 and in December of this year the Japan Church had gone on full self-support, releasing its appropriations for needier work in Africa. He was not unprepared for the report in June, 1933, that the Board was unable to make any appropriation toward the new work. He wrote the Secretary: "I do not blame them in the least, nor am I disappointed . . . not to say discouraged. . . ."

"Keep Praying About It"

"But this does not mean that I could forget them in their need."[5] A friend gave Haley $600 toward the project; the native church in South Africa raised funds to send one of their own number as a missionary,[6] and the Belgian Consul General agreed to accept a bank guarantee in lieu of the required four hundred dollar deposit for each incoming settler. So, concluded Haley, "Keep praying about it."[7] A year later, Haley reported that Barclay's Bank in Durban would give the letter of guarantee. The mission group in the Congo had agreed to "turn over to us one of the old German sites" for a Free Methodist mission. The people of the area "are pagans who know nothing of the great salvation our Lord purchased with His own precious blood. Help us praise the Lord for this wonderful opening."[8] Haley was working on visas and studying French between times. His faith is still strong as he remembers that—

"Beyond all these barriers, which are gradually giving way, is the little . . . mission, the only one in Urundi, with open doors waiting to welcome us. (We) . . . are looking to the Lord in persevering, believing prayer to see remaining obstacles removed and wheels of our chariot begin to turn."[9]

164

"Faith, Mighty Faith"

At Haley's suggestion, a small portion of the 2,300-acre Fairview Farm was sold for $2,400. This, with the special gifts received from interested persons, brought Board approval for the project with the understanding that the new venture was on a personal basis and that the Board could not be responsible for additional expense above what it would have had for him in South Africa. Another promise was given this persistent pioneer during these days:

"If the Lord delight in us, He will bring us into this land, and give it us."[10]

It was nine years after the founders of the C.M.S. in Ruanda received a call to work in this country that they received permission to do so. If Haley could go in 1933, it would be nine years waiting for him also. Actually it was ten. In his report the following year, Secretary Harry F. Johnson stated:

"... It is next to impossible to get permission for a Protestant missionary to enter ... the Congo Belge. ... Rev. J. W. Haley is leaving in November for the Congo where he is to establish Free Methodism in this new territory. His family is staying behind to enter the territory when the mission has been recognized by the government."[11]

In November we find Haley in Durban ready to sail for the Congo. On the evening before embarking a telegram from his home office was received: "Deposits unprovided." The Board treasury was low. The debt was considerable, and Hitler's rise to power was a threat, particularly to Belgium. The Secretary questioned the advisability of leaving a large sum on deposit with the Belgian government even if it were available. But Haley did not interpret the message as cancellation of the Congo plans. He wrote:

"I suppose it means that the Board thought they (deposits) would not be needed for the present. Had you meant for me not to go you surely would have said so long before this. ... I still plan to go ... leaving my family and all because Jesus said, 'Go ye,' and I trust the Lord and the church. ... May the Lord be glorified in this matter and thousands of souls won by our church."[12]

The Missionary Secretary's reply indicated his satisfaction over the trip, hoping that the new field would open so that "you could remain in Urundi. ... We promise to do our best toward your support and stir up our people to pray more earnestly for this new missionary project." [13]

"For Jesus' Sake"

Haley let nothing stop him in achieving the objective which God had put

165

in his heart. Short of funds, he wrote:

> "I am traveling third class on an old Italian boat to save money. It is really steerage, no chairs in the cabin, no bathtub, no soap, no bath towels, no sitting room or lounge, and very little deck room, but it is for Jesus' sake so I do it joyfully."[14]

He was "being alternately baked and stewed."[15] The locusts swarmed over the boat until one realized the uselessness of killing one or two.

Haley arrived in Urundi in mid-December and accepted the hospitality of the only Protestant mission in the country. He was busy "making rough furniture and window sashes and doors. . . ." The altitude was six thousand feet; the ridge forming the watershed for the Nile and Congo Rivers was only eight miles distant and in clear view. He pulled teeth every day, but taught a native boy how to do it, handling only the tough cases himself. Labor was cheap. Hospital buildings could be provided for less than one thousand dollars. The brick and tile were made on the job while logs were carried by the natives to be cut into lumber at the building site. He wrote:

> "We do not plan costly buildings . . . clean, proofed against the sun, comfortable and light and airy. What more do you want?"[16]

Haley thought that one nurse with trained native helpers could administer one hundred thousand treatments during the year. These were pioneer living conditions. It was seventy-five miles to the post office. He had not seen a newspaper since his arrival and thought it would be good to have a battery-powered "wireless." Perhaps someone with two sets could send one, but still, he had no money for duty, so he concluded: "I would rather it was not sent than to have a lot of expense to pay. I would rather put my money into the work here."[17]

Revival Comes

While living temporarily at the friendly mission station, he witnessed a remarkable movement of the Spirit.

> "Since Christmas," Haley wrote, "at every meeting people are confessing their sins. . . . The missionaries have been much in earnest prayer . . . three and four are on their feet at once waiting to confess. . . . All pray at once. . . . They come every day to confess to the missionaries. . . . They can hardly get their work done. . . . We are looking for a great infilling next and then a very aggressive campaign in the hills around that teem with people. . . . The missionaries have never seen anything like it, and are very thankful."[18]

This was Haley's modest report. It was too modest. It was not the whole

166

truth, as the author has another account from one of those missionaries through personal interview. He came to the Missionary Board office while on furlough to return a visit made by the Secretary while on his Urundi trip. There were a few items of business to complete—then prayer, and this friendly man was gone. A few minutes later he returned to the office saying, "I just had to come back and tell you something more about Brother Haley." He then reported his meeting with Haley and of their fellowship in the gospel. Haley's scriptural preaching and life of prayer put our brother under conviction. He confessed his spiritual need. "I came to the Congo," he said, "with the idea that I was a good missionary. We established a station and erected the needed buildings. A fine plantation was in production. We had a rug factory, a hospital, a school and church. The congregations were large. We attempted to establish hilltop schools through the country. Simultaneously, another group would file on the same locations. This happened several times. I was annoyed. It got on my nerves. I became impatient. I was difficult to live with. The missionaries and some of the natives found it hard to work with me. Then this dear Brother Haley came along. He made me hungry. He had just what I needed, and I told him. We read the Book of Acts together and prayed together. One day I saw that it wasn't necessary to be defeated. I asked the Lord to take all those 'un-Jesus-like' things out of my heart and give me the Holy Spirit. Well, the prayer was answered. When I asked forgiveness, others did too, and the revival began. In ten years we have opened hundreds of schools across the hills and thousands have been converted from lives of sin and filled with the Spirit." Tears were rolling down his cheeks and mine as he gave this wonderful testimony to missionary Haley's spiritual influence in his life and the great goodness of God in the redemption of these people. This man shared in baptizing and receiving into the Free Methodist Church 570 persons during the author's first visit to the Congo.

The First Station

On May 6, 1935, J. W. Haley could write: "I have taken possession of Muyebe." He had arrived on May 2 at one o'clock in the afternoon. He had exchanged his own small tent for a larger one. This was his new home at the Muyebe Station. In October the Secretary declared that the year 1935 would "go down in our missionary history as the year in which better days began for our work.... Receipts have increased this year and there is an awakening of missionary interest throughout the entire church. . . . The tide has turned."[19] In a later paragraph of the same report is to be found this terse statement: "J. W. Haley and family have occupied the Urundi Mission field."

Morning Glory Dispensary. Patients bring wood for medical fee

How wisely Secretary Johnson spoke, he could not possibly know at that time. He was aware of the fact that contributions were five thousand dollars above the previous year and that the debt was in process of liquidation. This was heartening to the entire church. What nobody could foresee was that this lone missionary in his tent on an Urundi hilltop was the harbinger of a mighty revival that would issue in the development of Free Methodism's largest conference, all within twenty years!

Mrs. Haley and the two daughters, Peace and Dorothy, arrived in August. Already a workshop had been completed and three of the four rooms finished in their 15x53 house. The men were making three thousand bricks daily. Wages were paid for work on Haley's residence. For the school and for God's house, all were to take time off to bring materials and erect such buildings. Teachers and evangelists were to be supported by the people from the first. A large bamboo stuck into an underground spring provided an abundance of clear, cold water. The Africans were learning to plaster with mud, make brick and tile. Daughter Peace started a small dispensary which was popular from the first. Patients stood for hours in the hot sun waiting for treatment—the sore eyes, the ulcers, the itch, the malaria. There was no money, so patients must bring a piece of wood at least four feet long and four inches in diameter. A large box of medical supplies received from America was appreciated. Haley always asked for more bandages. Mark them "Hospital Supplies," he said. They were duty free. While Peace operated the little dispensary, her sister Dorothy conducted a school. The students were learning the Lord's Prayer, the Ten Commandments, and the Story of Creation. There were 114 in attendance. Already they were learning to sing the Christian hymns:

"Some have already learned to sing several hymns and it is sweet to hear them singing praise to Jesus where a few months back there was no mention of His blessed Name."[20]

The earthen floors of the new mission house were still damp when the missionary family took possession. All were sick for a time but the floors dried and the missionaries resumed their work.

168

Haley was alert to the importance of his contacts with officials of the country. He had conferences with the Administrator, the postmaster, the great chief and the King of Urundi. The nearby local chief was very friendly and called frequently.

More missionaries must come to hold the field. Ila Gunsolus and the Frank Adamsons were transferred from South Africa. Haley thought that single men, just as in the early Portuguese East history, could help him hold the field. He needed a sort of "mobile squad"[21] to go where needed most. How modern this strategy!

Belgian officials approved his site and urged him to apply for additional land. Now it was safe to build the permanent residence. He started at once to make twenty-five thousand bricks and five thousand tile. They must burn four days. Then he could proceed with the building itself. Other station sites, Kayero and Kibuye, were granted the new mission.

In 1936, Secretary and Mrs. Harry F. Johnson visited the field, together with the Rev. and Mrs. E. E. Shelhamer and Attorney A. W. Baker from Johannesburg, the latter a friend of Free Methodist missionaries from the days of Harry Agnew. The visitors were deeply impressed with the field and its opportunities. A familiar note was sounded with Haley's appreciation of the Secretary's visit—he hoped that "their next visit will not be less than a month."[22]

Secretary Johnson's report of the same year was all optimism. "It is amazing," he said, "that in so short a time J. W. Haley and his staff could see so

Batutsi chief, Congo

First mission residence at Kibuye station

169

much accomplished. The gospel is welcomed here and the natives are not afraid to attend meetings. They attend by the hundreds."[23]

Depression Advance

There were ten missionaries assigned to the field and the appropriations at that time totaled less than $3,700. It was also noted that the missionary debt had been decreased from $111,000 to $78,603, and for the first time in the history of Free Methodist missions, there was a net gain of over one thousand members in one year! So the opening of a new field during depression days helped rather than hindered the work on other fields and elicited increased loyalty and sacrifice from the home churches as well.

The indigenous church principle of self-support was practiced from the first. A large box with padlock and two keys was provided for the offerings and two treasurers were appointed by the church. The box was kept at the mission house, but the missionary had no key! The "treasury" was carried to the church where the offerings were received and the pastors and teachers paid their allowances. A smaller box was later placed inside to receive special gifts for the support of African missionaries in unevangelized areas until a new church was established and able to care for its own ministry. This field has a great tradition of self-support. The church has been their responsibility from the first. The prayer and concern of the members have gone along with their material gifts. Little wonder the rapid growth and present significant program in Central Africa.

Section 2—TWO HUTS ON THE LUNDI

Portuguese East Surveys

Tribal wars in Portuguese East Africa many generations ago drove from the country the baHlengwes, a clan of the Thonga tribe among whom Free Methodist missionaries had been working since the 1880's. These people migrated across the border and settled in the southeastern corner of Southern Rhodesia. Nobody particularly challenged their presence as their villages were in the least desirable part of Rhodesia. It was a drouth area. Health conditions were bad; malaria was everywhere present and the heat almost unbearable. Even the trees were stunted from lack of adequate rainfall. The population was sparsely settled in an area one hundred miles long by approximately the same width. The language barrier and the unfavorable living conditions discouraged missionary activity and none of the Rhodesia missions had ever attempted work in this part of the country. Since these people were of the same tribe traditionally considered Free Methodist responsibility, it was natural that the Portuguese East mission and conference should feel a sense of obligation for their evangelization.

On representation of the mission through one of its furloughing missionaries, the Board in 1929 approved a trip of investigation. Accordingly Jules Ryff and Ralph Jacobs toured the area and on the basis of their visit the mission made a full report to the Board, urging the immediate opening of a mission station in this wholly unevangelized area. The financial crash of 1929 came after the October Board meetings when the first step was approved. The next year its severity was being felt. Missionary receipts had declined ten thousand dollars. The Secretary considered that Southern Rhodesia was not a new field, that the Free Methodist work would naturally develop north and west from Massinga, the northernmost station in Portuguese East. In due time "the natural development of the work" being done by the native evangelists would reach these of the same tribal family and language. There were only ten thousand people involved and no Rhodesia mission would consider starting work to serve such a small language group. So the matter was disposed of for the time. However, Portuguese East missionaries could not forget even ten thousand people living nearby without any opportunity to hear the gospel.

Another factor was important in their urge to enter new territory. Missionaries had been assigned to the Portuguese East field since 1885. Writing to his home Board, Ralph Jacobs, another pioneer of new fields, said:

"Your laborers in this field are missionaries with a call to establish a church and pass on to new fields. . . . We have been in the process for forty-five years and I feel the time has come for some definite policy along the line of caring for our old work and for an advance into new fields."[1]

Jacobs supplemented his statement with reports of increased self-support in the African church. The evangelists and ordained preachers understood the Christian message, especially the teaching on holiness. "Some of their sermons," wrote Jacobs, "were just as clear on holiness and as powerful as are preached by our best preachers at home. . . . We are about to place several extra burdens upon them hitherto borne by the white missionaries."[2]

Jacobs sent the Secretary a map showing the location of present work in Portuguese territory in its relation to the Southern Rhodesia field. The Sabie River district was far removed from the main Portuguese Conference work, so Jacobs thought that a Bible school just inside the Southern Rhodesia border could nicely serve both the new field and this Portuguese district, since all were in the same language area.

His inspection tour with Ryff deeply impressed Jacobs. He found ten thousand people "without any religious work among them." He wrote:

"The few days we spent there indelibly stamped the call on the hearts of your servants, and we trust and pray this same voice calling us will be heard by our home church."[3]

Jacobs proposed a station in Rhodesia and eventually one on the Sabie River to form "a line of stations from Inharrime (Portuguese East) to Rhodesia."[4] The following month Jacobs toured up into the Sabie River district where he found that "the need is overwhelming but God is already working up there. . . . We have villages where the gospel is being preached while other villages are calling for us."[5]

The Board was unable to take advance steps at this time, but the Portuguese East church continued to grow. It was becoming increasingly responsible for its own support. Over one thousand attended the annual conference, and a new district of twenty-six Christian villages was received into membership. Their leader "arose and eloquently and with much feeling said that they did not come for money but for a church home and for spiritual help."[6] This group had traveled one hundred fifty miles, much of the journey on foot, to attend the conference. No surprise that Jacobs could add:

"We can report that the mighty presence of God was with us."[7]

It was four years before anything more was done for Rhodesia. This time it was Laurence Arksey and Jacobs who made the trip. They interviewed government officials and applied for a lease of land. This was eventually approved by the government and the Missionary Board was requested to make an appropriation for the new station. By action of the Portuguese East executive committee and the home Board, Ralph Jacobs was requested to delay his furlough and take charge of building operations for the new station. The request came like "a bolt out of the blue, but there was no confusion, only a calm assurance that this was the will of God for us."[8]

Two Huts on the Lundi

On March 18, Jacobs wrote from Durban. He was still waiting for an official approval from the missionaries. He evidently received it. Ten days later he wrote from Lundi Hotel, Southern Rhodesia:

"Here we are safely landed about one mile from our building site. I saw the Assistant Commissioner this noon, and everything is in order to start building operations at once. . . . I expect to go on sixty-five miles further north tomorrow to Fort Victoria where I hope to arrange for our post. I will add our full address. . . . Fort Victoria, Private Bag, Lundi Mission, Southern Rhodesia."[9]

Just ten days from Durban! This explains the sentiments of a new missisonary

"Two huts on the Lundi"

working under Jacobs' direction. He told the author: "He doesn't make one unnecessary move; every step counts. If you follow him around for a day you know you have been somewhere."

In choosing the Lundi River location, attention was given to water supply, gardens, building materials, accessibility to roads and a large native population. Lundi fulfilled all these requisites. As for health, it was no worse than Portuguese East, probably no better. The hot climate and malaria discouraged European settlement. It was a beautiful spot. The sheer ruggedness of its mountainous rock outcroppings is hardly equaled anywhere. It was a big-game paradise. The hippo pools of the river were well stocked with the giant animals that on occasion are still a menace to the mission gardens. In the rainy season the river bed several hundred yards wide, normally sand and rocks with a few small streams, becomes a raging torrent from bank to bank, rushing to the sea. It was here that Ralph and Ethel Jacobs established camp, living in two huts "not yet . . . mudded, but it is still warm so we do not mind the fresh air." The heavy rains brought many mosquitoes but five grains of quinine daily kept the missionaries free of fever "although we have been bitten badly." The chief and his people were happy to have them. "Two men have already expressed the desire to become Christians and want to buy Testaments and song books."[10]

On instructions from the missionaries, the first residence was under construction and could be finished this "cool season" if the second thousand dollars could be sent soon. The foundation was of stone, the walls of cement

Rev. and Mrs. Ralph Jacobs

blocks. The second building was to be a combination church-school structure. Jacobs had received six New Testaments and song books. All were sold by night. "One man who bought a Testament and song book danced around with them and said, 'Today I believe' (become a Christian)."

The government officials exhibited great friendliness from the beginning. They urged the establishment of kraal or village schools throughout the area and offered government subsidy for the teachers' allowances. The standard government building plan, 16x40 of sun-dried brick walls and thatch roof, was followed in each school, the actual building being done largely by natives except the bricklaying. Three classes were taught in these primary schools. Pupils could read the New Testament when they had finished. Those showing superior ability were recommended for further training at the central school at Lundi. This school, too, was subsidized by the government. Both teachers and evangelists have secured their education here. The inspector suggested starting the school under a tree if necessary, for then "the people would be keener to build rather than if one started out by asking them to build first."[11]

"We Are Working . . . and God Is Working"

The Secretary urged Jacobs not to work too hard. "Conserve your strength," he wrote, "for the direction of the work, even if it takes several months longer."[12] In response to the Secretary's puzzled inquiry about his new pick-up truck, Jacobs replied, "The money came from our own accumulated tithe and a personal Christmas gift sent by my mother some time ago."[13] Concerning the building activities he said:

"My native men are working hard. . . . Early in the morning when I get

174

up, I find them around the campfire trying to read spellers or looking through the hymn book. . . . We are working hard at the building and God is working hard in many hearts."[14]

Sunday services were started soon after establishing camp on the Lundi. In the shade of the large trees that lined the river, large congregations gathered to hear the preaching of the gospel.

"At first curiosity brought out the people, then the Holy Spirit commenced to move on their hearts. Many were brought under conviction and from then on for over two years it was rare for a Sunday to pass without someone choosing the Lord."[15]

Bicycle Evangelism

The headmen and chiefs who saw the changed lives and villages of the new Christians begged for schools and evangelists. The field was ripe for harvest. To aid in the rapidly expanding work, the Portuguese East Conference appointed four experienced evangelists to assist Jacobs in following the new converts and in village evangelism. With bicycles they were able to cover long distances, bringing the gospel to the unreached heathen kraals. In 1944 a district was organized and several Rhodesians were licensed to preach! These men had repented of their sins, attended school, learned to read, had taken special classes in Bible and were ready to preach, all in five years! The writer heard one of them preach to a congregation of more than five hundred seated under the trees on a hot Sunday afternoon. He preached a powerful sermon. The people were deeply convicted. It seemed that not less than one hundred came forward in tears, repenting of their sins. These new preachers were appointed to the established circuits while the veteran evangelists were sent as missionaries to pioneer the opening of the next large native reserve, Matibi Number 2, to the preaching of the gospel and the establishment of churches and schools. Concerning these evangelists, Jacobs said:

"These men are entirely supported by the local churches they serve. What wonderful changes God can make in the human heart. . . . A few years ago these people were heathen, bound by beer and tobacco, unstable as water. Now they go forth preaching the gospel and doing it with no uncertain sound, their clean lives and good works bearing witness that they have been with Jesus."[16]

On June 8, 1939, the Lundi Station was officially opened. "Practically all the white people within a radius of fifty miles came to the service (thirteen) and the Assistant Native Commissioner brought a load of chiefs and indunas in his big truck."[17]

175

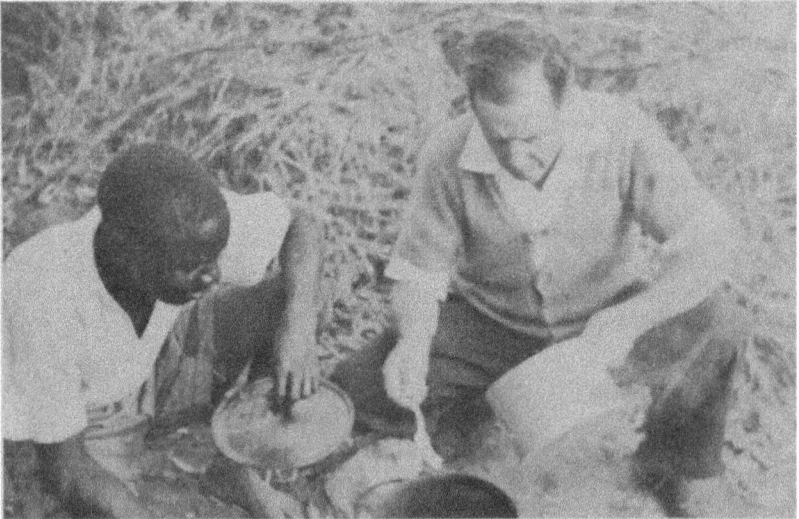

Ralph Jacobs, pioneer missionary

In 1944 Jacobs reported twelve outstations and 650 members! Since that time, the medical work has been expanded, two additional stations established, and a new Bible school opened.

Hardship

Life is not easy for the missionary on this field. The intense heat of the long summer is very trying. Now the thick asbestos-cement roofing makes at least ten degrees difference in room temperature and it is still hot. The first missionaries living in partially-finished houses had a most difficult time. "We have not been able to take our siesta," Jacobs wrote, "as the bedrooms are under a low iron roof with no ceilings over them and the heat has been terrific." They tried to sleep on a grass mat on the floor and on the army cot on the porch. "Our most comfortable chairs are two canvas veranda chairs." Jacobs made every effort to economize with Board funds "and will still continue to do so, but were it not for our faith in God and His love for us, we would be tempted in many ways." But there is the brighter side: "Souls are still choosing the Lord and the work is going forward."[18] A postscript to the same letter adds: "Mr. Jacobs came home from his faraway preaching places bringing the news of twenty-eight choosing the Lord." Returning from annual conference, Mrs. Jacobs brought some of the furniture from the Portuguese East station:

"A trunk of bedding, pictures, my sewing machine and one rocking chair. We were enjoying the rocking chair so much and Saturday night one of the house boys fell over it in the dark and broke one of the rockers. . . . We have opportunity of taking joyfully the spoiling of our goods, but I am afraid I was not very joyful."[19]

Because of the war, travel to the States was not advisable or possible in 1942, so the Lundi pioneers spent a few months in South Africa, their first furlough in ten years.

The transformation of lives and villages in this primitive area is almost unbelievable. To work with people who are hearing the gospel for the first time is a rare experience, even though to do so requires some hardship. People in darkness have seen a great light. The miracle of Lundi is being reproduced at other population centers of the area.

The World War II seemed very remote from Lundi Mission except for the soaring prices. The financial burdens of the Board were still heavy and general economic conditions were difficult. Things that matter most were happening in primitive native reserves—Matibi Number 1 and Matibi Number 2. Hundreds were hearing the gospel of Christ. Lives were changed, heathen customs broken, bodies healed, and minds opened to think the thoughts of God and read His Book. This was Venture in the Wilderness, changing it into the garden of God.

South America

The friends of Mexican mission work in Southern California pioneered the movement throughout the church to open a mission in South America. In 1936 the Commission on Missions took the following action:

"On motion, it was decided to request all Sunday-school boards that may be willing, to set aside their birthday offerings for the purpose of opening a new mission field in South America, such field not to be opened until sufficient funds are on hand to warrant its maintenance."[20]

The Commission on Missions took further action in 1939 while Jacobs was opening Lundi Mission and Haley was calling for workers in the Congo:

"It was on motion decided to make a survey of the possibilities of opening a mission in South America. The Missionary Secretary and one other member of the Commission who might be free to go are to make the proposed survey."[21]

M. L. Barton at first planned to go, but business matters made this impossible. The directors requested B. H. Pearson to take his place. Eventually E. E. Shelhamer joined the party. As a result of this trip that covered much of South America, the Commission in its 1940 meeting approved opening work in Brazil. Here members of the Japan Free Methodist Church had settled and were already at work. There were a few small Sunday schools and groups of believers. Missionaries were subsequently appointed, but due to war conditions, entrance permits could not be secured. Nothing more came of the South America venture until 1946. Thanks to the Sunday schools and the South America banks they used in collecting funds, there was on hand almost fifty thousand dollars for purchase of property and the equipping and sending of missionaries.

After ten years of sacrifice and sometimes frustrating and almost hopeless endeavor, the South America work was inaugurated. The rapid growth in this field should be ample reward to the pioneers of the movement.

Missionary Secretary H. F. Johnson and Youth Superintendent B. H. Pearson on survey trip, South America, 1940

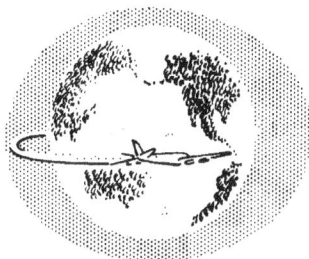

VII

Post-War

Expansion,

1944-1960

Section 1—VENTURES ON THE EDGE OF WAR

The treaty of Versailles at the end of World War I placed impossible reparations requirements on Germany. The seeds of another war more deadly than the first took root, giving rise ultimately to Adolf Hitler and World War II. By 1940 it was true that

"The outreach of war to every continent necessarily dominates the story of Christian missionary work throughout the world. . . . No country has remained unaffected."[1]

The year 1914 is usually considered the date of the beginning of the "New World." Likewise 1945 marked the dawn of a new era—the atomic age. This is another of those turning points in human history. The same year witnessed the feeble beginnings of the United Nations. In San Francisco, representatives of fifty nations solemnly pledged themselves to "employ international machinery for the promotion of the economic and social advancement of all peoples" by promoting "social progress and better standards of life . . . tolerance . . . and peace with one another as good neighbors . . ." and uniting "our strength to maintain international peace and security, and to ensure, by the acceptance of principles and the institution of methods, that armed force shall not be used, save in common interest. . . ."[2] Weariness from long years of war and cynicism over treaties so readily broken in the past, dampened what enthusiasm was generated at the time for this noble step. In 1950 the infant world organization survived the Korean conflict and is more strongly entrenched today as a force for peace in the world than at any previous time. War has been the dominant feature of this century. Two world wars and almost a third have sobered national leaders.

The economic and political decline of Europe has shifted world power to Russia and America. The overseas empires of the British, Dutch and French have been slipping away. The rise of nationalism with the appearance of independent nations, some loosely attached to their former rulers, has been occurring with breathtaking rapidity. The revolution in China was no "new deal for the forgotten man." It was a deep calculated destruction of religious and cultural foundations that meant a new way of life. The destruction of Europe in both wars left Europe impoverished. Millions lost every material possession. Improved means of communication, and especially the radio, gave the masses some understanding of a free world where poverty was not necessary. A great restlessness and discontent took possession of the common man. Communism and the messiahs of bread and plenty thrive under such conditions.

Revolutionary Age

It is a "revolutionary age." The underdeveloped nations want the gadgets of the Western world's assembly lines. However, the rapid increase of population in Asia without a corresponding addition to the food supply has actually lowered their standard of living during the last quarter century! Secularism, nationalism and Communism represent a revolt against the status quo of economics, politics and religion. Ancient systems of philosophy and religion, in failing to understand the problems that create this revolutionary age, reveal their helplessness in furnishing the right answers. Millions have turned from the gods of their ancestors in disgust. But these are people with eternity in their heart. They have great cavities of mind and soul. Their stomachs are empty, but the spiritual vacuum is even more acute. The gods of nationalism, the messiahs of heaven here and now, earthy ideologies demanding the total commitment of high religion, and promising bread and plenty, rush into these low pressure areas of want and misery.

Non-Christian Religions

Complicating the picture even further is the so-called revival movement in the great ethnic religions. Whether or not this represents a real increase in spiritual sensitivity, a hunger for that which high religion only can supply, or whether it is only the accompaniment of the rise of nationalism in areas where religion and government are traditionally wedded is not certain. There has been, especially in India, a tendency to revise Hinduism by the elimination of ancient teachings unworthy of the modern man's acceptance and at the same time introduce elements of Christian teaching. While this is a beautiful tribute to the influence of Jesus Christ in the world, it further complicates the situation. The Christian message, demanding complete loyalty, addresses itself to those who claim they already admire Jesus and follow His teachings more consistently than those of the Western world, while still professing their ultimate allegiance to the teachings of the Hindu holy books.

Secular Society

In Britain and Europe loyalty to the Christian enterprise, if gauged by the 5 or 10 per cent church attendance, is so weak that these countries may well be considered mission fields. The same is true in America where, in spite of mounting church membership, record-breaking church construction programs, and recent increased interest, attendance and generosity of financial support, society is progessively secularized and our religion too often seems of the exclusive country club variety. The church exists in a world of clever machines that are ever producing more things in less time. Society is heading for an order of shorter hours, higher wages, more leisure time, more luxury. The plans call for three times the present highway mileage and the increasing production of millions of automobiles. The travel, entertainment and luxury-oriented enterprises are prospering. In the minds of some economists it is a real concern just how long wall-sized TV, the endless "multiplication of goods and services, a radio in every room, the planned obsolescence of durable goods," and the "silly elaboration of packaging" will continue to satisfy. If this represents modern man's sense of value, to what absurdity may we expect him to go when incomes are twice their present level?

Undoubtedly the materialism and prosperity of the world is influencing the church. American churches are spending annually seven billion dollars for beautiful buildings. Their giving to overseas missions is equal to what they spend for themselves in ten days! So American idolatry is a fact and the pointer to one of our newest-to-be-recognized mission fields. If John R. Mott two decades ago could warn of America's growing extravagance, love of ease, softness and waste, what would he say if alive today?

The author finds it difficult for reasons of personal involvement to write from this point on. In 1944 he came to the secretaryship from a college church pastorate. This too was "venture." He had attended great missionary conventions over which a missionary-hearted mother presided. As a pastor he was concerned and at every opportunity promoted interest for the overseas work of the church. Some students of his former teaching days were on the mission field, and this was very satisfying. What surprises were in store for him as he came into the office and gradually began to understand the extent of the operation! Some felt that the situation was critical.

"Our General Missionary Secretary was elected at a crucial time, due

181

to the passing of two General Secretaries by illness within about two and a half years. . . . He seemed to know how to pick up the lines connecting the home base with the far-flung lines, developing them into strong departments. . . . Three times his offices have outgrown their quarters. . . ."[3]

Direct Relief

The conclusion of World War II was still eleven months distant. We were shocked by the suffering of Europe with its great concentration camps, its dispossessed millions. There was famine in both India and China about this same time. The missionary office promptly organized a church-wide clothing collection campaign for European sufferers. Approximately thirty tons of warm clothing were shipped by Free Methodist churches. Thousands of dollars were contributed for famine sufferers in India and China. In these countries Free Methodist missionaries took large responsibility in the administration of direct relief not only for their own denomination, but served as approved agents for Church World Service and other agencies which were at that time dispersing relief in large amounts. As much as ten thousand dollars was cabled to China in one day.

The period under review, 1944-1960, could well be characterized as life on the edge of war. The missionary program of these years must be understood in that frame of reference. Urgent appeals for China relief appeared in the 1945 numbers of *The Free Methodist*. The story of the Chengchow refugee school and the trek of six hundred students to western China to escape the war, under the leadership of our missionary Edith Frances Jones made the front pages of the newspapers of the world. The same was true of the remarkable conversion story of Jacob De Shazer, Doolittle bombardier, whose heart of hatred turned to love while still in the solitary confinement of a Japanese prison camp in China. Ultimately De Shazer engaged in missionary service in Japan where the newspaper reporters and photographers followed him as he told the simple story of his own conversion and witnessed to the gospel. Thousands of decisions were made for Christ in these great meetings.

Japan and China

At the close of the war, and before any missionaries could be sent, chaplains served as liaison with our Japan church leaders. Money was immediately sent for their regular support, together with hundreds of food and clothing packages. Meanwhile Missionaries Ashcraft and Schlosser were sent to China on a short-term assignment to re-establish the broken bonds of fellowship with the church and share in the administration of large scale relief programs then in operation. "Old China hands" Florence Murray, Kate

Leininger and Geneva Sayre returned during the summer of 1946. The war's end gave us one more opportunity to preach the gospel. New missionaries were soon assigned to the China field, but the political situation worsened during the next year. Evacuation from Honan was effected in 1948. Veteran missionary Pearl Schaffer reported the operation:

"Edith Jones, a party of sixteen Chinese, and I fled before the approach of the Communists (from Chengchow) today. The Lutheran Mission plane was sent for the emergency flight. . . . Miss Sayre went east on a special military train with a number of trunks."[4]

Three days later John Schlosser was—

"selling or giving away large quantities of supplies and household effects which we cannot take with us. Drugs, blankets, furniture, foodstuffs—we have a regular bazaar. And the filthy lucre that comes in! Torn and tattered bills by the thousands! A crew of men were working for hours sorting and packaging the stinking stuff so it can be turned in to the bank. It takes about six hundred thousand to equal one U.S. dollar."[5]

Ten days later the cable, "Honan evacuation completed. Ladies flew Chungking" indicated the turn of events. The mission re-established itself at Chungking, working an unoccupied field of a sister mission, and Florence Murray established on a limited basis the Szechwan Bible School.

Missions in Red China

In June and July Geneva Sayre made trips to Chengchow to deliver appropriations and collect supplies left at the mission. The Kaifeng Bible School was still operating under the direction of Chinese leaders. In October there was a complete "turnover" in Kaifeng. Geneva Sayre was there with relief supplies. After a short house arrest she was permitted to continue with her work. The schools were to remain open. No civics was to be taught. Since Kaifeng was one of the earliest larger cities to be taken over, a "soft" policy toward foreigners was employed. Miss Sayre was given free plane travel and encouraged to continue with her relief work. She had previously been appointed director of Honan relief for "The United Nations International Children's Emergency Fund" (UNICEF). Large quantities of supplies began arriving at about the time of the turnover. On an international pass she was free to travel on both sides of the line and for some time carried on the distribution of rice, milk powder, margarine, vitamins and cloth. The Honan allotment was two hundred tons of rice with other staples in proportion. She reported that "the Communists are furnishing beans, vegetables, and fuel to match the UNICEF supplies."[6] Later in the year the Kaifeng Bible School was opened with more than one hundred students. By Communist order, it must be "self-supporting." An industrial program was organized. The Friends Service Unit contributed old sewing machines which were repaired and put in service in the tailoring department, specializing in military and office uniforms. Miss Sayre wrote:

> "Another group is taking raw sheep wool, washing, carding, spinning, dying and knitting it into garments to sell. We are giving each student six pounds as a starter. . . . We wanted to buy some stocking-knitting machines but this will have to wait. . . . I am straining every nerve to try to catch up by the end of the year, but I am almost crushed at times. . . ."[7]

The Commission on Missions heartily approved the projects and forwarded funds to Miss Sayre as long as this was possible. Still hopeful that the mission would eventually be outside this crisis, as had been the case previously, Miss Sayre reported later:

> "Our industrial work keeps us buzzing, with no idle time. I believe we are on the right track teaching the industrial work. We have ten sewing machines, one stocking-cap knitting machine, five stocking machines in use. . . . Others are learning dispensary work. . . ."[8]

The machines were kept busy all day in three shifts with classes arranged accordingly. By January near-famine conditions existed. Some of the people, including the pastors, "are digging up grass roots for fuel to cook with, selling clothing, or anything they can, to live."[9]

In early 1951 Miss Sayre and Friends Service Unit workers were placed under house arrest. After extended negotiations she was allowed to proceed to Hong Kong. Here Miss Sayre plunged into the refugee school work with her characteristic vigor.

Philippines—"Uncivilized Area"

Meanwhile, our chaplains and missionaries were in Japan, delivering hundreds of food packages, distributing shipments of clothing, and vitamins, and assisting in the repair and construction of war-damaged churches. Walter Groesbeck surveyed possibilities for mission work in the Philippines. Ultimately he located an area in the northeast part of the island of Mindanao. On the map it is marked "uncivilized area." Both Groesbeck and Schlosser transferred to the Philippines, the latter assisting at the Far East Broadcasting Station in Manila for one year before going with Groesbeck. At first these missionary families rented native-type houses. There was no way to make them fly- or bug-proof. Open toilets and other unsanitary conditions made dysentery a normal part of life. There were no highways to unite the various parts of the field. Travel was by infrequent coastal steamer or up the rivers in dugout boats propelled by outboard motor.

Jungle evangelism in the Philippines

Here the missionaries were out on the frontier again, opening up the interior "barrios" to the gospel. Many were hearing the gospel for the first time. Special problems beset the new workers. There was no unified language, the people speaking "a mixture of three smatterings—English, Visayan and Manobo. No adequate study helps were available. . . . Manobo is a language not yet reduced to writing." The climate was difficult. Even though it was a hot, swampy area, settlers were moving here. The big lumber companies were cutting giant mahogany trees, land was being cleared for small farms, and surveys were being made for a highway to connect the population centers. In 1950 the missionaries were "laying the foundations for a long-time permanent program."[10] They arrived before the great influx of population, in advance of roads and cities, to assist in establishing "a genuinely Christian civilization in what now is marked on the map as an 'uncivilized area.' "[11]

The Missionary Secretary visited this field in 1952. Like the other passengers disembarking at Lianga, he jumped from the coastal steamer to the lifeboat bobbing alongside. When the boat stuck in the surf he waded ashore in the darkness to meet pioneer missionaries stationed here. Some long trips on steaming rivers under a merciless sun will not be forgotten. The rice breakfast and the bad egg, the attempt to sleep on the bare floor, still recall the rough life of the interior. But out in these places missionaries are leaving little hand-wound phonographs with gospel recordings in the language of the area. Teachers, storekeepers, policemen, soldiers, mayors of towns are being converted. Some have been given local preacher's licenses and are helping carry the gospel to these needy places.

Mindanao is still an "uncivilized area." With a Magahat guide and a certificate from the 15th Judicial District Court, Butuan City,[12] to assure

---

REPUBLIC OF THE PHILIPPINES
COURT OF FIRST INSTANCE OF AGUSAN
15th Judicial District

Office of the Clerk of Court
Butuan City

CERTIFICATE

To Whom It May Concern:

This certifies that according to the records of this office, the persons herein below mentioned have not been convicted of any crime, nor is there any pending criminal case filed against them in the Court of First Instance of Agusan:

1. Datu Taglion Kogit, of Sitio Mingkyapi, Langasian, Loreto, Agusan.
2. Datu Delhagan Kogit, also of same residence as above.

Issued upon request of Rev. W. Walter Groesbeck, Missionary of Free Methodist Mission in the Philippines of the City of Butuan, Province of Agusan.

Butuan City, Philippines, August 9, 1956.

Macario C. Conde,
Clerk of Court

(Seal)

---

the leader of the Killer Tribe that he would not be charged with past crimes, Groesbeck undertook this difficult and dangerous mission into the uncharted wilds of the island. It was a long day of travel, first on the Agusan River with the large outboard motor, and later by dugout canoe and small motor up the I-hao-an River, a branch of the Agusan. Then an impossible hike along the river no longer navigable by reason of rapids and boulders. Groesbeck described this trip:

"... Sometimes we were able to wade in the river ... other times we scaled cliffs; we passed through gorges beautiful to behold but almost impassable. A few times we went around an out-cropping of rock just holding on by our fingertips and by toeholds chipped out in the rock. As I looked down at the rocky river bed, I knew that if we fell it would mean death."[13]

Missionary Groesbeck and chief of killer tribe, Philippines

Here Groesbeck contacted the tribe and at last the chief. Through his interpreter-guide, the missionary apologized for not coming sooner. He explained that he was there to tell him and his people about God. Chief Taglion said he wanted to become a Christian. Preliminary negotiations concerning the relocation of the tribe in an area where the government could provide a school for the children and where land suitable for gardens was available were instituted. Groesbeck arrived home with cuts, bruises, and a heavy heart. Such is missionary life in the Philippines.

187

Life Is Difficult

Americans live in a tiny island of luxury and privilege. Relatively, most of the world is a slum. It is a dangerous world. Life is not easy. In China it was war and starvation. In the Philippines, climate, primitive living conditions, dangerous outlaws. A policeman at Bunawan was killed by his prisoner the day before the writer's arrival at the Bunawan Station. Jacobs' helpers in Southern Rhodesia fought lions and elephants in bringing building materials for the new mission station. The undernourished, hungry Japanese were grateful for the hundreds of American food packages. De Shazer was burdened for the salvation of Japan. Too many seemed not to understand, or care. He ate no food for forty days, spending the time in prayer and Bible study. This was followed by a great campaign in Osaka with hundreds of decisions.[14] The same month our newly-arrived Congo nurse, Berdina Beckwith, died of complications following a surgical operation. In September a typhoon struck Osaka and completely wrecked the Maruyama Church, and in Congo lightning destroyed two of the village schools. In the Dominican Republic, Mrs. Amy Willard had put her ten-day-old baby to bed and retired for the night. When her husband came home from a late committee meeting, she was dead. Her passing was unexpected. Meanwhile, a severe famine was raging in Southern Rhodesia where the missionaries were importing food for the pastors and evangelists. Ten-year-old children were hiking to Johannesburg, hundreds of miles south, hoping to procure food. Rev. and Mrs. Tillman Houser visited their widely separated outstations in wild Southern Rhodesia, sleeping at night in the box of their pickup truck. And Paul De Shazer in Osaka, through prayer and a chance surgical procedure, was cured of a violent case of sleeping sickness, to the amazement of the doctors who called it a "miracle."

The list could be extended. We have selected these instances from a few short weeks as a sample of missionary life. This is the kind of world and the sort of people we mean when we use the terms "mission field" and "missionary."

Ventures in Planning

An unusually large number of missionaries were detained on furlough because of World War II. During one year almost one-third of the entire force was at home. For purposes of understanding the missionaries and their problems, and for joint planning in the face of a changing world, missionary planning conferences were scheduled in various parts of the country. These were closed meetings for planning and later recommendation to the Commission. The India discussions were held in Buffalo in the midst of the city's

188

biggest snowstorm. Planning for China was done at McPherson, Kansas, to accommodate Doctor Green and the West Coast missionaries. Similar considerations fixed the Japan discussions at Seattle where several former Japan missionaries were in residence. At Rochester, New York, and Los Angeles, California, seminar discussions with an invitation to the public were a sort of compromise between the missionary convention type of program and the planning conference. Missionaries from various fields participated in these. One of the main topics for discussion was the indigenous church and how to translate the theory into action on the field.

Section 2—TRAVELS

For several years there had been little field visitation. Two Missionary Secretaries had been sick and were not able for such trips. Furthermore, travel was practically impossible because of the war. The Commission was eager for the Secretary to visit all of the fields. However, there were some priorities. The Dominican Republic trip is a short one and good orientation for further foreign travel. This was the Secretary's first air-travel experience. It was a memorable trip meeting the missionary friends, attempting to use the Spanish forgotten from college days, meeting government officials, pastors and the people. Travel on the crowded narrow-gauge train, the crowds, the altar services, the early morning prayer meetings, the communion service on a dirt floor administered by a barefoot preacher, the pastor with thirty-two preaching points reporting over fifty conversions at just one of these places, the horseback ride that was not forgotten for weeks—this was the Dominican Republic. Yes, one preacher rode his horse seventy-five miles in one day to attend the district meeting. The weary Secretary had already retired. But this dear man had come to see the new Secretary. He would be content with nothing less. That Dominican pastor probably remembers the Secretary as a rather sleepy, uninteresting, non-communicative person, hair slightly disheveled, shoes unlaced, and necktie missing. At that moment a large scorpion started crawling across the living room floor, but the long-experienced foot of Superintendent Mills took care of the situation. It was a good trip. The two-motored DC-3 was quite satisfactory, but the ancient three-motored Ford plane with overhead wing, cabin suspended below and nothing but the fresh air beneath rather worried the tenderfoot traveler.

The old thatch-roofed classroom building has now been replaced by a modern, three-story, reinforced concrete structure. The Santiago school is at the very heart of the work. Here preachers and laymen are prepared for the work of the church tomorrow. Even now gospel teams from the school regularly assist in the evangelism crusade that is in progress all the time.

189

Not next, but early in his term of service, the Secretary spent almost four months in Africa visiting the Free Methodist work, largest of Free Methodist mission fields.

Africa Visit—1946

Because of its insight into mission field activity and some of the concerns of a Missionary Secretary as he makes an executive visit, a report of the first Africa trip is included.

First impressions are always more vivid and since this report is quite typical of executive visits to other parts of the world, full account of trips to each field will not be given here. This report, a rather personal one, was prepared for the Commission and not for publication. Its informal style has been retained:

I arrived in New York Wednesday noon, July 10. It was a sweltering hot day. There was enough time for lunch, a final inoculation, the purchase of a DDT bomb, and that one last transit visa. The Airways limousine took us to La Guardia Field at 4:30 p.m. Here was more ticket-checking and waiting. While I was securing insurance for the trip, a telegram came from Mabel Cook and I dictated reply over the phone. Finally we went through the gate and filed out to the big four-motored, much-publicized forty-one passenger "Constellation." It was my first experience on a plane of this size. We left the field at 6:30 p.m. for the smoothest, fastest, longest, most unexpectedly stopped ride in my short experience with air travel. . . . Our plane landed at Dakar, 4:30 a.m. of the second day. There was a light breakfast of assorted cold meats and cheeses, hard French bread and nasty coffee. A radioed message instructed the crew to check the fire extinguishers. One was broken and two days were required for the repairs. At 9:30 a.m. we were taken to a partly-evacuated army camp and placed temporarily in the Officers' Club. Some felt that there was more to the grounding order than just fire extinguishers. We were on a rocky cliff overlooking the Cape Verde lighthouse, and there was a bit of a wrecked ship showing above the breakers. This was Friday, July 12. We slept in army barracks with the crew and had our meals at the army mess—a little sloppy, but enough, and quite good.

On Sunday we arranged for religious services in the Club. Dr. Goodall was good enough to give us a sermon on the "Use of Disappointment." We enjoyed singing the Christian hymns. In the afternoon the Pan American agent brought us a report of the serious accident at Reading, Pennsylvania, with loss of life, and the grounding of Constellation planes by order of the C.A.A., together with the information that Air France would take us to Leopoldville on Tuesday. . . .

The next two days at Leopoldville were busy ones, attending the sessions of the West Africa Missions conference. There were two hundred in attendance from Angola, French Equatorial Africa, and the Belgian Congo. Thirty nationals were present. All addresses and reports were translated from English into French and Portuguese.

South Africa

Pan American had arranged reservations for me to Johannesburg, so I got off on the first plane. Many of my fellow-travelers were stranded in Leopoldville. It is a two-day flight to Johannesburg. The agent, in error, told us that we stopped over Sunday in Elizabethville, so the wrong information was wired to Jules Ryff. He was greatly chagrined when the taxi delivered me at his door one day before schedule. But the welcome was genuine, and the hospitality generous. The next afternoon I left by train for Durban, arriving at nine o'clock, Tuesday morning, July 23. After tea and a visit to Miss LaBarre's home, I went by car with A. E. Haley and Doctor Rice to our Fairview Station. It is a beautiful drive, this seventy-five miles along the coast, through sugar-cane plantations, small towns, seaside resorts and native villages.

We arrived at the Fairview Farm house where Rev. and Mrs. A. E. Haley live, at 2 p.m. The farm extends from the Indian Ocean inland for approximately one and a half miles, and is about three miles long. Originally it was 2,250 acres, but the Missionary Board has contracted to sell a portion to our own members. They have been buying this property over a period of fifteen years and the last payment is to be made this fall. From the front porch of the Haley house there is a grand view of the Indian Ocean, and at night one can hear the breakers pounding on the beach a mile and a half distant.

After lunch with the Haleys I was taken to the teacher's house of the Fairview Girls' School. The school building is in disrepair, but this large residence has been kept in quite good condition to serve vacationing missionaries. Dr. Rice, who lives here while awaiting passage to America, has recently made several nice improvements. Here again is a wonderful view of the Indian Ocean—if anything, even better than from the farmhouse. These houses are about a quarter of a mile apart.

The next morning Doctor Rice and A. E. Haley took me to Izingolweni, the rail station for Edwaleni Industrial School.

This was a great morning, my first real view of African villages and African transport. I actually saw a woman carrying a baby on her back, and a large load of wood on her head, being followed by her husband riding on the horse. A woman will bring the horse to the train for the husband, and return home carrying his suitcase on her head while he rides. It is a man's world.

We started our mission meeting that evening, July 24, and continued the following day. On Friday at 6:30 a.m., on invitation of Rev. J. Cele, our pastor at Fairview. I had the privilege of preaching my first sermon in Africa. The church was full, my heart was full, and the Lord helped me. My interpreter broke down in tears, and we had a wonderful altar service. Brother Cele asked me to hold a revival meeting for him. Our people seem to be hungry for a real spiritual awakening.

After breakfast we were off to visit Pondoland. I saw deserted mission stations at Greenville and Critchlow, a sad and sorry sight. This was a full day. We arrived late at Itemba for the quarterly meeting. Miss Hartman had a real meal waiting for us. It was cold and windy, but there was a good congregation. I heard the evangelists' reports the next morning in quarterly conference. Altogether there were nine conversions reported since conference.

In the afternoon we visited the Ebenezer Hospital. I expected to see something falling into decay; reports had been so gloomy. Here was the one really fine building in all our South Africa work. There are sixteen rooms. The walls are concrete, and the roof is of tile. Some repairs are needed. There is a fine electric lighting plant and one hundred acres of land. There is a small chapel, and buildings for tools, a house for the caretaker, and the usual farm buildings. Both bus and train stop at the station just across the road from the entrance, and this is the center of our work. Itemba Mission Station is about two miles across country. We have eight hundred acres at that station.

Sunday was a busy day. The Kresges and Miss Current came, and a truckload of boys from Edwaleni. After the morning sermon, A. E. Haley conducted the communion service. It was a cold day, but there was a fair congregation. According to plan, I returned to Edwaleni with the Kresges. This is about twenty-five miles from Itemba and the Ebenezer Hospital. We have 1,063 acres, including two beautiful hilltops. A good river forms a great

Edwaleni Industrial School

bend around three sides of our property. It is a scenic location.

Edwaleni means "on the rock." It is literally true. There are four major buildings here—the school building, the principal's residence, the teacher's house, and the shop building. Doctor Rice has worked hard during these difficult years. He has farmed a large piece of land down by the river, to augment the food supply for a dormitory of one hundred fifty. A pump at the river sends water up the new pipeline to the school for irrigation and washing. Tin roofs and large cisterns provide the drinking water. The shop is very large, being constructed by Doctor Rice after the storm that almost totally destroyed the first building. The government assisted us in this. Smaller buildings include the blacksmith shop, the leather shop, the tannery, the garage and storehouse. The large school building contains the chapel, the dining hall, boys' dormitory, and tailor shop. This is a substantial building, with concrete foundation and steel girders beneath the floor; but everywhere there is need for a thorough repair and reconditioning job. Everything is worn down—steps, floors, walls, furniture and equipment. . . .

On Friday, August 2, we made the trip to Ebenezer Hospital for the conference evangelistic rally. A. E. Haley took me on to Edwaleni for lunch and the special chapel in the afternoon. I thrilled with the opportunity to address one hundred fifty select Christian men. I believe there is great work to do at Edwaleni in the days ahead.

We returned that afternoon for a week-end evangelistic conference at Ebenezer, August 2-4. Services were held in the mission tent, which was pitched on the front campus. Saturday afternoon I had a conference with the evangelists and pastors. They are few in number, and advanced in years, for the most part. Few new recruits are coming on. After hearing all the reports, which were more or less routine, I asked, "What can be done to have a revival in this area? Things are not going well. You have fewer members than you had years ago. Why are you not having success? What can the Missionary Board do to help you win more souls? What do you need?" No answer. Finally, one of the pastors asked, "What are our rights?" I arranged a meeting after supper to read them the chapter of the Discipline on the South Africa Mission Conference. I made a few comments. Then we adjourned for the evangelistic service.

I have come to the conclusion that the only thing that is basically wrong in South Africa is the thing that is wrong any place where the Lord's work is not succeeding. We need a revival in South Africa. Some may attempt to remedy matters by doing some external things, such as changing the Discipline. Possibly some changes are necessary, but these will fail of their purpose without the undergirding of a mighty revival. . . .

We had good meetings, and some conversions at the altar services. Monday and Tuesday we continued the mission meeting at Ebenezer. I think some good work was done.

Tuesday night I met with the purchasers at Fairview. They presented a program of music, readings and speeches. These are the best educated and probably the most ambitious of all our African people. It requires tact and a progressive philosophy of missionary work to successfully guide such people.

August 7 I visited Adams College, which is sponsored by the American Board. I preached to a full house that night in Durban. The next day was a busy one, arranging the bank account for the Board, checking on transportation for Doctor Rice, and having a last meeting with the missionaries.

Arriving the next morning at Johannesburg, I was met by Jules Ryff. He is all business. He rushed me off to Pretoria, the capital, some forty miles distant. Here I had my passport visaed for return to the Transvaal after the Portuguese East Conference. While at Pretoria I interviewed the Assistant Superintendent of Public Health regarding the government plan for health work in the Ebenezer Hospital area. That night the little Germiston Chapel was filled with Europeans for a welcome service and missionary meeting. Mrs. Ryff, assisted by the two daughters, sponsors the work among the Europeans.

The next evening I spoke for Jules Ryff at one of the mine schools. There were over two hundred enthusiastic men present. Sunday morning Frederic Ryff was my interpreter. There were more than three hundred men, and we had a great altar service. Sunday afternoon Frederic took me to his home at Witbank, and the next morning at four o'clock we were ready to leave for Portuguese East Africa. We arrived at our lovely Inhamachafo Station long after midnight. . . .

Portuguese East Africa

The Portuguese East Conference opened at 2 p.m., Thursday. Frederic Ryff was my interpreter. Conference opened with the sacramental service. When I started to get the business under way, there was some confusion. A committee came forward to make speeches. They had everything planned to greet their "grandfather the Bishop and their father the Missionary Secretary," so they went through with it all, reading their speeches and presenting their gifts to us both.* After the gifts came the list of requests. When the "Great One" visits them they do not honor him unless they ask him for something. If you do not ask for something, it means that you do not think the "Great One" is able to do anything for you. Well, it was an interesting

---

*Changing the date of the trip made it impossible for Bishop Ormston to make the visit to Africa.

list, and after a meeting with the missionaries, was easily answered two days later.

During the conference I visited the Portuguese Administrator. He received me cordially and we had a most pleasant exchange of views. He, as every other person, wanted to know about conditions in America.

Sunday was a great day. While I was preaching Sunday morning, the Spirit of God moved on the people—about fifteen hundred under the trees in front of the church. They stopped the service by rushing forward for an altar service. After a great season of prayer, I continued with the sermon, until I saw the congregation start to leave me. They were running for the church. I looked around. The rain was coming. So we all crowded into the church, that is, about one-third of the congregation, and I finished the sermon. Then we had another good season of prayer.

There was a grand missionary meeting Sunday afternoon. Men and women reported our new work in Northern Mozambique and Southern Rhodesia, and the offering, which was given to the Missionary Board, amounted to seventy-five dollars in our money. This was something, in a country where the highest paid preacher receives thirty-six dollars for the year!

On Monday, August 19, we visited our Massinga Station, one hundred fifty miles north. This is primitive country. We have a fourteen-thousand-acre plantation here. There are fine mission buildings. The two wells do not furnish enough water for the mission needs. If we can drill deeper to a large supply of water, then we can go ahead with another evangelists' school. This is the center of a new revival movement. Many young people were in the service. This is the base for operations through undeveloped, primitive, unevangelized country for hundreds of miles west and north to our Southern Rhodesia field. . . .

Transvaal

Early Wednesday morning, August 21, I left with Frederic Ryff and his family for the Transvaal, and I was with him all week, over Sunday, and until the following Wednesday. We passed through a large game reserve to reach our first appointment. This half-day looking for wild animals as we were driving along is really the only release from work I had on the entire trip. I have never worked harder, but I enjoyed every bit of it. Everything seemed so necessary, so long overdue, so needing an answer, and it was unto the Lord, and I was blessed in the doing of it. But this one afternoon, we saw all manner of deer, antelope, elk, giraffe, baboons, buffalo, hippopotami, and zebra. We came to a spot where three lions had made a kill, but actually missed seeing them by a few minutes. There were elephants, but we missed them, too.

195

I will not detail the trips with Frederic Ryff. In general it can be said that our Transvaal work is with the Portuguese East boys who have come up to the Rand to work in the mines. Jules Ryff works the nearby mines east but mostly those west from Johannesburg, over a total spread of one hundred miles. Frederic is located at Witbank, eighty miles east of Johannesburg. Besides the large mining area near Witbank, he has schools and preaching arrangements for very large numbers of mines east and north. He has a preaching plan which is printed so that each evangelist and teacher knows exactly his assignment each week. I was impressed with the excellent organization worked out by Jules Ryff, and used also by Frederic. These men both have the happy faculty of knowing how to assign responsibility and check results. Through a system of deacons, inspectors, and evangelists, a record is kept of each member, his church attendance, school attendance, contributions, spiritual condition. When he moves from one mine to another, or returns to Portuguese East, the evangelist at that place is notified, and his record is transferred. I have never seen anything like it. You understand that these men are hundreds of miles from their homes. The average period of work is one and one-half years. The mines are glad to have us organize these schools where the men learn to read and write. They are taught to read the Bible and the hymn book, as well as other Christian literature. It was my privilege to preach in several of the mines, and there was always an excellent response. This was my heaviest schedule. We had several services each day. It was always a rush to make the next mine by the appointed time. Sunday,

Jules Ryff plans work with district elders

196

August 25, called for a district meeting in the morning at eleven, but in addition we had three other preaching services, 9 a.m., 3 p.m. and 7:30 p.m. I was very weary, but we were up at four the next morning, to meet the next appointment.

The Ryffs are so busy caring for our own Free Methodist people from Portuguese East that they are unable to do anything for the permanent residents of the Transvaal native locations. This might be attempted, with additional personnel. But our men are learning while they earn, and when they return to their homes they become real spiritual leaders. Some have opened up new work on their own initiative. To my great satisfaction, I found that in the Portuguese East Conference we have many more circuits and churches than some other boards. Our church does not know how really strong this work is. But we are very short of staff. One man is now principal and teacher of the Evangelists' School, and also superintendent of over three hundred churches!

Southern Rhodesia

The last service in the Northern Transvaal was at Messina, ten miles from the Southern Rhodesia border. Next morning, by previous arrangement, we met Ralph Jacobs, superintendent of our Rhodesia work, at the Customs and Immigration office. After brief passport checking, my bags were carried across the line, and we bade dear Frederic Ryff fond adieu. We pray for additional staff, to assist Frederic in his extensive field.

We left the border at 10:45 a.m., and arrived at the new station, Matibi Number 2, at 5 p.m. The government and the local chiefs urged us to bring schools and missionaries to this area. After much prayer, the missionaries felt that the new work should be opened before the Jacobses leave on furlough. The site was carefully selected and a government grant of one hundred acres received. A permanent garage and storeroom are just completed. The school is temporarily housed in a lean-to, beside the garage. There is a hut for the evangelist, a dining hut and a sleeping hut. During the afternoon drive we encountered abundant supplies of wild game. This is the land of the lion and the elephant, too. I was outwardly brave when appointed to the thatch-roofed, mud-walled and mud-floored hut, as my detached bedroom for the night, but I made two mistakes. I failed to carry a flashlight, and I sprayed thoroughly with DDT. I did a thorough job, as there was no screening, and I promptly fell asleep. Some time later I was awakened by singing at the evangelist's hut. Several bugs had fallen on my pillow. I brushed them off, crediting DDT properly. Just as I was dozing off, a heavier object plumped down on my covers. I hastily shook off the nocturnal visitor, pulled my head under the sheet, and repented my use of DDT. How much better to leave the poisonous things in the thatch than to have them fainting and falling from their nests to my bed! Somehow, day finally arrived, and with it the discovery that the "scorpion" was only a big fat beetle. My friends, the missionaries, seem to enjoy this story.

New Station—Nuanetsi

During breakfast, news came that water is in the new well. There was heartfelt rejoicing. How earnestly prayer for water had been made the night before! We went to see another charge of dynamite set off. At 9:30, the heathen began arriving from all directions, the most primitive people I have ever seen. The chief who walked seventy-five miles to ask for schools is there. They sit on the ground with blank looks, five hundred of them, naked and near naked. They cannot sing; they cannot read; they have never heard the gospel. What an hour! The text is, "I declare unto you the gospel . . . how that Christ died for our sins." When I am through, the evangelist jumps up and exhorts, repreaching part of the sermon. The old chief says "Amen," and then makes his address of thanksgiving for schools, the three already started, and for missionaries. He calls attention to several places where more schools are needed. It is his big day. I feel that God and the Free Methodist Church will hear this Macedonian call, and do something about it.

Lundi

After lunch we leave for Matibi Number 1, eighty miles north and west. It is dark, seven o'clock, when our headlights fall on the new hippo-proof gate at the mission boundary, and something new overhead, large cardboard letters spelling out the word WELCOME. What a welcome it was—seventy-five young people, besides teachers and some from the Christian village, standing at the driveway in front of the "big house" to sing their songs of welcome. They promise to return after dinner with more songs. And dinner it is, turkey dinner for all the missionaries, Jacobs, Sayres, Mae Armstrong, Ruth Smith and Miss Frederick. The chorus returns, so we retire to the lovely screened-in front porch. The harmony is wonderful. Their school song in English, "The Lundi Central School," to the tune of "The Church in the Wildwood," was most excellently done, and had real heart appeal. The contrast to Matibi Number 1 will never be forgotten. "I am not ashamed of the gospel!"

We were off early. Jacobs, Sayre, Smith and Armstrong, to visit the schools. They are located at strategic population centers from twelve to fifteen miles apart. There is a teacher and an evangelist at each location. The school buildings are of brick, with thatch roof and mud floor. Desks and benches are locally made. This is the school during the week, and the church on Sunday. In the mid-afternoon we found groups of our people loaded heavily with their food and camp equipment, traveling on foot to the district meeting at Lundi. They arrived the next day. Some traveled forty miles. Our members are young people, and young married people—a real youth movement.

A Gospel Preacher

Saturday morning the crowd is too large for the church, so service is held under the trees. One of the evangelists is preaching. His coat is well worn. He wears shorts, no socks, and patched shoes. His face is all aglow as he preaches on the Last Judgment. He reads the story of the flood. He tells of the government action regarding herds of infected cattle. "They were not sick, but they were infected. They were killed, and the bodies burned. This is a picture of the Last Judgment. Sinners will go to the outer darkness. But the veterinary has an injection against disease. Herds that have been inoculated are safe. Jesus also has an injection, a power, the gospel, that He can apply to our hearts and keep us free from sin." You should hear the whole-souled "Amens." Six years ago, this man and this congregation were as pagan and sinful as the Matibi Number 2 crowd, but the gospel of Jesus Christ works miracles. The preacher handled his Bible like an expert, and he preached with unction. Saturday afternoon I had a conference with the preachers and teachers. Sunday was a full day, 9:30 a.m. communion, with five hundred in the congregation; 10:30 a.m., preaching and altar service, followed by testimony meeting; 1:30 p.m., baptism of forty-seven and reception of fifty-eight church members; 7:30 p.m., service with missionaries. I had no sleep, for it was necessary to leave by car at midnight to reach the Bulawayo airfield in time for the morning plane to Urundi. . . .

Congo

At Muyebe there were two hundred fifty gathered to sing their welcome. This meant another speech, but it is getting simpler each time. It is good to be at the Haley House, even if but for a night. Next morning we go thirty miles to Kibuye, visiting village schools on the way. Enthusiastic reception by the hundreds everywhere! Betty Cox and the Bilderbacks are at Kibuye. The government has approved a hospital for this station. The location is ideal, with more level land than is usually found. There are two good brick-walled, thatch-roofed missionary residences, a guest house, servants' quarters, garage, brick-and-tile school, 40x120, dispensary and infirmary huts, a church which was formerly a drying shed for tile, but Allen Bilderback has put in brick walls, and a platform at one end, and it will seat one thousand people. It was filled for our one o'clock service! It is here that a wonderful revival

199

movement is in progress, and on the last Sunday of September six hundred members were received into the church. Our missionaries here are young, enthusiastic and happy, and the Lord is giving them success, even though they are still learning the language.

Thursday, September 12, we returned to Muyebe. At 3 p.m. our meeting with the Free Methodist missionaries began, and continued Thursday night, Friday and Saturday. . . . Saturday we met with twenty preachers and twenty delegates of the Congo-Nile Mission. They have no conference, but operate according to the Free Methodist Discipline. The missionaries were unanimous in requesting ordination for three really sanctified and spiritual leaders. All of them have taken everything offered in the preacher's course of study. This was approved by the preachers and delegates, after I had asked the disciplinary questions.

Muyebe—Largest Church

Sunday at Muyebe will never be forgotten. I had already seen the evangelists at work. They spent Saturday questioning candidates, checking membership lists, making sure there were no mistakes. Services started at 8:30 Sunday morning. Try to believe me when I say there were three thousand seated on the ground in the patio between two wings of the school building. Who could have dry eyes? Eleven years ago there were no Christians and no schools here. Then came a man sent from God, and his name was J. W. Haley. Today there are these hundreds of humble followers of Jesus Christ. After the benediction the great congregation hastens down the hill to the river. There are two hundred twenty candidates for baptism, women on one

Muyebe church has largest membership in world Free Methodism

side of the river, men on the other. The congregation lines the bank and the hillside to witness the service. I have the privilege of sharing in the baptismal rites. In addition, three hundred fifty probationers are received, making a total of five hundred seventy members coming into the church in one day. A few more than this were ready to be received at Kibuye, but time and strength made it impossible to do it all the same day. Think of it, nearly twelve hundred ready to join in one day! I felt as if I were back in the Book of Acts. Really, I did not dream that there was any place in the world where such numbers were coming into the Kingdom. I have talked with other mission secretaries, and missionaries, and I am convinced that this is the ripest field for evangelism in the world today.

Monday, Tuesday, and Wednesday were spent at the Danish Baptist Mission, where the Ruanda-Urundi Alliance was in session. About thirty missionaries, representing the missions at work in this area, met for spiritual fellowship and business. J. W. Haley has pioneered this organization and every mission feels indebted to him. It was good to find things in such a state. These people are really stressing spiritual things. They pray for revival in good old Wesleyan terms. The Anglican missionaries seem like old-time Methodists. I reminded them that John Wesley was our spiritual father. When hearts are one, heads can get along quite well.

The best of the wine had been saved for the last of the feast. It was a weary body, carrying a light and happy heart, that reluctantly said "goodbye" to Urundi.

I feel very unworthy of this great experience. I have been privileged to see God at work in Africa. The Free Methodist Church does not know how really great the work is, what golden opportunities face us on every field, how terribly understaffed and overworked we are and how desperately urgent immediate action is. The time is now. And Africa is only one of our fields!

Lessons from Trip

The Secretary summarized his conclusions from the trip, writing while stranded for three weeks in Leopoldville awaiting the resumption of the "Constellation" flights. He said:

1. My ideas regarding missionary candidates have been changed. The mission field is no place to orient inexperienced youth to the work of the Lord. Every missionary candidate should have successful pastoral, educational, medical or industrial experience in this country before appointment to the foreign field. The need is so great we may be tempted to rush candidates off, immediately upon graduation from college or seminary, but I am persuaded that this is usually not the best plan.

2. I am satisfied, too, that we need to give more attention to the method

of missionary work. Some of our missionaries do have a real insight into the missionary task of the church. They know what they are doing and why, and they have success. In other places, there is little evidence of any program being consistently followed. There are meager results and a tendency to place blame on the Board; on the natives; on conditions. We must study our missionary program, and see that new missionaries go to the field with a philosophy of missions that will work. It is not enough to raise and appropriate money and send missionaries. What is the missionary to do with his time and our money when he arrives? That must be our concern.

3. The missionaries are a unit in begging for closer contact with the home Board. They want a representative from the Board to preside over their annual sessions and help them follow a consistent policy of development on the field through the years. We have monuments on every field to "strong-willed" missionaries. Many of these projects are now idle and in decay. We have wasted money. With the right sort of general leadership, I feel that it will be only a few years until our mission membership will equal that of the homeland. I honestly think that the saving in unwise and costly ventures, the special projects of some sincere missionary who does not see all the field, would more than pay the cost. Besides this, a forward move under God into these whitened fields would doubtless turn thousands to righteousness, and no money value can be placed on this achievement.

4. The church in America does not know how large and how important our work is. It is staggering to discover that in large areas we have the leading mission work, judged by numbers of churches and members. Other missions look to us for leadership. Somehow we must do a better job of telling the Free Methodist Church what the Lord is doing around the world. Also, we must have a balanced picture. Some missionaries are good publicity agents. They spend more time at the typewriter than in the native villages. The various fields need full and proportionate representation.

5. The missionaries stress the importance of censoring reports from the field. No material critical of the colonial governments or of other churches should appear in print or form a part of a missionary's deputation addresses. Our work depends in large measure on friendly relations with the government. It is therefore most important for Belgian Congo missionaries to have residence in Belgium en route to the field. Likewise, appointees to Mozambique should reside in Lisbon for some time. The purpose of such residence is two-fold: first, to gain a speaking knowledge of the official language of the colony; and second, to develop an understanding of, and an appreciation for the institutions of the home government, as well as to make personal contact with government officials, which will prove of inestimable value when residence is established in the colony.

The Secretary had been in Africa almost four months. Delayed on the return by mechanical difficulties, he finally reached Winona Lake less than ten days in advance of the annual meeting in October.

Section 3—AREAS OF SERVICE

Missionary pioneers not only venture to the new geographic areas but undertake new and different methods of work in fields already occupied. The Secretary, at the conclusion of his first Africa trip, keenly felt the necessity of giving "more attention to the method of missionary work." Of course, missionary policy and method must be grounded in a sound philosophy of missions and an understanding of the nature of the church. The Christian worker will need insight into the special forms the malady of sin takes in the part of the world he serves. He must be able to speak of man's awful lostness in understandable terms. Man's deepest needs and most devious wanderings must be grasped for what they are, a degradation for which there is no cure apart from the gospel of Christ. The ambassador for Christ needs to understand his gospel. First, having experienced this miracle power in his own life and observed its working in the lives of others, he will have an ever stronger faith in its adequacy for the needs of the least, the last, the lowest and the lost. He can affirm that when men repent of their sins and believe the gospel, they will be saved. If this did not happen, he would never preach such a gospel again. His is a higher pragmatism.

> "Go and shew John again those things which ye do hear and see: the blind receive their sight, and the lame walk, the lepers are cleansed, and the deaf hear, the dead are raised up, and the poor have the gospel preached to them."[15]

This is the final test of the validity of the Christian faith. Is it coherent with the facts of life? Are its teachings in harmony with all we know about the nature of the universe and the character of man? We know of no way to amend the affirmation: "The wages of sin is death"[16] to bring it in line with truer truth. Just as valid is the gospel offer: "If we confess our sins He is faithful and just to forgive us our sins, and to cleanse us from all unrighteousness."[17] The experience of multiplied thousands through all the Christian centuries gives witness to this truth. In this confidence the Christian worker ever seeks ways to make relevant and meaningful the great message of salvation. The mighty acts of God which He wrought in the birth and life, the death and resurrection of Jesus Christ, must become understandable in the situations where men live.

> "And Jesus went about all Galilee, teaching in their synagogues, and

203

preaching the gospel of the Kingdom, and healing all manner of sickness, and all manner of disease among the people. . . . And they brought unto him all sick people that were taken with divers diseases and torments, and those which were possessed with devils, and those which were lunatic, and those that had the palsy; and he healed them. And there followed him great multitudes."[18]

It was a sick world. Men were tormented by fear. They were insane and devil-possessed. Their nerves were shattered. This is a picture of the world then and the world now without Christ. Jesus came to this world with a message and a miracle. He changed that world, by healing the sick, giving His peace to the fearful, casting out the devils of greed and jealousy, hate and uncleanness, and filling those same lives with love and service, forgiveness and purity. To the palsied nervous wrecks, harried with a bad past, immersed in a nasty present, He promised:

"Whosoever heareth these sayings of mine and doeth them, I will liken him unto a wise man, which built his house upon a rock.

"And the rain descended, and the floods came, and the winds blew, and beat upon that house, and it fell not; for it was founded upon a rock."[19]

The Christian miracle makes men strong on the inside so that they can stand anything that may happen to them.

What are the needs of our world? How do we implement the essential message of Christ, bringing it into miracle-working contact with that need? In times of crop failure, famine relief has been dispensed in Portuguese East Africa, Southern Rhodesia, China, India and Japan. Such programs of direct relief are at best temporary. Efforts are made to develop training centers where on a long-time basis people living in these low-income-producing areas may be trained to better care for themselves. In times of sudden catastrophe, however, Christians must always remember to "bear one another's burdens."

Medical Missions

At the beginning of the period under review, there were neither doctors nor nurses assigned to the India hospital, although for many years the buildings had been completed. Today there are two missionary and two Indian doctors working full time. The nursing is handled by an all-Indian staff. A mobile medical unit is in operation on regular schedule in the villages, this work being correlated with the ministry of the local church. Recent improvements include staff quarters, a second doctor's residence and a water system to replace the bullock cart and tank arrangement. The heroic efforts of John Benson, Plant Manager of the Free Methodist Publishing House, to provide water for Umri Hospital is a full chapter in our missions story.

Staff at Umri Mission
Hospital, India, 1960

Water system—yesterday, India

Inauguration new water system at Umri Mission Hospital, India

Benson drew the plans with specifications, raised the needed funds for the materials and his own trip expense to India, where he supervised the project, bringing it to completion in 1959. He lost twenty pounds in the process and appeared to be several shades darker upon his return.

During World War II our South Africa doctor was pressed into service as principal of the Edwaleni Industrial School. He has been released for full-time service in the medical program. With government assistance, the Greenville Hospital has been constructed. It is located in a needy area where Free Methodists have sole responsibility for the evangelization of the people. The hospital is already crowded. A nurse's training program is operated in connection with the medical program. A new residence for the doctor has recently been completed. The construction of buildings in areas so far removed from sources of supply for materials increases the missionary's difficulties. Area Secretary C. H. Zahniser was sent by the Commission to assist the already overworked doctor, J. Lowell Rice, in bringing the project to completion.

The primitive area of Southern Rhodesia where Free Methodist missionaries work is one of great need. Here, as in South Africa, a friendly govern-

Missionary doctor, Paul Embree, assisted by missionary nurse Nina Detwiler and African nurse, treating patients, Southern Rhodesia

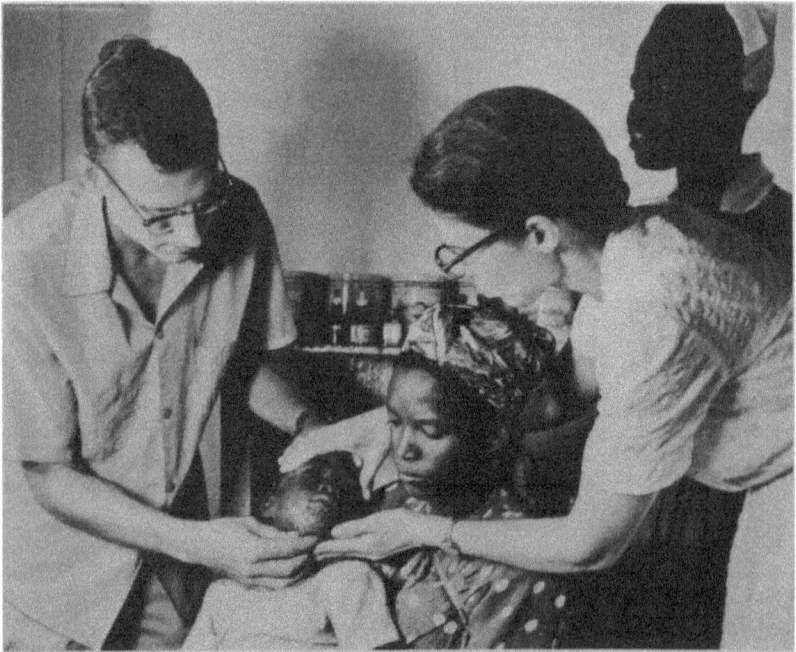

ment grants subsidy for current operating expenses as well as capital grants for buildings and equipment. The Lundi Mission Clinic is the outgrowth of medical work done by non-medical missionaries from the opening of the mission. The present clinic serves a wide area and is presided over by a registered nurse with regular visitation by the missionary doctor. At the Chikombedzi Clinic (Nuanetsi Hospital), ninety miles southeast of Lundi, several buildings are complete and in use. Other buildings have been approved and will be financed jointly by mission and government funds. A mobile medical unit operates in the villages, with an effective evangelistic program. This is the big game country, the land of lions and elephants. Travel is ever dangerous under such conditions. Calls are answered, day or night, sometimes to distant villages where the seriously injured or the sick cannot be moved. A stretcher on bicycle wheels has been most useful. The writer assisted in the dedication of a new tuberculosis village and in ground-breaking for the second unit of the hospital. The latter is now complete and in operation.

A large hospital with several buildings has been established in the Congo. Dispensaries are in operation at most of the mission stations. The Kibogora station clinic is the largest of these and should be developed into a regular hospital program. The government has made regular grants for medical supplies and has assisted with certain equipment, the largest project being the installation of a large water system to serve the entire hospital area. Bricks and tile for the buildings were made on the job. Friends in America have been moved to assist in providing these facilities. At one missionary convention a man came to the writer expressing the conviction that he should build one of these hospital units. He would talk with his wife. Soon both returned. Although seated in different parts of the church, both had been challenged to provide the funds for this building. This was only the beginning of their generous gifts.

Other medical programs have been established in Portuguese East Africa. Two maternity centers here have been favorably received by the government officials. Good work is being done in Paraguay at the Asuncion Clinic. Registered nurses are located at the school centers in the Dominican Republic and in Japan, where they care for the medical needs of the students. In the Philippines our registered nurse renders limited service as prescribed by law.

There are thirty eight Free Methodist doctors and nurses serving in twenty-one hospitals and dispensaries. Approximately three hundred thousand treatments are administered each year at an average cost to the church of ten cents each.* The Umri Mission Hospital, India, reports:

"Powdered milk and cheese have been given out to literally thousands

---

*Government subsidies assist in keeping the costs low.

in the past year through the hospital. It is our practice to give free milk to all in-patients and poor tuberculosis and leprosy patients, and malnourished children.

"Case No. 1. She is the laundryman's wife. She had been coughing up blood for a considerable length of time and losing weight. Intensive investigation revealed the presence of the dreaded tubercle bacillus. This means a long hospital stay with treatment by expensive anti-tuberculous drugs amounting, even with our lower mission hospital rates, to $6.50-$8.50 per month. Besides this, the woman is six months pregnant.

"To make the situation even more difficult, the laundryman's wage is equal only to the basic minimum charge necessary to care for his wife in the hospital. Also, the Government of India, except for special government employees, offers no financial help for such sufferers.

"However, there is available the *Compassion Fund* sent out by the Free Methodist churches of Canada and the United States. The laundryman's wife was admitted to one of the tuberculosis huts on the hill, and with rest, good food, milk, cheese, wheat gifts sent out by the government through Church World Service, and the anti-tuberculous drugs, the patient is showing definite progress.

"This is just one isolated case. We cannot begin to meet the need. Therefore we have to pick selected cases for this help. Truly, the tuberculosis problem of India, like their population problem, is, as it were, a never-ending stream.

"Case No. 3. Marcus was sent by Miss Helen Rose, one of our missionaries who is doing public health work in the villages. He was suffering from tuberculosis of the bone. With prolonged rest and medicine and a few simple surgical procedures, Marcus became well physically. Also, he was baptized as a new creature in Christ several weeks before he came out of his caste. From all we can observe, both his physical and spiritual healing have lasted, and at present he is a profitable worker for the hospital.

"The important thing is that all these patients hear the gospel message as they come to the hospital and most of them purchase a Gospel portion to take back to their village. We were encouraged recently to talk with a missionary of another denomination who has a work two hundred miles away from us, as he told us that upon coming to a certain village in his area for the first time and beginning to talk about Jesus, he was gladdened to hear the immediate reply that they had already heard about Jesus when they visited Umri Mission Hospital."[20]

Ventures in Farming

Dr. Frank Laubach, literacy missionary and world Christian, says: "Our chief problem today is not Communism, it is the *hunger* which gave birth to Communism—the hunger of body, mind and soul. We are running a race between compassion and suicide."

Millions have been robbed on our Jericho roads. There are the economically hurt. In Asia there are more people who have never once had enough to eat than the total population of North and South America. One-half of the world has never seen a bed or a doctor or a dentist. With 9 per cent of the world's population, North America has 43 per cent of the world's wealth. Asia with 53 per cent of the world's population has only 11 per cent of the world's wealth. The life expectancy in North America is sixty-seven years; in Asia it is twenty-seven. Broken men and women by the millions lie along the Jericho road.

In Jesus' familiar story, the priest and the Levite represent the type of church that thinks primarily of itself. Jesus said, "Ye are the salt of the earth." We are to function as salt, as saviors. The priest and the Levite were more interested in being "salted" than in being "salt." They had a security complex; they were neutral. They acted on the basis of the law—the letter of the law, and not on love. The church in Russia became robes and ceremony and theology and creed. For a thousand years it conceived its function to engage in prayer and develop its holiness separate and apart from the life of the nation. The church became cold and unresponsive to the needs of the Russian people. It stopped being salt and the world came in and trampled it under foot. The priest and the Levite represent what the church ought *not* to be.

The good Samaritan acted on the principle of love. He gave until the need was met. He gave himself. He gave time, talent, courage, physical strength, money, good will and friendship. Love goes beyond the rules, between the rules and under the rules.

The good Samaritan church must share. It happened in a small East African city. The hotel was crowded and guests were asked to "double up" on the rooms. One woman was overheard telling the hotel clerk, "I can't share; I never have shared." The priest and the Levite didn't share, but the good Samaritan did share. He is the picture of what the church *ought* to be. . . . There are bandages to roll, there is clothing to collect and send to our missionaries for distribution to the needy. The church must underwrite the support of doctors and nurses, hospitals and clinics. We must provide vitamins, medicines, medical instruments, and food supplements. We will continue to support the classes in agriculture and trade school education. We will encourage the people of Kentucky to raise strawberries instead of tobacco on the barren hillsides for a cash crop. Missionaries teach the rotation of crops in Africa and the use of good seed. We want to help men everywhere to cooperate with the laws of God so that they may have enough food for themselves and for their children.

Missionary Rolland Davis in India has been experimenting with soybeans

Agricultural missionary Edwin Clemens inspects corn dwarfed by drought

to discover the type that grows best in the soil and climate of central India. He has prepared careful reports on twenty-five varieties, laying the foundation for a better food supply from impoverished land in an overcrowded country. Edwin Clemens, professionally-trained agriculturist in Portuguese East Africa, is teaching pastors and Christian village leaders the secrets of fertilizer, cultivation, good seed and crop rotation. Already there is a noticeable difference in the crops of the heathen and the Christian villages. The non-Christians are asking, "What makes the difference?" Here is a new field for evangelism. The earth, the rain, the sunshine come from God. We belong to God. God's laws for all of life must be obeyed. This includes the moral law as well as the laws of growing corn and cotton and beans. In the 1956 India famine the people of the Free Methodist area were eating leaves and fodder. Grants of aid for shipments of food to the area assisted our missionaries in dealing with a stubborn situation. Hand-operated seeders and the "stab corn planter," along with Laubach literacy charts and the "Story of Jesus" in words of one syllable, are an integral part of mission equipment. The Christian church believes that women must no longer follow the herds of water buffalo picking up the fresh-fallen manure from which they screen the undigested grains to cook for the next meal. The big trucks should no longer rumble through the streets of Asia's big cities, picking up in the early morning those who have starved to death on the sidewalks during the night. It is a ghastly picture. The luxury, the softness and purposeless extravagances of our society mock us in this tragic hour of man's plight—man's hunger.

Bible Schools

Pioneer missionaries recognized from the first the necessity of training the native and national leaders to evangelize their own people. Agnew in Portuguese East Africa picked out men with qualities of leadership whom he thought would make good preachers and evangelists after they were converted. Laid low with the malarial fever, Agnew persisted in his translation of simple theology for his Bible school students. He never expected to see America again, but his evangelists must have a book on Bible doctrine! Without a Bible school, Lucy Hartman called the district evangelists to the station each week for one day of intensive Sunday-school lesson and Bible study. In Formosa, the mountain preachers from the aboriginal tribes churches, with meager educational background and a different language, are unable to profit from the regular classes at the Holy Light Bible Seminary. Special instruction is given these men for one week each month. They then return to the mountains, put into practice all they have learned and then return the following month for another "short course" in Bible. There is no other way just now, considering the urgency of getting the gospel to all these neglected peoples.

Geneva Sayre risked her life in Honan, China, after the political turnover, to establish the Kaifeng Bible School on a firm, self-supporting basis. The Bible school continued its work after all missionaries were forced to leave the country. Temporarily re-established in Chungking, the missionaries first of all started a Bible school! Amid the ruins of churches and parsonages, Japan placed priority on rebuilding its Bible school. On the island of Awaji thousands of New Testaments were distributed with a Christian testimony by these students. They also aided Kaneo Oda and De Shazer in their tent evangelism campaigns. The huts and gardens of the Evangelists' School in Portuguese East Africa is the most prized investment in the conference. Here are trained for larger service the men who will be leaders in the church tomorrow. They come with their families, live in a typical village, cultivate their fields in the early morning hours, then attend classes until late at night. It is a self-supporting program, one of the finest we have seen. Nogales Bible School students have week-end assignments, assisting pastors in Mexico with the regular church program and in opening new Sunday schools and preaching points. In Formosa, the Bible school has priority in field planning. To-day almost forty students are in classes, with definite evangelism assignments each week. In primitive Southern Rhodesia a new Bible school was opened

211

Men's chorus at Bible school, Egypt

in 1957. Here the evangelists make blocks and otherwise assist in the building program during the morning, then attend classes in the afternoon. All have field work assignments. The Congo Bible school with its sixty-five students is none too large for the rapidly expanding work. The Egypt Bible school is far too small in a conference with over eighty churches. Property and enlarged facilities for this important school must be provided.

The most significant development of the period is the increased number of Bible schools and their enlargement. In India, on our Bible school campus, fifteen evangelical groups are cooperating in the operation of Union Biblical Seminary. The Free Methodist campus has been turned over to the Seminary Board of Governors on a long-term lease. The twelve students of our own Bible school are now included in a student group of one hundred. The unity of this fellowship is grounded in the Bible, prayer and evangelism. The evangelism morale is high. Recently thirteen teams returned from their vacation period evangelism crusades. Graduates have gained entrance into Nepal, where missionaries may not go. They labor as self-supporting missionaries in that difficult field. Asbury Seminary professors Harold Kuhn and Wilbur T. Dayton have each spent a sabbatical leave at Yeotmal. Incidentally, the Free Methodist Church in India has had more conversions and accessions to the church during the last decade than in the preceding seventy years of its history! There are other factors, but the work of the Seminary is certainly partially responsible for this forward move.

The day the writer arrived in India on his 1958 trip the newspaper in a nearby city carried this item:

"A Hindu priest has informed us that two learned Christian preachers are carrying on their work amongst the learned people with great force, and a large number of these educated people are in danger of changing their faith. They are not offering any material benefits but they are saying that after death they will certainly receive an inheritance in heaven, and they are saying this with all their conviction and with great force, and this eternal inheritance no one can receive outside of Jesus Christ. That is their meaning.

"I call on you, the people, heroes of the Hindu faith living in _____;
I call on you, rise up and combat this wild and foolish turning from the Hindu faith. Will you do this? Will you rise up?"[21]

Who were the "learned Christian preachers"? Two graduates of Union Biblical Seminary, members of the India Conference. Here is an insight into the value of sound Biblical education where prayer and evangelism are properly related. It is also an index, a sort of pointer to the weakening of the foundations, the working of the leaven, the promise of the new day when "every knee shall bow." This is the "cutting edge" of evangelism in an immediate encounter with the religions of mankind. This is "venture."

The training of an adequate national ministry is an integral factor in the development of the indigenous church. During this period the number of Free Methodist Bible schools has increased from four to fourteen.

Ventures in Evangelism

The recent shift in emphasis from the institutional work to that of direct evangelism by the larger denominational boards tends to confirm the im-

Evangelistic team, Union Biblical Seminary, India

portance Free Methodists have always attached to such work. We have seen
that Free Methodists are essentially missionary, not merely reformers. Their
foreign-field emphasis has been in the same direction.

"Our line of work has been . . . evangelistic, educational, the ministry
of healing, industrial and social uplift. Evangelism takes the first place.
Meetings in tents and halls and in the open air are the regular order.
Sunday schools, children's meetings and work among the women furnish
a large field which we are entering with great success."[22]

Since World War II, growing out of De Shazer's remarkable campaigns in
Japan where many thousands of serious inquirers made definite decisions,
the crusade method has become an important factor in our world-wide
strategy. At different times college quartets have visited the Dominican
Republic for evangelistic tours. An evangelist has been employed full-time to
conduct revival campaigns on our Spanish-speaking fields. Twice the denomination's youth organization has spearheaded a crusade movement in
the nearby Dominican Republic. The most recent of these continues to
bear fruit. Cooperation with evangelicals in city-wide campaigns in Japan,
India, Africa and Latin America is regular procedure.

De Shazer's campaigns in Japan are too well known to bear detailing at
this point. The Associated Press in Tokyo credited him with "thirty thousand converts during his first year in Japan. Recently, following his forty-
day fast with prayer for revival in Japan, Mr. De Shazer with Mr. Oda had
four thousand decisions for Christ in a fifteen-day campaign in southern

Missionary De Shazer telling Japanese policemen about Jesus and the Christian gospel

Japan. Night after night the altar services ran until early morning."[23] At Sendai in northern Japan Oda reported one hundred conversions. He organized a new church. A gospel radio program was broadcast from Osaka each week and new believers were being registered almost daily. Oda toured Brazil in 1955. Here he preached in most of the Japanese colonies and was most effective in presenting the gospel to the Buddhists. Mitsuo Fuchida, leader of the Pearl Harbor bombing squadron, was converted through the ministry of De Shazer and he too has become an effective evangelist.

Meanwhile, the work of evangelism proceeds on other fields. Frederic Ryff reported one hundred fifty at the altar during one trip visiting the mine schools and churches of the Transvaal. In Natal, South Africa, the Laymen's Convention was the occasion of seventy-five "repenting." Many decisions were made by young people at their youth camp. The next year (1957) three hundred hospital visits were being made in Durban each Sunday, while Edwaleni Technical College reported fifty-three conversions in their October revival. As these lines are written, our recent graduates of the Biblical Institute in South Africa are working in aggressive evangelism programs at Durban and the rural Ebenezer area.

In the Congo gospel teams have been used extensively from the first, holding short two- or three-day meetings in the school-church locations. They have been employed in opening up new areas, and loaned to other missions in times of special need. In 1955 the first converts, sixty-five lepers at the Nyankanda Colony, were baptized, and the following year sixty-seven were baptized at the Usumbura convention. That same year 821 were received

Pioneer missionary James H. Taylor, Jr., walks fifty miles in one week, visiting mountain churches, Formosa.

215

in church membership on the Kibogora district. In Southern Rhodesia and Portuguese East there is a strong urge to establish a line of churches across the hundreds of miles now separating the two fields. In 1954 the Portuguese Conference at their annual missionary meeting collected $160 to send their missionaries to this wild and dangerous section. New villages are frequently opened to the gospel through the medical services. In one of these, thirty prayed at the time of the missionary's first visit. Recently Portuguese businessmen have been converted through the faithful witness of the African Christians.

Revival meetings have been normal procedure on the new Formosa field where there has been an annual increase in membership of from 25 to 35 per cent. Mrs. Carolyn Winslow was permitted to preach in the Buddhist temple precincts. A radio program was established in 1954. At Fengshan, a new point in 1957, there were forty-three baptisms. One missionary walked fifty miles one week in an evangelistic trip to the mountain churches. Presently reports are being received of a continued revival movement and frequent baptismal services.

In India, the hospital creates an atmosphere favorable to the gospel. There is a Christian bookstore and reading room. The local pastor, serving as chaplain of the hospital, visits the patients, distributes Gospel portions, tracts and other Christian literature, conducts daily worship services, and follows the patients to their villages in a systematic way. This organized effort is bearing fruit with conversions regularly reported. In the villages the jeep with its public address system, the gospel films and slides, the preaching and singing team, arouse great interest. At the beginning of this period, only small groups listened to the gospel. At some villages there was no response. Today from five hundred to a thousand gather to hear the gospel and there are more calls from new villages than the workers are able to answer. An Indian superintendent recently reported to the writer of a village calling for the gospel but the officials had so far refused him permission to enter. He requested prayer that the situation might be changed.

Latin America has traditionally been unresponsive to mass evangelism efforts. Converts in these lands have usually been hand-picked, the fruit of personal witnessing. Here, too, conditions are changing. In the Dominican Republic one of the most experienced missionaries is in the field with a small team most of the time. The pastors, too, are learning that this "new" method bears much precious fruit. There were 113 converts in 226 services held. Gospels totaling eight thousand copies were distributed. Many have completed the Bible correspondence course. This, too, has led to conversions. More than thirteen thousand Gospel portions have also been given to the people. A goal of one thousand conversions was set for the team this last

Open-air evangelism in Brazil

Hong Kong evangelism

year (1959). There were thirty-seven decisions in the three weeks' meeting at one church. The Santiago crusade previously referred to registered not less than one thousand decisions and our nearby churches have been filled constantly since these meetings.

In Brazil there is a conference evangelism fund supplemented with mission funds. The best pastors consider it an honor to be sent to a new field where they have the privilege of opening up a new work! At one new preaching point there are already sixty "listeners." Open air and street meetings in the cities are very fruitful. One church with nearly two hundred young people in its membership has twenty-two Sunday-school and preaching assignments each week. There were conversions on Sunday morning when the writer recently preached for this congregation.

The Philippine field hitherto has recorded relatively small gains. The villages are widely scattered, the population sparse, and the working force inadequate. Reference has been made to Groesbeck's hazardous trip to the "Killer Tribe." Actually three trips were made. Datu Taglion and twenty of his followers were baptized in 1957 and have moved down from their wild mountain refuge to fertile land where they can raise food and where the government can provide schools. Others will continue to move down to the valley. The Bible school students are required to spend one year in directed evangelistic service as a part of their graduation requirement. As these lines are being written a city-wide crusade is in progress at Butuan. Prayers of Free Methodists around the world are supporting this great effort. Laymen, pastors and Bible school students received special training in personal evangelism, the use of the Bible, and above all, prayer, in preparation for the campaign. An organized follow-up was planned at the conclusion of the special services.

In Saskatchewan, Canada, there were eighty campers at the first Indian tent meeting in 1957. Thirty were baptized during the camp. In Mexico, the situation does not conform to a regular pattern. Some churches seem to have a continuous revival in their regular services. Others concentrate on district conventions. At the close of one special campaign at the Chandler, Arizona, church, twenty were received into membership.

Hong Kong, an overcrowded refugee city at the crossroads of the Far East, lends itself to special revival meetings. Besides the roof-top evangelism program, special campaigns are scheduled in the churches. In 1958 two such meetings resulted in sixty-seven conversions. More recently refugee Bible schools have been held on the flat tops of the resettlement apartment buildings. This program is accompanied with evangelistic services. Within recent weeks more than fifty have been baptized. Hundreds are hearing the gospel for the first time.

The writer assisted in the dedication of a new church in northern Japan in 1958. Several requested prayer at the morning service. In the evening, Oda preached a clear gospel sermon from the familiar text, "For I am not ashamed of the gospel of Christ, for it is the power of God unto salvation to everyone that believeth; to the Jew first, and also to the Greek."[24] He asked the people to remain in their seats and engage in silent prayer. Unexpectedly a fine-appearing gentleman jumped to his feet and began praying very fervently. The tears were rolling down his cheeks. Suddenly great peace came to him. There was a radiant smile on his face. From every corner of the room men hurried to welcome him into the "fellowship." He was the banker of the city and he had found Christ as his Saviour. This man is no exception. Thousands in every land are discovering the truth of the ancient promise, "For whosoever shall call upon the name of the Lord shall be saved."[25]

Literature

Accompanying the evangelistic emphasis and supplementing it is the work of literacy and literature. The immensity of the task may be realized by noting that at least one-half the people of the world are unable to read or write their own language. In Japan the literacy rate may be higher than in the United States. In India and Africa over 90 per cent are illiterate. In Egypt literacy campaigns are being promoted with unusual vigor. In the village of Deis Al-Baraha one such has been concluded with graduation exer-

Elizabeth Cox and total literature available in Ruanda-Urundi, 1956

cises. After prayer and singing an old man came to the platform. He said: "I am a new literate. Only four months ago, I started to learn reading and writing, and now listen to my reading." He then read a portion from the Sermon on the Mount. He was followed by a young man who reported what he had read about germs: ". . . Be careful not to walk with bare feet in the wet ground for the Nile water is full of germs as well. We must use pump water for drinking and washing. This we have learned from the Solih books, and we are trying to practice what we have read."

A woman shared in the program, telling what she had learned about flies. She knows now how to keep her children clean. A second woman read from "The Life of Christ." Through this reading she came to know Christ and has committed herself to the Christian way.[26]

In the Congo, on the occasion of the Secretary's visit in 1946, the total literature for three million people was not more than four or five little brochures. Our missionary Betty Ellen Cox is a pioneer in the Ruanda-Urundi literature movement. She has produced textbooks in geography and arithmetic and at the present time is finishing copy for the very first dictionary of the language! Laubach literacy methods are employed here as on other Africa fields. Miss Cox trained a small group of what she considered less than likely prospects for reading. After a few days she gave them a simple story about Jesus. She happened to be near as one of the slowest in the group jumped to his feet and, rushing to a few men standing near, exclaimed, "Look! See what Jesus did. He made that sick woman well. It says so. Why, fellows, that's our Jesus—that's our Jesus!"

After people learn to read, the real work begins. They must be supplied with literature. Too often we are weak at this point. Sunday-school literature must be prepared and books of sermons and theology provided for the pastors. Interesting literature in attractive format for the young people is desperately needed. Inter-mission cooperation is essential in such an undertaking.

Where suitable materials are not available, our missionaries have produced them, as in the Transvaal, Portuguese East, India, China, Formosa, Brazil, and the Spanish-speaking countries. This is not something new for Free Methodists. Ward was preparing a grammar for the Korkoo language and helping reduce it to writing in 1887. Four years later the Board declared that it had "no right to use mission funds to publish books."[27] That day has long since passed. In 1920 an appropriation of two hundred dollars was made for "newspaper evangelism" in Japan. Assistance has been given for the publication of devotional classics, theological and sermonic material. The Book of Discipline and the Catechism have, of course, been printed in the major languages.

Radio evangelism in Brazil

District superintendent using hand wound phonograph with gospel recording, India

Audio-Visual Methods

There is no substitute for the Christlike life of a devoted Christian. In harmony with our concern for the church we seek to establish, it is not wise to establish institutions or employ equipment that in the foreseeable future the people we serve will be unable to secure and maintain. Over against this consideration is the race against time and the legitimate desire of every Christian to extend his influence just as far as possible. The influence of the modern missionary is extended by the use of portable electric generators, gospel slides and films, projectors, public address systems, tape recorders, hand-wound phonographs and gospel recordings in the various dialects. These and many more mechanical aids are being employed by Free Methodist missionaries. More recently radio broadcasts, using the talents of the national church leaders, have been successfully produced. In primitive areas, the little hand-wound phonograph with gospel recordings is very effective. Left in the possession of the most qualified person in the village, the phonograph is a source of continual astonishment to the people. Day after day the records are played. Gradually some little understanding of the way of salvation is received. When the evangelist or missionary returns with the burning gospel message on his own heart, it is better understood than would otherwise be the case. The Board has shipped as many as fifty such machines at one time to a single field, but this is not adequate. Consider the Free Methodist area in India of some two thousand villages. It is safe to say that in the

221

past twenty-five years not half of these towns have heard the gospel message even once!

Where Christian radio stations are in operation, pre-tuned battery sets are placed in villages, usually under the supervision of the "head man." At the appointed hours for their language program, the villagers come for the broadcast. This again is just one more ally of the missionary in sowing the good seed of the gospel.

The Missionary Schedule

What do present-day missionaries do? We have already detailed the work of the earlier pioneers. Here is the story of an unusually big week in the life of Jake De Shazer in Japan.

"One Saturday he was invited to give his testimony at the Memorial Hall in Tokyo. Ordinarily this hall would hold thirteen thousand people; but this evening 'it was jammed to the rafters by 6:30 p.m., and five thousand people were said to be waiting outside.' Upon finishing his testimony of love to this crowd, De Shazer was ushered outside where he preached from the top of a sound truck. Although it was raining, the people stood and listened, and many accepted Jesus when given the invitation.

"Upon arriving in Osaka twenty-four hours later, De Shazer immediately began working with the Japanese young people in the street meetings and distributing literature.

"Rev. and Mrs. Jacob De Shazer spent the mornings of the next five days of the week in language study. The afternoons were filled with attending board meetings and prayer meetings, and passing out literature. Two or three hundred people immediately gather around when an American begins to speak. Each person receives a Gospel of John and an invitation to our church.

"A hospital service where forty responded to the invitation, and a preaching service filled Friday afternoon and evening.

"Saturday morning was full of preparation for the afternoon service in Osaka, which began at 2:30. After testimonies by the young people, De Shazer talked to them on repentance. When the invitation was given by the local pastor, eighty of the three hundred present accepted Christ as their Saviour. After a showing of the film, 'God of Creation,' the service ended. It had lasted from 2:30 to 8:30."[28]

Section 4—NEW FIELDS

The period under review began during the closing months of World War II. As in the previous struggle a quarter century earlier, there was a high level of prosperity attained during the mobilization period. Contrary to the expectations of many and certainly unlike the former post-war era, economic conditions steadily improved, with only one or two minor recessions. The great increase in population created a demand for the construction of vast housing facilities. Enormous grants of foreign aid through Point Four, the World Bank, and other agencies, set in motion extensive improvement and reclamation projects, not only in the war-devastated areas, but also in the undeveloped countries, particularly those of Middle and East Asia. Also, the largest peace-time army in our history with enormous appropriations for new kinds of atomic weapons, together with the necessary research to properly develop the same, kept the government budget at a high level and further stimulated the expansion of our economy. The United Nations was the great new fact. Here nations might shout but not shoot. As long as they could keep talking, somehow we could get along. The United Nations, the world travel of hundreds of thousands of young men and women of the armed services, the steadily shrinking globe—all tended to save America from another spell of isolationism. Foreign policy was taken out of politics and put on a bi-partisan basis. America became a citizen of the world.

All this had its effect on the church. Again youth responded to the call of the mission field and contributions increased to unbelievable levels. Eventually several new fields were opened and the missionary force almost tripled. Still needed to fill actual vacancies were some fifty young people with professional training in the fields of education, agriculture, nursing, medicine, evangelism and church administration. The generous budget of $800,000 lacked $200,000 of meeting the minimum needs of workers on twenty-three fields. The missionary program in its year of greatest prosperity (1959) had its most difficult budget-making experience. It was patent that Free Methodist missions were suffering from success.

NEW FIELDS ESTABLISHED—1943-1960

1943   Northern Ontario, Goldlands, Timmins, jointly with the East Ontario Conference, R. E. Goheen.

1946   Brazil, Lucile Damon, Helen Voller.

1946   Paraguay, Harold Ryckman, Evalyn Ryckman, Ruth Foy, Esther Harris (Mrs. Reinaldo Decoud).

1948   Texas Latin-American, Sixto Tarin.

1949   Philippines, Walter Groesbeck, Gertrude Groesbeck, John Schlosser, Ruby Schlosser.
1951   Hong Kong, I. S. W. Ryding (Mission turned to Canadian Holiness Mission, 1956).
1952   Formosa, Geneva Sayre.
1952   Saskatchewan Indians, Lloyd Robertson, Bessie Robertson.
1959   Hong Kong, Alton Gould, Phyllis Gould. Started under auspices of the Holiness Movement Church of Canada in 1954. Merged with Free Methodist Church, 1959.
1959   Egypt, founded in 1899 by the Rev. H. E. Randall of the Holiness Movement Church of Canada. Merged with the Free Methodist Church in 1959.

Miss Helen Voller, left, and Miss Lucile Damon traveling to annual conference, Brazil, 1947

Miss Geneva Sayre and Miss Kate Leininger, Fengshan, Formosa.

The Budget

The budgets for the new fields established during the period now claim 36 per cent of the total field expenditures and 26 per cent of the missionary personnel. It is interesting to note that 22 per cent of the total overseas membership is located in these newest fields. Relatively higher investments are always required in the early years of a field's history. There are non-recurring expenditures for land, buildings and equipment. Usually, too, there is a higher ratio of missionaries to members. However, this was offset by the one field, Egypt, acquired by merger. It had a large membership. It also had a relatively small missionary staff. Even so, it is quite remarkable that these new fields should account for more than one-fifth of the total overseas membership.

The opening of new fields and the expansion of programs already in operation on the larger established mission fields required the appointment of additional missionaries. The total staff under appointment in 1944 was sixty-two. In the centenary year there were 201 missionaries in active service and 23 retired.

The addition of eight new fields together with the tripling of the number of missionaries in service has required an unprecedented building program. Since building costs are still relatively low on most fields, the figures may not be impressive, judged by American standards. Almost two hundred major buildings have been purchased or built. Land has been purchased, lighting and water systems installed. The total expenditure for these improvements was $848,727.86. Comparable buildings in America would doubtless require three times this expenditure. This construction program includes schools, hospitals, clinics, residences, churches, light plants, and water systems.

Sunday school, India

Statistics

During this period of advance the number of organized churches increased from 165 to 582. The mission churches were taking ever-increased responsibility for their own maintenance and outreach. At the beginning of the period

225

New school building in Usumbura, Ruanda-Urundi

only $30,000 was contributed by the overseas congregations. In the centenary year their giving totaled more than $340,000. The 421 Sunday schools have multiplied seven times. The total is 3,065 schools at the centenary landmark. The only education available in certain areas is through the mission day schools. Often these are aided by government subsidy. The importance of such schools where under Christian influence young people learn to read and write their own language cannot be overemphasized. One of their first reading books is the Bible. On some fields missionaries report that 90 per cent of the students have "chosen the Lord" by the time they have reached the sixth grade. Including the boarding schools, there are more than eleven thousand students securing a Christian education in overseas institutions under Free Methodist auspices. The number of day and boarding schools is more than two hundred.

The number of doctors and nurses has doubled, while the total missionary staff has tripled. The development of Bible schools is a significant feature of the period. There are now fourteen such schools in Africa, India, Japan, Formosa, the Philippines and Latin America. Included is Nogales Bible School, located on the American side of the Mexican border, but serving primarily students from Mexico.

The membership gain is impressive. Without counting the new fields, there has been a gain of 21,107 in mission church membership. The 8,656 church members reported from the new fields practically equal the 8,950 membership on all fields in 1944. The total gain on fields old and new is 29,713. This represents a 332 per cent increase. The grand total in mission church membership at the centenary stands at 38,719. When one superintendent was first asked if his field could set a definite goal for church membership in 1960 he replied, "No, unless we have a revival." From reading the hundreds of letters that annually come from the fields, the Secretary must say concerning many areas, "Revival has come." The key to such success is

226

the same as in 1947 when the Secretary stated in his report to the General Conference:

"I know there are hungry, undernourished, sick and dying Free Methodists around the world today. I know there are about fifteen million people in the areas assigned to the Free Methodist Church who are wholly dependent on our missionaries and our native pastors for the message of full salvation. I know that what we are doing is only a drop in the bucket of human need. Whatever we do is that much more than nothing. If we were not there, no one would be there! And when I think about those things, despair would overcome me were it not for my faith in the gospel and in the living Christ, alive and working throughout the world by the power of the Holy Spirit. More and more I am being forced back to the conviction that our greatest need right now is intercessory prayer.

"If through prayer we can release God's power on the mission fields, making missionaries and native pastors more effective than they would otherwise be had we not prayed, then we must conclude that the salvation of the world is somehow contingent upon us and our prayer life. 'Lord, teach us to pray.'"[29]

Section 5—A POSITIVE PROGRAM

When Peter and John were at the beautiful gate of the temple confronted by human need in the form of the crippled man, a careful, correct and complete diagnosis of his case and their own liabilities would have spoiled one of the best stories in the New Testament. It would have been perfectly true for them to enumerate a long list of deficits. They were strangers in the big city, horny-handed sons of toil from Galilee. They had no prestige or social standing. They had no contacts with the Community Chest and had not seen the hospital. They didn't even know where the ambulance was located, and they had no money. All too true, and not enough power in the whole recital to cure a headache—just enough to give one. But these representatives of the Christian church in that first century faced their "crippled" world with a positive program. They lived in a positive frame of mind. "Silver and gold have I none." They could extend the list, but they didn't. They stopped right there. "Such as I have, I give." This is the basis of strength then and now. The "crippled" world doesn't care what you do not believe, what you do not possess, what you cannot do. What do you believe? What do you have? What can you do?

It has been in this spirit that the missionary work of Free Methodism has gone forward. There are problems, but it is dangerous to become too problem-conscious. The enemy of the kingdom would keep us so busy repairing fences and pumps, debating colors of barns and shapes of silos, that little time or energy remains to plant and harvest the crops. As already intimated, from the very first of this period, priority has been given to planning with the missionaries regarding aims and objectives, the next possible steps, and the kind of people needed to carry forward specific projects.

Forward Movement

The Secretary in his annual report of 1947 summarized the world advance of Free Methodist missions. This statement was prepared after consultation with the missionaries. Objectives for Africa included the appointment of missionaries to long-vacant mission stations, new personnel to the cities such as Durban, and to strategic rural areas of possible advance as Massinga in northern Mozambique. Here a line of outstations was envisaged reaching to the Rhodesia field. Medical programs, including the location and erection of hospitals with suitable personnel, were recommended for South Africa, Southern Rhodesia and the Congo. The development of more adequate Bible teaching in the South Africa day schools was urged. Congo hoped to fully occupy territory for which it was responsible. India envisaged a three-point program including plans for a Bible college, return of a doctor and reopening of the hospital, intensive village evangelism with a "roof fund" to encourage the construction of churches. For China it was repair of war damage, adequate personnel for the new Shensi field, self-support in the long-established Honan field, and adequate budgets for the Bible and middle schools and the hospital. In the Philippines there was the pious hope expressed of opening work when personnel was available. The Dominican Republic needed several churches, an administration building at the "Instituto," an evangelistic program for its unreached areas, a new constitution for the conference built on the expectation of ultimate full self-support. In Brazil the lay-revival movement was encouraged. Appointment of additional missionaries and the provision of residences for them, together with assistance in securing suitable church buildings were stressed. Paraguay proposed a Bible school program for the orphanage campus, together with an aggressive evangelistic advance. Mexican Missions needed a new campus for its Bible school, more self-supporting churches in the States, and a greater evangelistic advance in Mexico. The review of these early statements of purpose is rewarding. In almost every case the goal has been reached and surpassed.

Centenary Goals

In 1951, the General Conference, looking forward to 1960 as the centenary of the church, approved the following goals for the decade:

1. An American church of 60,000 members; a world church of 100,000 members.
2. Every local church to establish another local church.
3. Every annual conference to hold one or more city-wide evangelistic campaigns where groups of our churches are located.
4. The Commission on Evangelism to establish new churches in new fields remote from established work.

To reach the goals, the Conference requested the cooperation of each department of the church, called for increased publicity to clarify the objectives in the thinking of the church, and wisely added an "urgent call to prayer for a baptism of the Holy Spirit to accomplish these objectives through divine power."

According to this action it was expected that membership in North America would increase by 20 per cent, whereas for the overseas churches a 100 per cent gain was proposed. It seemed entirely impossible. A membership goal was established for each mission field, based on membership and its normal rate of growth. However, to reach the General Conference objective, it was necessary to ask most of the fields to report gains more than twice their recent accomplishments. Admittedly all were too high. But the importance of a definite goal cannot be overemphasized. The following letter was sent to each missionary:

"This is one of the most important letters that I have ever written to you. It deals with the Forward Movement and the Centenary Goals adopted by the General Conference. For more than a year now I have been stressing evangelism and soul-winning in my letters to the field. We are trying to arrange our business matters to consume the least time possible and devote ourselves to planning and prayer for world revival. The end of all our work is the establishment of the church whose purpose is the salvation of a lost world. May the Lord bless you in this endeavor.

"Enclosed you will find the statement of Centenary Goals and the announcement of certain literature available. Some of this you may wish to adapt and translate for your work.

"The membership goal is 100,000: 60,000 in North America and 40,000 on the mission fields! We have a terrific assignment! Careful and wise planning with prayer and spiritual renewal will make real an otherwise impossible objective.

1. I suggest that each of us search his own heart and then dedicate himself anew to this great task.
2. Let the missionaries and the national church workers pray and plan together for a great advance.
3. Enlist the schools, young people, WMS, Sunday schools—all, in this great work.

4. Elect a small committee composed of nationals and missionaries to direct the Forward Movement. Work with and through the church.
5. Let us have a report on your specific Forward Movement plans just as soon as possible.
6. Advise us regarding literature or other evangelism materials needed.
7. Be sure to surround all the planning with an atmosphere of *prayer*.
8. Expect the Holy Spirit to give guidance.
9. Don't be afraid to cut some new trails—try a new method—such as literacy, gospel films, radio, PA systems, gospel distribution, gospel teams, campaigns, etc.
10. Send us frequent reports of your successes."

On the basis of membership statistics in October, 1959, Southern Rhodesia, Formosa, the Dominican Republic, Brazil, Texas and Saskatchewan Indians have exceeded their quota. The largest conferences found it difficult to maintain the same percentage of gain as the smaller ones. All worked hard and to the astonishment of many, the total membership has reached 38,719, very close to the centenary year goal.

The missionaries proposed other objectives. Included were the more liberal use of audio-visual techniques, less emphasis on institutions, with greater mobility for evangelistic thrust in areas of special need and opportunity. More regular field visitation to promote better understanding and more effective cooperation between the missionaries and the home board was recommended. More attention was given to the work of the missionary, better training for such work and orientation in practical service after the completion of training and before proceeding to the field. Self-help programs in underdeveloped countries and areas subject to drought and famine were recommended for Southern Rhodesia, Portuguese East Africa and India. More attention was to be given the needs of young people, their world, and more adequate preparation for living in it, with stronger challenges to Christian service. Crusade team suggestions grew out of this proposal. Greater sense of mission for the extension of the Kingdom of Christ to every inhabited corner of the earth was made emphatic. Involved in the last objective was stewardship and tithing education.

Section 6—VENTURING INTO THE SECOND CENTURY

In the last year of the centenary decade, our missionaries have been praying and planning for the work of the first quadrennium of the new century. Our portrait of overseas Free Methodism would be nostalgic and static if we concluded with only the backward look. We have needed this to understand our nature and destiny, our gospel and its power. Facing the new day, we once again are required to evaluate the special needs, the peculiar forms of sin and degradation that overcome men at this hour, that we may better bring to bear on such lostness the gospel miracle of Jesus Christ.

The new emphasis coming from every field urges strengthening the church, nurturing its spiritual life, developing lay leaders, self-support and evangelistic outreach. Camp meetings, correspondence courses, literature, extension courses, enlisting capable young men for ministerial training, full-time national evangelists, training courses for converts preparing for church membership, and the translation of holiness literature are a few of the means to be employed.

Along with this is a strong urge to evangelize—to carry the gospel to unreached areas. One field has prepared a map locating its unreached areas. On another, the establishment of a new station in a city with no evangelical mission, approximately 150 miles from our present work and central to a new government-sponsored colonization program, is urged in strongest terms. On another field a station is proposed near government headquarters to facilitate mission business and at the same time supervise a new area developing northward toward the next mission field. Each missionary is to have a definite assignment where under pastoral direction he assists in youth and Sunday-school work and conducts Bible study classes. Crusade teams are recommended in individual churches and in cooperative city-wide campaigns. One field hopes to have a crusade later when the spiritual condition of the church is improved to properly conserve results. A survey committee composed of nationals and missionaries is constantly seeking new opportunities for evangelistic outreach. New work is to be established in two important cities in Brazil. The Japan program calls for opening work in fifteen population centers. City churches are to develop branch Sunday schools, Bible study groups and preaching stations. There is to be liberal use of lay workers. In Brazil a mission station is being turned over to a conference-appointed evangelist. When the missionary returns from furlough, he will spearhead the opening of work in a new field, to be determined by the survey committee. Egypt aims at a 10 per cent gain annually. The same is true in the Transvaal, where four full-time district evangelists supported by the church are envisaged. One full-time national evangelist is planned for Egypt. A village crusade team in Egypt will promote literacy, health and youth work, with prayer meetings and gospel preaching. Fifteen new churches are planned in Egypt and thirty new points in the Transvaal.

Youth work includes the strengthening of the present educational institutions, daily vacation Bible schools, summer camps, gospel teams and evangelism crusades. One field requests a specially trained youth worker.

Byron S. Lamson, Missionary Secretary since 1944, Habeeb Boctor, Hanna Attia, W. J. Stonehouse immediately after the church in Egypt voted to unite with the Free Methodist Church, May, 1959

To accomplish its objectives, India will require a bookstore, a central conference office, a conference campground. A lay-leaders' training center is needed for each district. A missionary couple for the seminary is requested, and another for the conference work. It is anticipated that the seminary will shortly have an Indian as its president. Every effort will be made here and on all other fields to fully indigenize the work and place additional responsibility on national leaders.

The proper emphasis comes in the conclusion of India's report:

"It has seemed to this committee that the main task of the church in India, and yea, the church anywhere, is to obey Christ's command to be sure of the infilling of the Holy Spirit (tarry), actively witness to the saving power of Jesus everywhere that the gospel has not been heard ("go" and "preach"), and patiently work at the task of making disciples of Jesus everyone who believes on Him ("teaching"). All the above plan and goals

232

revolves around this Commission of our Lord. No mention is made of goals in membership, baptisms, or the establishment of new churches. It is their conviction that when the church sincerely and diligently seeks to obey and carry out this command of Jesus, the Holy Spirit's power produces fruit. Jesus says that He will build His church."[30]

The Pilgrim Life

So the Free Methodist overseas church goes forward into the new century marching on its own feet. Missionaries will still be needed, but they will work in full cooperation with and, in some instances, under the direction of the national church. They will turn over their tasks just as soon as they have trained leaders competent to assume their responsibilities. They will "venture" into new areas of service, open up new cities to the gospel message, continue to be pioneers of the mind and spirit in the exciting days that lie ahead in our second century. Mission Board funds will be used only to open new work and pioneer projects for which the young church is unprepared. The missionary will be ever pressing on to bring the transforming gospel of Christ to the half of the world for whom no present provision is made. Conferences will establish their own evangelism and church extension funds, to match Board gifts. It will be an exciting experience to serve as a missionary under these conditions. It is the pilgrim life. He will be out on the cutting edge of the church's evangelistic thrust, where the religions of men challenge the advance of the gospel of Christ. In some isolated sectors, the battle may not seem so successful, but concerning the finality of his message and its full adequacy for the needs of men and nations, he has full assurance. All other messiahs with their earthly kingdoms are marching to their own funerals. By faith the ambassador of Christ understands that even now the eternal victory has been won; that the prince of this world has already been judged. He knows that the living Christ is patrolling the Jericho roads of life, binding up the hurts and bruises of men, healing the broken-hearted and setting the captives of sin free. It is in this enterprise that he has a share.

The Power of God

In 1948 when the Secretary visited Kibogora station in the Congo, it was only recently opened. The missionaries were meeting with an unexpected opposition from local chiefs. A rival medical program seemed to detract from the health services offered by the mission. There were probably forty present for the morning preaching service. Two men were at the altar "repenting of their sins." They not only confessed to God, but also to man. Their lives were dirty and wicked. Their family matters were all mixed up. Some of the missionaries winced as their confessions involved so many others,

233

frankly feeling that they had gone too far, and fearing a negative reaction to the service. Ten years later the same station was visited. Again it was Sunday morning. Now not forty, but possibly two thousand were in the congregation out under the trees. After the introduction the missionary asked, "Are there any here who can remember seeing the Missionary Secretary when he was here ten years ago?" Fifteen or twenty did remember. A man with a shining face seated near the platform jumped to his feet and began to talk very rapidly. My interpreter gave me his testimony. He said, "Yes, I remember when the Missionary Secretary was here. I repented of my sins that morning and I haven't gone back since. You know me. I did repent. I haven't gone back!"

There were nods of approval. This was one of the two men of ten years before. He had repented, and his wife, too. Their family affairs were fixed up. He was called to preach the gospel and had recently graduated from the Bible school. The next week at the annual conference the Secretary had the privilege of ordaining this man as a minister of the gospel in the Free Methodist Church. This is the gospel of which we are not ashamed—"the power of God unto salvation."

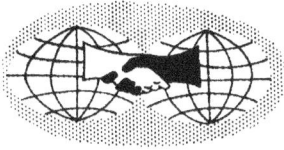

World Fellowship of

Free Methodist

Churches

Nationalism

We are ready now to have just a glimpse of the great "venture" of the centenary year, the Asia Fellowship Conference of April, 1960. This is a pointer of things to come. More than two years ago the Secretary replied to an important question concerning nationalism and its effect upon missions. He said:

"By nationalism we mean efforts of subject peoples to achieve independence and the attempts of small and weak nations to become larger and stronger, independent of aid from the outside. . . . This drive toward nationalism has a tendency to splinter the world up into atomistic states each going its own way. . . . Newly independent nations look with suspicion upon missionaries coming from the Western world. They are trying to free themselves of foreign influence. They feel that the Christian church is a foreign import. If there is to be a Christian church in these countries they want it to be truly indigenous, without support and the paternalistic pressures from the older churches of the West.

"We, too, want the church to be truly indigenous. . . . The church is there as truly as it is here or anywhere.

"This means that missionaries will go to these fields upon invitation of the mission churches, and will take appointment under the mission conferences and work as partners and servants of the church. The influence that they bring to bear in a mission conference will be on the basis of their own personal membership in the conference, and not as representatives of the mission. Ultimately the mission itself as a mission will disappear. The missionary will work in and through the national church."[1]

Free Methodist World Fellowship

With this as a background for their thinking, the Executive Committee of the Commission on Missions have for many months been considering this matter of a developing church around the world. A special committee was appointed to consider this matter and to make some recommendations to the Commission and the Board of Administration. On October 15, 1958, the Commission on Missions made its first representation to the Board of Administration.

The Commission on Missions reiterated its objective to assist in the development of an indigenous church on every mission field just as rapidly as possible, and expressed appreciation for the increasing capacity of our overseas church leaders in carrying forward the work of the church.

The Commission on Missions petitioned the Board of Administration to set up a world planning council for Free Methodism and to appoint an American Panel to study various plans of world fellowship. The American Panel was given authority to affiliate with national panels of Free Methodists throughout the world in planning for a Free Methodist world fellowship.

Following this action by the Board of Administration, a news release stated that "After seventy-seven years of missionary activity around the world, the Free Methodist Church has taken the first step toward bringing the present mission conferences into the full fellowship of a world-wide Free Methodist organization.

"The Board of Administration in annual session at Winona Lake, Indiana, October 15, 1958, approved a World Planning Council for creating a new type of world church relationship. A North American Panel was elected and it is expected that other national panels will be organized for study, consultation and joint planning.

"This action points to the early organization of largely autonomous national churches which are now under the direction of the missionary department of the North American church, and will apply in those countries where the nationals have developed capacity for such responsibility. This is in line with the missionary policy of the Free Methodist Church to develop as rapidly as possible self-supporting, self-propagating and self-controlling churches in foreign mission fields.

"It is hoped to have a comprehensive plan for the structure of world Free Methodism ready for the presentation at the next General Conference in 1960 when Free Methodists will observe the one hundredth anniversary of the founding of their denomination."

The North American Panel elected an Executive Committee that has been active. They have carried forward the work assigned in the spirit of Bishop Stephen Neill's statement:

236

"We must help our brethren as individuals and as churches to a fuller surrender to Christ, to a richer experience in the life of Christ.

"We must bring the younger generation to a personal experimental knowledge of the grace of Christ, to guide them to the place of victory over sin.

"We must help them to rely more fully on the guidance of the Holy Spirit who was sent to guide us into all truth. Scholarship, technical qualifications, organizing ability, are all useful in their place; not one of them can be considered a substitute for the one essential thing. Perhaps the church in China hit the nail on the head in its famous prayer of twenty years ago: 'O Lord revive Thy church, beginning in me.' "[2]

The panel also considered the report of the All-Africa Church Conference entitled "The Church in Changing Africa." This conference was held in Nigeria in January, 1958.

"We are one in Him who was born a Jew in Bethlehem, fled from Herod into Egypt, grew up in Nazareth, died in Jerusalem, arose there and lives today in Ibadan and in every other city and village in the world that His Father created.

"A church does not develop self-government, self-support, and self-propagation—the goals to which the mission long gave lip service—if it is treated as a child for a hundred years. There are in the Church of Christ young churches, recently called into being, but there are no younger churches, despite the fact that we Westerners want to call them so and to treat them as our juniors. Where two or three are gathered together in Jesus' name, he has promised to be in the midst of them. They are then meant to be a church, part of the Church, Christ's body, the agent of His mission of reconciliation."

Overseas Free Methodist churches and the place of the missionary was viewed in the light of D. A. McGavran's views on church growth. He says:

"The thesis of this book may now be fully stated. The era has come when Christian missions should hold lightly all mission station work, which cannot be proved to nurture growing churches, and should support the Christward movements within peoples as long as they continue to grow at the rate of fifty per cent per decade or more. This is today's strategy.

"By 'growing churches' we mean organized cells of the movement of a people. Folk join these cells by conversion without social dislocation, without entering a new marriage market, and without a sense that 'we are leaving and betraying our kindred.' "[3]

With this background in mind the panel proceeded to study the problem. Missionaries on furlough were brought into consultation and on the basis of valuable suggestions received from them several preliminary decisions were made.

Jundo Uzaki, Free Methodist minister from Japan doing graduate seminary work in the United States, was made an associate member of the North American Panel. He assisted very much in the discussions of the panel.

Asia Conference

It was decided that there should first be an Asian conference rather than one with world-wide representation. On invitation of the church in Japan, it was decided to hold the conference there.

The panel also suggested the organization of study panels in Africa and in Latin America with a view to later conferences in these areas. It is hoped that lessons learned and decisions made at the Asia Conference will be of great value to the Africa and Latin America consultations, and also that possibly some recommendations would go to the General Conference in June, 1960.

The discussions revealed the fact that the missionaries present strongly urged the importance of a spiritual emphasis in the Asia Conference as a basis for fruitful planning on an organizational level. Revival is needed throughout the world. The need of the world is one. We are living in a time of change and crisis. It was urged that the conference deal with the question, "How can we best harness all of our resources for evangelistic advance throughout the world?" It was hoped that there would be a fresh empowering of the Holy Spirit enabling our churches to meet the present challenges and opportunities. It was also the expectation that plans for closer cooperation and a better utilization of resources in carrying forward the work of the Lord would result from the Asia Conference and that definite plans could be formulated for a Free Methodist World Fellowship.

The conference was definitely for work and counsel and would make no attempt to hold public services except possibly at the conclusion of its work. Delegates to the conference were assigned on a membership basis as follows: Hong Kong, two; Philippines, three; Formosa, three; India, three; Japan, six; Egypt,* three. In addition to the above, there was one missionary representative from each field. This in addition to a delegation of six from North America made a total of approximately twenty-six. It was asked that each country cooperating in the conference set up its own study panel which would include the national delegates to the Asia Conference and an equal number of reserve delegates to be elected by the annual conference or by the highest interim governing body. If possible, at least one layman should be included in each delegation. One delegate from each field was designated to serve on the program committee.

It was agreed that it would not be necessary for members of the delega-

---

*Since the church in Egypt had already become autonomous, it was felt that they should be included in the consultation.

tions to be English-speaking; however, one member of each national delegation was expected to be able to speak English, since the English language would be used at the conference.

In October, 1959, Bishop L. R. Marston, Chairman of the North American Panel, outlined the work of the conference:

"Questions relating to essential doctrines of the church, its organizational genius, and its life witness have been forwarded from the North American Panel to the study panels of the various countries. In turn, questions are being proposed from the overseas churches. These questions involve the church and its challenge to youth, and its approach to Communism. The overseas churches are concerned with the basis of ultimate authority for Christian faith and practice. Practical concerns, such as the need for literature, books for the libraries of educational institutions and ministers, have been proposed."

The general features of the Asia Conference deliberation will be:

1. Welcome address will be given by the leader of the Japan delegation.

2. Keynote address will outline the basic considerations that led to the holding of the conference. The hopes of the mother church for the conference will be presented by the senior Bishop of the Free Methodist Church, Leslie R. Marston.

3. Following this first service the representatives of each country will be in charge of the program in succession until each field represented has opportunity to express its hopes, needs, plans, and suggestions for the conference. This sharing of insights by each of the consulting groups should produce a mutual understanding and a sense of unity and fellowship.

4. Each delegation will give a short, comprehensive, and authoritative history of the Free Methodist Church in its area.

5. The conference will consider the need for and the possibility of joint action in world evangelism.

6. Consideration will be given to the status of each church in relation to the parent church and to other Free Methodist churches throughout the world.

7. An attempt will be made to define Free Methodism. Such questions as the following will be considered: What is the portrait of a Free Methodist church? What are the essential characteristics that qualify a church for membership in the Free Methodist World Fellowship?

So again we see that "venture" is the symbol of that which is truest and finest in Free Methodism. It is at once the key to understanding our heritage and the pointer to our future tasks. It is the spirit of the Asia Conference, of the centenary General Conference, and of every Free Methodist, world-wide, as he marches along the tomorrows' highways on kingdom business, "spreading Scriptural holiness over these lands."

"Is there some desert, or some boundless sea,
Where Thou, great God of angels, wilt send me?
Some oak for me to rend, some sod to break,
Some handful of Thy precious corn to take
And scatter far afield,
　Till it shall yield
Its hundredfold
　Of grains of gold
To feed the happy children of my God?

"Show me the desert, Father, or the sea;
Is it Thine enterprise? Great God, send me;
And though this body lies where ocean rolls,
Father, count me among all faithful souls."[4]

IX

"A Praying, Suffering, Witnessing People"

Greatness of the Task

One half of the world has not heard the gospel. The world population has an annual net increase of twenty-five million! Strong revival movements in both Buddhism and Hinduism are a new challenge to the Christian movement. The present century has been one of suffering and cruelty. There is in wide areas a conviction of hopeless "wayoutlessness," a cynicism and despair. The world is plagued with racism, economic tensions, unprecedented military expenditures, while the dread of a civilization-destroying nuclear war hangs ominously over our heads.

There is moral decline in unexpected places. Large-scale dishonesty in the television industry, cheating on university campuses, the corruption of police forces in cities large and small, add to our sense of futility. To some it seems to be the soggy butt-end of Western civilization where the phonies have inherited the earth, and it is always three o'clock in the morning with never a sunrise!

We cannot complete the picture in detail. It is a world of lost faith. There is fear, despair and fatalism. There is a decline in the sense of personal responsibility due to over-emphasis on society and man's involvement in group sinning. There is a "lostness" that lives without God, an idolatry of assembly-line gadgets, a search for a heaven here and now. It is a wistful, lonesome, sad, lost age, desperately in need of salvation. The condition is so serious that mild inoculations of the real remedy will not satisfy. Neither the social gospel's optimism nor the irrelevant pessimism of Barth will meet the need of lost men here and now. Hot-house churches that have retreated from the inner city to comfortable suburbs, bitten by the "security complex,"

241

intent on saving themselves, do not have the answer. The church as a "fellowship," a human grouping of the religiously like-minded, more "country club" than "life-saving station," will never transform the world. Once again the church with all the implications of the gospel, unafraid and daringly aggressive, is needed.

The Hour Has Come

At the General Conference of 1903, the committee on the state of the work declared that—

> ". . . the foreign work makes a better showing than the home work in every particular. The amount of money raised, the number of missionaries employed, the results in the conversion of the heathen, and the extension of the missionary field is very encouraging."[1]

We know now better than when this observation was made that the overseas church is growing more rapidly. In 1914 there were scarcely two thousand members on all the mission fields. However, in 1944 this number had increased to almost nine thousand overseas communicants. The total is now slightly under forty thousand, a gain of 1,742 per cent! In the same period there has been a 58 per cent membership increase in the North American churches. To witness the growth of these small mission churches and conferences until some of them far exceed in size their North American counterparts, to discover that two of every five Free Methodists in the world are members of the overseas churches, and that the number of members in full connection in the United States approximately equals the overseas membership of all classes, is a profound and moving experience.

The obstacles faced by these tiny islands of Christian faith are almost unbelievable. They are located in the midst of a complex of ancient culture, philosophy and religion. Frequently they are almost overwhelmed by primitive witchcraft and the superstition of animistic tribes. Not infrequently they are subjected to fanatical persecution inspired by a fascist ecclesiastical hierarchy. The whole culture, government, social and economic order is so organized as to practically disenfranchise the Christians in given areas. The opposition, persecution and downright bestial physical violence visited on some of the younger Christians is unbelievable. The lack of trained leadership, social prestige, long-established Christian traditions, a social, political and legal system based on Christian assumptions—such conditions make the task seem hopeless. Yet it is in this sort of world that the church records its greatest triumphs.

The churches of Canada and the United States with personnel, institutions, finance, a praying, suffering, witnessing people, with proper direction in the best use of present facilities, could, we believe, far surpass the overseas churches in accomplishment. The following suggestions are based on such faith, and are submitted humbly and in the fear of God. Many have burdened hearts these days, hoping for a greater advance in soul winning through the varied ministries of the church. Our prayer is that a new infilling of God's Holy Spirit may once again make the church terrible as an army with banners for the pulling down of the strongholds of Satan. We list three great needs of Free Methodism today.

1. *More coordinated activity based on cooperative planning by the several agencies of the church.*

As indicated previously, there has not been the same centralized planning and administration of the home evangelism work as has of necessity obtained in the overseas program. When the general evangelists worked under the direction of and in harmony with the planning of the General Missionary Board, there was the nearest approach to such planning. Free Methodism made its greatest gains during those years. Gradually the work of general evangelists as missionaries, pioneering new fields, ceased, as their responsibility more and more became one of cultivation in established areas under conference direction.

The list of home mission enterprises, started by individuals, churches or conferences, is a long one. The fatality rate is high. The investment in personnel and finance is beyond computation. That list indicates not only the great concern of the church, its attention to human need, its eagerness to respond to every opportunity for extending the gospel witness but at the same time reveals a sad lack of planning. In the main, those programs that were carefully considered and planned jointly by the General Church and local agencies and for which the denomination assumed responsibility have prospered. Many others have ceased to exist. This is frustrating, wasteful and self-defeating.

United acting and planning is essential. We have caught a glimpse of good men divided over plans and personalities. A spirit of division always destroys a revival movement. The church in dealing with its radical extremists overcompensated for what seemed to be fanaticism. In so doing, Free Methodism became less than its true self and the fires of revival cooled down. The church is too small and too weak to afford the luxury of planless activity. We want local initiative, but more coordination in planning and action by the several departments of the church is essential if the total Free Methodist influence is to be effectively released in those areas of greatest need and where the church has special responsibility.

2. *Free Methodists need a positive program.*

In dealing with the Pentecost Bands, the conferences in 1889 and 1890 passed resolutions on the subject. Such action was largely negative. They would give no support to independent missions, no services were to be

243

held by such missionaries, no funds raised for them; there was no approval of their projects. E. F. Ward was warned not to join them. Criticism was leveled at their theology and an issue was made of their failure to render responsible financial reports. Assuming the truth of these charges, the strategy was doubtless wrong. It put the church in a negative and weak position. In the end, only a positive program that is in line with human need and the heart of the Christian gospel will survive. Negative legislation may bolster up weakness for a time, but not forever.

The church must recapture a sense of the awful lostness of this age, and at the same time experience a new faith in the redeemability of a lost world. Old General Booth used to say to the young officers in his training classes: "I wish I could send you to hell for about two weeks!" Crude? Yes. But the General knew that his workers needed a concern for the lost based on a "feeling" deeper than mere creedal statement of the fact. The significant and elemental features of man's predicament to which the gospel addresses itself must be understood and felt. The essential Christian message with its special word for the needs of men in this day must be more clearly grasped. Further, the church must discover new ways to make relevant the eternal gospel of Christ to modern man's lostness. To do this will require united prayer and consultation, cooperative planning and action to challenge all our resources in the most significant venture of our times.

The church cannot possibly do all the good things that need to be done. Only the presentation of priority items jointly agreed upon should be allowed to engage our attention. The time is short. Our efforts must be directed to the places of greatest need, where there is the least competitive activity and where we have the greatest probability of success. That such overall planning and considerations have not guided our heterogeneous home evangelism and home missions enterprises none will deny. Positive action to implement these suggestions can be taken, without much modification of present organization. The decisive factor here is the human equation. Do we have the will to act?

This is the cure for disloyalty, division and idolatry. Free Methodists have a great gospel and program. It must be translated into action. The highest idealism of the New Testament must take on flesh and blood. These great insights must be brought down from the mountaintop of spiritual experience and placed on the calendar pad of today's agenda.

3. *The Challenge of the Largest Cause.*

The wearisome repetition of ill-conceived projects with their drain on personnel and finance can be avoided. Less time should be devoted to handling problems. Problems are self-made. People with a small program become problems. Many church workers do not have enough significant activity to engage their full attention. Some church programs are too petty. Christianity is more than folding Sunday-school papers or attending board meetings. Division over little issues indicates a lack of a great overarching purpose large enough to challenge men to sacrifice and suffering. We will recover this or die.

Our world is on the brink of damnation and needs desperately a salvation from all sin.

Lost men collapse and seek an escape in alcohol or commercialized amusement. Many become hardbitten materialists. Spiritual ideals are scrapped. They enter the "rat-race" for things; they become squirrels grubbing for nuts. Others turn to religion, remembering something of early religious training or through personal contact with some radiant person discover life with hope and meaning. Man still has eternity in his heart. He has hungers and thirsts in the realm of the spirit. Our great cities are crowded with lonesome people. There must be a way for loving friends with vital faith to radiate and share the things of the spirit that give life its true dimension.

At the conclusion of a gospel service at Osaka Christian College a young atheist asked me several searching questions. Then I asked him, "Why are you becoming interested in Christianity?" His reply was very revealing: "Oh, your happy Christians and your wonderful Book!" Is this an insight into modern man's need with a suggestion for today's strategy? Where did this man see happy Christians? In the factory? Where did he find the "wonderful Book"? Did he listen to a gospel broadcast?

" . . . The church must follow in the footsteps of Jesus . . ."

Jesus Christ is our pattern! This is the affirmation of our Book of Discipline: ". . . The church must follow in the footsteps of Jesus. . . ."[2] The "store-front churches" tell us that we must have a new concern for the underprivileged. Little Rock asks us: "Are there still 'free seats' in the Free Methodist Church?" We haven't opened wide our doors in this crisis nor have we been doing very much to tell this race-conscious age that we both believe and practice "free seats"! We need adequate churches, but not too fine for those who "labor and are heavy laden." We need a new sense of God, a vision of His present activity in all the work of the world. We must enter more fully into sympathy with our Lord who declared: "The Son of Man is come to seek and to save that which was lost."[3]

The Free Methodist Church has never toned down the matchless character of Jesus Christ. In this hour Jesus Christ is a Person whom modern cynics, sad and lonesome young men and women, can know better than they can know anyone else!

We have the Book of books recording the mighty acts of God which He wrought in human history in the birth, life, death and the resurrection of Jesus Christ our Lord. These are among the best-attested facts in history. Here also is the story of the early followers of "the Way" going everywhere

245

sharing the good news about this Person and the new life through Him. There is recorded the establishment of tiny cells of believers and followers. There are letters of instruction to young Christians on how to live this new life in a wicked and unbelievably hard and cruel world, both general principles and specific details. Here is the atmosphere of confident assurance of an eternal significance for life. Man is made in the image of God. There is meaning and purpose for him in both time and eternity. The resurrection of Christ is the vindication of the finality, the truth and the ultimate victory of this Way. Pentecost is a personal assurance to believers, a sort of added witness to the resurrection. The resurrection vindicates Jesus, the experience of Pentecost validates the resurrection.

The experience of Pentecost is not on the level of mere emotion. Emotions are chaotic, transitory and weakening. The experience of God in the life of man gives insight, strength, direction and coordination. It is an undergirding that modern man needs. Lives are changed by the outworking of this inner transformation. It is for this that J. G. Terrill could ride horseback forty-five miles in a snowstorm and call it the "happiest day"! An inner conviction of the ultimate worthwhileness of this way led a Grace Allen to say even before the South Africa work was officially started:

"... I believe I am willing to suffer a good deal in order to get our work started here. I intend ... to visit from kraal to kraal and do personal work with the people. I have a horse and saddle which I have bought with the money I have earned teaching here, and I mean to be a regular circuit rider."[4]

Living by the same faith in the awful heat of Southern Rhodesia, without benefit even of refrigeration or screens for the half-finished, unceiled, oven-like house, Ralph and Ethel Jacobs invested not only their tithe but personal funds as well to lay the foundations of this new field. In the midst of these hardships they sent to the home office their victorious testimony:

"Greetings to the Commission on Missions:
> "It is great to be out where the fight is strong,
> To be where the heaviest troops belong,
> And to fight there for man and God.

> "It seams the face and dries the brain,
> It strains the arm till one's friend is pain,
> In the fight for man and God.

> "But it's great to be out where the fight is strong,
> To be where the heaviest troops belong,
> And to fight for man and God."*

---
*Author Unknown.

246

Now is the time for the church to dedicate itself unreservedly to the work of our Lord—seeking and saving the lost. It is an age of rapid social change. We call it a "revolutionary age." Men and nations are susceptible to change. The gospel message, "Repent," really means, "Change your mind." These mind-changing days are harvest times for the church. We are called anew to these opportunities by the spiritual hunger of those still in darkness, by the failure of man's idols, by the urge of the Holy Spirit and the command of Christ. Changed lives around the world—bad men made good by the power of Christ, confirm our faith in the complete adequacy of the gospel. It is indeed "the power of God unto salvation."

Let us not worry too much over the fact that the overseas churches are growing so fast. Only 7 per cent of the people of the world live in Canada and the United States, whereas 55 per cent of the Free Methodists live in these countries. There are fewer Free Methodists per million population outside North America. Humanly speaking, the forces opposing the advance of the gospel seem insurmountable. But where the opposition is most intense, the growth of the church is most vigorous.

The only cause large enough to save the church is paradoxically that of saving the world. The world is really lost. However, we are convinced of the complete adequacy of the Christian gospel. Christ can satisfy every man on the North American continent, the Holy Spirit fill every empty life in the Western world, and there will be no less of Christ or the Spirit available for Asia and Africa. He is waiting this moment to meet every need of every man on this planet. As we lose ourselves for Christ and His gospel, seeking above everything else to save a lost world, God will save the church.

> "Spread, O spread the holy fire,
> Tell, O tell what God has done,
> Till the nations are conformed
> To the image of his Son."[5]

CHRONOLOGIES

BELGIAN CONGO

1935 J. W. Haley and family occupied Urundi mission field
      Muyebe dispensary, Peace Haley
1936 Rev. and Mrs. Ronald Collett
      Miss Ila M. Gunsolus (transfer from South Africa)
      Rev. and Mrs. Frank Adamson (transfer from South Africa)
1937 Miss Esther Shelhamer (Mrs. Gilbert James)
1938 Margaret Holton, R.N.
      Marjorie Peach, R.N. (Mrs. J. Lowell Rice)
1939 Rev. and Mrs. Burton R. McCready
1940 Miss Peace Haley (Mrs. Oddvar Berg)
      Muyebe school, Ila Gunsolus
1942 Kibogora dispensary, Hazel Adamson
1943 Rev. Oddvar Berg
      Kibogora school, Ila Gunsolus
      Rev. and Mrs. Emanuel Wegmueller
1944 Miss Elizabeth E. Cox
1945 Rev. and Mrs. Allen Bilderback
1946 Kibuye Hospital plans approved
1947 Berdina Beckwith, R.N.
      Esther F. Kuhn, M.D.
      Elizabeth Van Sickle, R.N.
1948 Miss Aster L. Derry
      Rev. and Mrs. Paul W. Orcutt
1949 Kivimba Normal School opened in cooperation with Protestant Alliance
1950 Mweya Bible School opened by holiness missions
1951 Miss Evelyn Rupert
1952 Rev. and Mrs. Merlin F. Adamson
1953 Merton J. (M.D.) and Arlene (M.D.) Alexander
1954 Clara M. Sparks, R.N.
1955 Large area, including Usumbura, added to Free Methodist mission
      Myra Adamson, R.N.
      C. Albert (M.D.) and Louise Snyder
      Constitution of Congo-Nile Provisional Conference approved
1956 Doris Moore, R.N.
      Miss Eileen Moore
      New church, seating 1,800, built at Kibuye, funds provided by local
        church
      Muyebe dispensary reopened, Margaret Holton
      Government builds residences, schools, church for Protestant Center at
        Usumbura, new mission headquarters
      Usumbura schools, Estelle Orcutt
1957 Rev. and Mrs. James F. Johnson
      Two-room baby clinic and maternity building, and two new wards, all
        of brick construction, completed at Kibuye
      Applications made for forty locations for churches and schools in area
        between Usumbura and Kibogora

248

Seven buildings completed for new headquarters station at Usumbura. New school opened, Elizabeth E. Cox, principal

Dr. Esther F. Kuhn released to Nyankanda Leper Colony for two-year period

Second doctor's residence completed at Kibuye

Rev. and Mrs. Gerald Bates

1958   Olive M. Bodtcher, R.N., appointed and released to Nyankanda Leper work

New child welfare building completed at Kibogora

1959   Stanley R. Lehman, self-supporting builder, commences work in Ruanda-Urundi

Girls' Home Economics school, Muyebe (cooperative with Protestant Alliance), Estelle Orcutt

Miss Martha Pedigo

Miss Marie Rothfuss

Leonard H. (M.D.) and Martha Ensign

BRAZIL

1928   Rev. Daniel Nishizumi (from Japan)

1941   Financial help from Missionary Board given to Rev. Daniel Nishizumi

1946   Miss Lucile Damon

Miss Helen L. Voller

1947   Rev. and Mrs. James Junker

1951   Rev. and Mrs. Donald H. Bowen

1952   Rev. and Mrs. Harold Ryckman (transfer from Paraguay)

1953   100-acre campus purchased for seminary

James Chapman, short-term missionary helper

1954   Seminary at Mairipora and day school in Sao Paulo under construction

1955   Rev. and Mrs. C. W. King

Constitution of South American Provisional Conference approved

1956   Two dormitories, mission residence and classroom building completed on seminary campus

Mirandopolis Day School founded by Helen Voller

Seminary classes opened in Sao Paulo, Donald Bowen, director

1957   Second missionary residence and caretaker's cottage completed on seminary campus

Two-year lay workers' course offered

Two churches built. Three properties purchased

Rev. and Mrs. Clancy Thompson

1958   Rev. and Mrs. Clarence T. Owsley

Sao Paulo First Japanese church divides its membership (400) and starts new church in another part of city

1959   Rev. and Mrs. Clancy Thompson open new work at Atibaia

Rev. and Mrs. Roy Kenny (1955) from Holiness Movement Mission

New churches opened at Mairipora and Caieiras

Two churches added to the field from Holiness Movement Church

CHINA

1904   Rev. Floyd Appleton

Rev. and Mrs. N. S. Honn

Rev. George H. Scofield

1905	Miss Edith D. Graves
	Miss Clara Leffingwell
	Miss Florence R. Myers (Mrs. G. H. Scofield)
1906	Rev. and Mrs. Frank Millican
	Miss Laura Millican (Mrs. C. F. Appleton)
	Miss Lily M. Peterson
1907	Orphanage opened
	Rev. and Mrs. Fred J. Fletcher
	Miss Lucy Tittemore (Mrs. Frank Perkins)
	Miss Edith Frances Jones
1908	Miss Mary Ogren (Mrs. George Schlosser)
	Rev. George Schlosser (transfer from South Africa)
1910	Bible Training School, C. F. Appleton
1911	Miss Maud W. Edwards
1912	A. L. (M.D.) and Maud Grinnell
1913	Miss Letitia Chandler
1914	Orphanage turned over to Mennonites
	Grace M. Stewart, R.N.
1915	Kate P. Leininger, R.N.
1916	Rev. and Mrs. E. P. Ashcraft
	Miss Bernice M. Wood
1917	Rev. Thomas J. Beare
	Rev. I. S. W. Ryding
	Rev. Jacob Schaffer
1918	Miss Minnie Honn (Mrs. Earl Burr)
	Rev. and Mrs. Glade L. McClish
1919	Grinnell Memorial Hospital opened
	Miss Mattie J. Peterson
	Miss Florence M. Murray
1920	Bible school buildings erected, Kaifeng
1921	Miss Geneva Sayre
	Grace Somerville, R.N.
1922	Mrs. Jacob (Pearl Denbo) Schaffer
1923	Rev. and Mrs. H. R. Leise
	Rev. and Mrs. E. L. Silva
1925	Harry and Mrs. (Alta Sager, M.D.) Green
	Miss Bessie Reid (Mrs. Luther Kresge)
1926	Grace M. Murray, R.N.
	Rev. and Mrs. James H. Taylor
1929	Mission conference organized
1932	John D. (M.D.) and Lydia Green
1934	Pearl M. Reid, R.N.
1935	Hospital reopened
1936	Rev. and Mrs. Harold Winslow
1937	Miss Frances Schlosser (Mrs. James Scherer)
	Gain of 227 members
1941	Northwest Bible Institute, Fengsiang, James H. Taylor, Sr.
1942	Kate Leininger and Geneva Sayre under guard in occupied China
1943	Kate Leininger and Geneva Sayre released from internment. Returned to United States on SS "Gripsholm"
1945	Rev. E. P. Ashcraft, returned for short term

	Rev. John H. Schlosser
1946	Mrs. John H. Schlosser
1947	Rev. and Mrs. W. W. Groesbeck
	Rev. and Mrs. Elmer E. Parsons
	Irva G. Wickman, R.N. (Mrs. Floyd Rush)
	Miss Geneva Sayre (returned)
	Kate Leininger, R.N. (returned)
	Miss Florence Murray (returned)
	Mrs. Mary Schlosser (returned)
	Mrs. Pearl Schaffer (returned)
1948	Bible school, Chungking, Florence Murray
1951	All missionaries safely evacuated

DOMINICAN REPUBLIC

1889	Mr. and Mrs. Samuel E. Mills
1893	Miss Esther D. Clark
1907	Rev. J. W. Winans
1908	Rev. and Mrs. Roy Nichols
	Miss Nellie M. Whiffen
	William C. Willing, M.D.
1912	Rev. and Mrs. E. H. Stayt
	Lincoln School for Girls, San Francisco de Macoris, Nellie Whiffen, director
1913	Miss Ethel Newton
1915	Miss S. Belle Avery
1916	Boys' School, Macoris
1917	Rev. and Mrs. George W. Mills
1919	Helen O. Abrams, R.N.
	Land for school at Macoris
1920	Miss Doane Avery
	Miss Clara M. Hayden
	Rev. and Mrs. L. E. Hendren
1921	Miss Eva Whiffen
	Rev. and Mrs. Harry F. Johnson
1922	Bible School (Santiago) established, Harry F. Johnson
1923	Rev. and Mrs. Wesley O. Smith
1925	Miss Lorena M. Smith (Mrs. Cecil L. Morris)
1927	Jessie Ragatz, R.N. (Mrs. A. W. Booth)
	Instituto Evangelico founded, Harry F. Johnson
1929	Rachel M. Smiley, R.N.
1931	Rev. and Mrs. E. C. Snyder
1936	Rev. and Mrs. Nahum E. Perkins
1940	Rev. and Mrs. Ralph Thompson
1942	Miss Ruth D. Hessler
1944	Rev. and Mrs. Eldon R. James
1945	Rev. and Mrs. F. Burleigh Willard
1950	Y.P.M.S. Crusade, Ernest Keasling, director
1951	Rev. and Mrs. Wesley Stickney
1953	New building completed at Instituto Evangelico
	Mrs. F. B. (Alma Gregory) Willard
1955	Rev. and Mrs. John G. Gilmore

1957　Mr. and Mrs. M. D. Bonney
　　　　Two churches built
　　　　Evangelistic campaign, one month, with Lowell Billings and Greenville
　　　　　College quartet
　　　　New church at Ciudad Trujillo
1959　F.M.Y. Crusade, Mervin Russell, director; B. H. Pearson, evangelist;
　　　　　Elwyn Cutler, publicity
　　　　Rev. and Mrs. Donald M. Vesey (transfer from Mexican Missions)
1960　New residence for superintendent

EGYPT

1899　Rev. Herbert Randall, Assiut
　　　　Miss Edith Burke
　　　　Miss Cora VanCamp
　　　　Miss Carrie Reynolds
1900　Girls' School, Cora VanCamp
1901　Miss Elma Cannon (Mrs. W. C. Trotter)
　　　　Rev. Wesley Trotter
1903　*Bugle of Holiness* established
1904　Miss Lydia Bradley (Mrs. A. A. Caswell)
1906　Miss Emma Barkley (Mrs. P. C. Bennett)
　　　　Miss Ethel Clarke (Mrs. A. Joyce)
1907　Training School, Rev. Wesley Trotter
　　　　Conference established
　　　　Miss Sarah Longhurst
　　　　Miss Clara McLean (Mrs. F. C. Kendall)
　　　　Rev. Allan Moore
1908　Girls' School, boarding department added
　　　　Rev. F. C. Kendall
1909　Mrs. Allan Moore
1910　Miss Jennie Sinclair (Mrs. J. Burgess)
1911　Rev. A. A. Caswell
1912　Miss Annie Werry
1920　Rev. and Mrs. J. C. Black
　　　　Miss Elma Brown
　　　　Miss Bertena Greene
　　　　Miss Albertha Roe (Mrs. W. A. McMillan)
1922　Miss Catherine Fraser
　　　　Rev. R. L. Mainse
1924　Mrs. R. L. Mainse
1925　Rev. and Mrs. S. A. Graham
1926　Miss Lois Pritchard (Mrs. W. H. Hall)
1930　Miss Nellie Douglas
1931　Miss Edith Burke transferred to Sudan
1933　Summer camp on Cyprus secured
1936　Miss Louisa Baulke (Mrs. Torance Alexander)
　　　　Miss Olive Cooke (Mrs. Lorne Kenny)
1938　Rev. Lorne M. Kenny
　　　　Miss Mildred Cooke
1944　Miss Marion Greenleese
1946　Miss Catherine Graham

252

1947	Rev. T. W. Alexander
1950	Miss Jean Burns
	Miss Naomi Lindsay
1951	Egypt Bible School, Lorne Kenny
1954	Rev. and Mrs. Norman Cooke
1959	Rev. and Mrs. Earle Hawley
	Miss Irma Ergezinger
	Merged with Free Methodist missionary program
	Rev. and Mrs. T. W. Alexander
	Rev. and Mrs. Norman Cooke
	Miss Naomi Lindsay

FORMOSA

1952	Geneva Sayre (transfer from China)
	Kate P. Leininger, R.N. (transfer from China)
1953	Rev. and Mrs. James H. Taylor, Sr. (transfer from China)
	Mrs. Carolyn V. Winslow (transfer from China)
	First Free Methodist church organized
1955	Holy Light Bible School opened at Kaohsiung
	Rev. and Mrs. James H. Taylor, Jr.
1957	Nine graduates from Holy Light Bible School receive appointment to full-time pastoral and evangelistic work
	Church built in Lower Ping Tung
	Membership increases 66 per cent
1958	Rev. and Mrs. William Bicksler
	Thirty-five registrations at Holy Light Bible School
	Three new churches built
	Five new areas occupied as regular preaching points
	Purchase of land and building (dormitory, dining room) for Bible school

HONG KONG

1953	Rev. I. S. W. Ryding established mission preaching center, including Christian day school and evangelical literature center
1956	Mission turned over to Canadian Holiness Mission
1959	Rev. and Mrs. Alton A. Gould and work of Canadian Holiness Mission merged with Free Methodist missionary program
	Roof-top evangelistic campaigns in government resettlement estates. 744 decisions

INDIA

1881	Rev. and Mrs. E. F. Ward
1885	E. F. Ward asks General Missionary Board to serve as advisory committee
	Miss Louisa Ranf
	Miss Julia Zimmerman
1890	Miss Celia Ferries (Mrs. V. G. McMurry), first superintendent under General Missionary Board
1892	Miss Anna Jones
1894	Miss Mattie Miller
1896	Miss Emma Appling (Mrs. T. H. Gilpatrick)

1897	Famine
	Rev. and Mrs. H. L. Crockett
	Rev. V. G. McMurry
	Rev. H. L. Crockett, superintendent for India
1899	Seventy-five orphans if Secretary secures support
1900	Prospect of great famine
1901	Miss Ethel H. Clarke (Mrs. August Youngren)
	Miss Rose Cox
	Miss Effie L. Southworth
	Rev. and Mrs. J. T. Taylor
1902	Miss Mary E. Chynoweth
1904	Rev. and Mrs. E. F. Ward added to staff at request of India mission
1905	About 100 orphans receive instruction at orphanage
1906	Miss Gertrude Alcorn
	Miss Mata D. Allee
	Rev. and Mrs. S. D. Casberg
	Rev. and Mrs. G. G. Edwards
	Yeotmal Industrial School
	Famine Fund, industrial school building
	Boys' orphanage and industrial school
1907	Miss Edith M. Santee
1908	Industrial school, theoretical course, carpentry and cabinetmaking. 800 visitors inspect work. Government official recognizes superior work of school
1909	Miss Louise Calkins (Mrs. Harry Love)
	Mr. and Mrs. H. M. Damon
	Frederick G. Mynett
	Forty members. New station, eighteen acres, Umri
1910	Abraham A. Lind
1911	Miss Ethel Ward
1913	Rest Home
	Miss Ella Becker (Mrs. J. E. Cochrane)
	Rev. and Mrs. Clyde Foreman
	Lorena Marston, R.N.
	Miss Elizabeth Moreland
	Day schools
1914	Miss Effie G. Cowherd
	Mrs. E. F. (Elizabeth Tucker) Ward
1916	Miss Grace Barnes
1917	Miss Evangeline Crockett (Mrs. W. N. Thuline)
	Miss Helen I. Root
	Rev. Winfred N. Thuline
1918	Dr. and Mrs. F. A. Puffer
1919	Rev. and Mrs. R. N. Davis
1922	Ida Mary Menter, R.N.
1923	Umri Hospital completed, S. D. Casberg. Used as dispensary
1932	Persis M. Phelps, R.N.
	Rev. and Mrs. Elmer S. Root
1936	Dr. and Mrs. Frank J. Kline
	Two new stations opened
1937	India Provisional Conference organized

254

One hundred converts baptized
1938 Lois Kent, M.D.
1939 195 baptized in year
     Yeotmal Biblical Seminary, F. J. Kline, principal
1940 Melvin (M.D.) and Olive Casberg
1941 Umri Hospital opened, Melvin Casberg
1943 Mrs. R. N. (Muriel Abell) Davis
1945 Umri central schools and hostels, new campus
1950 Mary L. Luffy, R.N. (Mrs. S. C. Crawford)
     Helen L. Rose, R.N.
     Paul W. (M.D.) and Jessie Yardy
1951 Umri Hospital reopened, Paul W. Yardy
1952 Rev. and Mrs. Claude Vaucher
1953 Union Biblical Seminary (Yeotmal) under sponsorship of cooperating
     evangelical missions
1955 Indian national presided over annual conference for first time
1957 Melvin K. (M.D.) and Betty (R.N.) Pastorius
     Rev. and Mrs. Elmer Root pioneer in training courses in lay leadership
     Union Biblical Seminary receives authority to grant degrees
1958 Rose Memorial Wards at Umri Hospital completed

JAPAN

1895 Paul Kakihara
1896 Rev. T. Kawabe
1902 Rev. and Mrs. August Youngren
1903 Rev. and Mrs. W. F. Matthewson
1904 Two main centers, Sumoto (Awaji) and Osaka. "Our most rewarding
     mission field"
1905 Mission property secured on Awaji Island
1906 Rev. and Mrs. Sherman E. Cooper
1907 Miss Minnie K. Hessler (Mrs. W. A. Morse)
1908 Rev. and Mrs. Matthias Klein
     Rev. and Mrs. W. L. Meikle
1909 Miss Ruth Mylander
1911 Rev. and Mrs. R. W. Millikan
1913 Bible School and Boys' Training School in operation
1914 Osaka Bible School begun
1917 Rev. and Mrs. Oliver R. Haslam
     Osaka Bible College completed
1918 Miss Lillian O. Pickens
1919 Rev. and Mrs. H. H. Wagner
1920 Miss Gertrude Aylard (Mrs. W. F. Matthewson)
     Osaka Bible School rebuilt
1924 Rev. and Mrs. Frank Warren
1930 Church built without Board assistance
     Kindergarten built and paid for. Self-supporting
1937 Miss Frances M. Hart
     Church built at Akashi, work opened at Nagoya
1941 Japan church reorganized for recognition by Japanese government. "The
     Japan Wholly Sanctification Church"
     Rev. T. Tsuchiyama made General Superintendent

1948	Rev. and Mrs. Jacob De Shazer
	Miss Alice E. Fensome
	Rev. Oliver R. Haslam (two-year term)
1949	Rev. and Mrs. Elmer E. Parsons (transfer from China)
1950	Pearl M. Reid, R.N. (transfer from China)
	Articles of Incorporation approved for Japan church
	Many thousands of converts in De Shazer campaigns
1951	Miss Myrtle Anderson (transfer from Kentucky Mountains)
	Rev. and Mrs. Harry A. Bullis
1952	Rev. and Mrs. Norman Overland
	Rev. and Mrs. Edward Skudler
	Osaka Christian College buildings completed
	Japan church returned to full membership in world family of Free Methodist churches
1956	New administration building completed at Osaka Christian College, entirely with Japanese funds
	Rev. and Mrs. K. L. Snider
1958	Nine new churches completed
1959	De Shazer reopens work at Nagoya
1960	Asia Fellowship Conference held, Kyoto

PARAGUAY

1946	Rev. and Mrs. H. H. Ryckman
	Miss Ruth N. Foy
	Miss Esther Harris (Mrs. Reinaldo Decoud)
	Clinic established in Ryckman home, Evalyn Ryckman
1949	Elizabeth Reynolds, R.N.
	New church and Bible school completed
1950	Articles of Incorporation approved for Paraguay church
	Clinic building completed
1951	Rev. and Mrs. Wesley G. Hankins
	Rev. and Mrs. Donald M. Vesey
1953	Bible School opened, Wesley Hankins
1954	Two new preaching points opened
1956	Rev. and Mrs. Ernest Huston
	First youth camp held
1957	Two graduates from Asuncion Bible School
	Property purchased at Loma Pyta
1958	New Japanese settlements reached (with help of Brazil district)
1960	New work opened at Encarnacion, Ernest Huston. (Japanese and Paraguayan)

PHILIPPINES

1949	Rev. and Mrs. Walter Groesbeck (transfer from China)
	Work opened at Bunawan, Walter Groesbeck
	Rev. and Mrs. John Schlosser (transfer from China)
1950	Mission station opened at Butuan City
1952	Rev. and Mrs. Raymond E. Streutker
	Naomi Thorsen, R.N.
	Butuan becomes mission headquarters
1953	Miss Belva I. Wood (Mrs. Leonardo Puspos)

256

1955	Headquarters residence built in Butuan
	Light and Life Bible School opened at Bunawan, John Schlosser
1956	70 per cent gain in membership
	New work opened among primitive Manobo mountain tribes
	Rev. and Mrs. James W. Spurling
1957	Elsie Apling, R.N. (transfer from Kentucky Mountains)
	Light and Life Bible School relocated at Butuan
	Five acres land purchased for Bible school campus
	Chief and several members of Manobo tribe baptized and brought into fellowship of church. Regular services held with Manobos
	C.Y.C. leadership training course given by Mrs. Ruby Schlosser
	First annual conference with delegates. Fourteen churches reported. 68 per cent membership gain
1958	First permanent Bible school unit completed
	Registration at Bible school increased almost 100 per cent
1960	Butuan Crusade
	Bible school and church completed

PORTUGUESE EAST AFRICA

1885	G. Harry Agnew
	Rev. and Mrs. W. W. Kelley
1888	Rev. and Mrs. J. D. Bennett
	Mr. and Mrs. A. Y. Lincoln
	Miss F. Grace Allen
1892	Mr. and Mrs. Frank Desh
	Mr. and Mrs. J. J. Haviland
1895	Mrs. G. H. (Susie Sherman) Agnew
1897	Mrs. G. H. (Lillie Smith) Agnew
1902	Rev. J. W. Haley
	Rev. and Mrs. Carroll Smith
1903	W. A. (M.D.) and Mary Backenstoe
1904	Inhamachafo Clinic, Dr. Backenstoe
1905	Miss Esther Hamilton (Mrs. J. W. Haley)
1906	Portuguese East Africa students supported from U.S.A.
1907	Miss Ethel Cook
1908	New school building, Inhamachafo. Twenty evangelists registered
1910	Rev. Jules Ryff supervises Inhambane work from Germiston, Transvaal
1911	Mr. and Mrs. E. H. Wells
1912	Miss Ida B. Rice (Mrs. Charles Weaver)
1913	Miss Margaret A. Nickel (transfer from South Africa)
	Girls' Boarding School, Mabile, Margaret Nickel
1916	Miss Mae P. Armstrong
	Rev. and Mrs. Gilbert Pine
1918	Miss Ethel Davey (Mrs. Jules Ryff)
	Lydia O. Gaudin, R.N.
1920	Rev. and Mrs. Ralph J. Jacobs (transfer from South Africa)
	Inhamachafo property acquired
	Miss Adelaide Latshaw
1922	Rev. and Mrs. Gerald H. Bullock
	Miss Nellie Reed (Mrs. L. D. Bohall) (transfer from South Africa)
1923	Miss Ruth Moreland (Mrs. A. D. Zimmerman)

1924	Girls' Boarding School transferred from Mabile to Inhamachafo
	Teacher training school, Inhambane, Mac P. Armstrong and Adelaide Latshaw
	Provisional conference formed
1926	Rev. and Mrs. Herbert M. Roushey
1927	Rev. and Mrs. L. M. Arksey
1928	Miss Edna Mae Hoyt (Mrs. J. M. Dickinson)
1931	Theodore (M.D.) and Lois Thomas
1933	Well drilled at Massinga, abundance of water found
1936	Rev. and Mrs. Victor W. Macy
	Gain of 352 members. Thirty new stations opened
1937	Rev. and Mrs. Wesley C. DeMille
	Membership gain of 485
1947	Miss Lily Horwood
	Kathryn R. Smith, R.N.
	Miss Verna Tite
1948	Rev. J. M. Dickinson
1949	Florence M. Carter, R.N.
1950	Rev. and Mrs. Edwin S. Clemens
	Georgia Slosser, R.N.
1955	Marguerite L. Palmer, M.D.
	Maternity clinics, Inhamachafo and Massinga, completed
1957	Rudimentary school, Inhamachafo, has enrollment of five hundred
	Youth Bible School established
	Medical work expanded to include nurse's training program at Inhamachafo and Massinga
1958	Leona Carlson, R.N.
1959	All conference committee chairmen are Africans

(handwritten annotation in left margin: 1 9 3 8)

SOUTH AFRICA

1885	Rev. and Mrs. Robert R. Shemeld
1888	Miss Ida Heffner (Mrs. Spalding)
1889	Miss F. Grace Allen (transfer from Portuguese East Africa)
1891	Rev. and Mrs. A. D. Noyes establish Fairview farm and station
1898	Rev. and Mrs. J. P. Brodhead
	Miss Lucy A. Hartman
1900	Mr. and Mrs. W. C. Gray
1902	Miss Margaret A. Nickel
	Mr. and Mrs. Nathaniel Smith
1903	Rev. and Mrs. Jules Ryff
1904	Rev. Albert E. Haley
	Government grants secured for Fairview station school and Girls' School
1905	Mrs. Albert (Matilda Deyo) Haley
	Rev. and Mrs. W. S. Woods
	Miss Nellie A. Reed (Mrs. L. D. Bohall) stationed at Fairview
1906	George D. Schlosser
	Rev. and Mrs. N. B. Ghormley
	Rev. J. W. Haley opens training school at Greenville
	High school and Bible training school at Edwaleni, N. B. Ghormley
1907	Mr. Ole Kragerud
1908	Rev. and Mrs. A. M. Anderson

Rev. and Mrs. G. G. Kessel
Miss Luella M. Newton
W. A. (M.D.) and Mary Backenstoe transferred from Portuguese East Africa
1909 Harriet Sheldon, M.D. (Mrs. H. E. Barnes), associate to Dr. Backenstoe
1910 Edwaleni, manual training teacher requested
1912 Edwaleni, twenty-five scholarships
1913 Rev. and Mrs. J. S. Rice
Industrial department added to Edwaleni school
1914 Chapel building at Edwaleni, J. S. Rice. Twenty-five scholarships
1915 Rev. and Mrs. Ralph Jacobs
Miss Alice Evans (Mrs. W. J. Hampp)
1917 Rev. and Mrs. J. W. Haley (transfer from Portuguese East Africa)
1919 Rev. and Mrs. William Caldwell
Rev. and Mrs. William S. Hoffman
Rev. and Mrs. Gilbert Pine (transfer from Portuguese East Africa)
1922 Miss Daisy E. Frederick
1923 Ebenezer Hospital, Dr. W. A. Backenstoe
1925 Edwaleni school changed to industrial school to secure government grants
1929 Rev. and Mrs. Frank Adamson
Miss Ila Gunsolus
1932 Fairview Girls' School closed because government grant withdrawn
1937 Miss Margaret LaBarre
1941 J. L. (M.D.) and Marjorie (R.N.) Rice
1942 Cyclone damaged Edwaleni buildings
1945 Mr. and Mrs. Luther Kresge
Mary E. Current, R.N.
1947 Miss Laverna Campbell (Mrs. David Madgwick)
Miss Mamie B. Matson (Mrs. John Larkan)
Miss Gertrude Haight
Rev. and Mrs. John M. Riley
Rev. and Mrs. Frederic J. Ryff (transfer from Transvaal)
Ebenezer Clinic reopened, Mary Current, R.N.
1951 Rev. and Mrs. Warren H. Johnson
1953 Rev. and Mrs. Phillip S. Kline
1954 Greenville Hospital dedicated, September 26
1955 Laverna Grandfield, R.N.
Kathryn Hessler, R.N.
Mission cooperation with Sweetwaters Bible Institute
Authorized sale of portion of Fairview farm
Rev. and Mrs. Elmore L. Clyde
1957 Greenville Hospital begins training program for African nurses. Nine students enrolled
Youth camp held at Fairview. Attendance of one hundred
1958 One new preaching point opened on Edwaleni circuit
New churches built at Izora and Mbodia outstations
1960 New church and youth building in South Durban completed

SOUTHERN RHODESIA
1938 Rev. and Mrs. Ralph J. Jacobs (transfer from Portuguese East Africa)

1940	Miss Daisy E. Frederick (transfer from Portuguese East Africa)
1941	Lundi Central Primary School, Daisy Frederick
1944	Miss Ruth E. Smith
1946	Rev. and Mrs. Eldon B. Sayre
1947	Nina G. Detwiler, R.N.
1948	Rev. and Mrs. Tillman A. Houser
	Naomi E. Pettengill, M.D.
	Virginia I. Strait, R.N.
1949	Miss Frances R. Folsom (Mrs. Clarence Curtis)
1950	Dumisa station opened
	Chikombedzi Clinic (Nuanetsi Hospital) dedicated
1952	Ruth E. Morris, R.N.
	Ruth Ryff, R.N.
1954	Paul W. (M.D.) and Esther Embree
1956	Tuberculosis wards completed at Chikombedzi Clinic
1957	Cooperative agreement made with Brethren in Christ Mission for advanced training of African teachers
	New unit completed at Chikombedzi Clinic
	Government grant of one hundred acres secured adjacent to Lundi station for Bible school. School opened, Eldon B. Sayre, fifteen registrations
1958	Rev. and Mrs. Philip L. Capp
	Miss Donna M. Grantier
	Miss Ellen Jespersen (Mrs. Clarke DeMille)
	One new missionary residence completed
	Two residences for Africans built at Bible school
	New industrial building completed at the central primary school
1959	Mr. Clarke DeMille

TRANSVAAL

1905	Rev. and Mrs. Jules Ryff (transfer from South Africa)
1938	Rev. and Mrs. Frederic J. Ryff
1948	Rev. and Mrs. Clifford O. Guyer
1949	Rev. and Mrs. Wesley DeMille (transfer from Portuguese East Africa)
1955	Rev. and Mrs. Frederic J. Ryff (transfer from South Africa)
	New district opened in Orange Free State
	Mission residence purchased at Klerksdorp
1956	Cumming Farm purchased for Bible school
	F. L. Baker Memorial Bible School authorized for Cumming Farm
1958	Rev. and Mrs. Donald Crider
	F. L. Baker Memorial Bible School, Frederic J. Ryff
	Farm, Bible school, clinic and day school all operated on Baker Memorial Bible School campus

MISSIONS IN NORTH AMERICA

FLORIDA SPANISH MISSION

1941	Mission opened, Rev. and Mrs. E. E. Shelhamer

260

1942	Miss Ruth Landin
1945	Becomes part of the program of Commission on Missions
1948	Rev. and Mrs. Philip J. Calkins
	Kindergarten opened
1951	Friendship School opened, Helen Crawford, director
1952	Name changed from Tampa Spanish Mission to Florida Spanish Mission
1953	Free Methodist church organized among Spanish-speaking people
1954	Additional property purchased for expansion
1955	Rev. and Mrs. John Baker
1956	New classroom building completed. Registration 125
1958	Rev. and Mrs. Robert Cranston
1959	Another classroom building completed
	Miss Ileen Hawkins
	Miss Edith Gish

KENTUCKY MOUNTAINS MISSION

1912	J. M. Moore, M.D.
1919	Miss Elizabeth O'Connor
1921	Oakdale Christian High School, Elizabeth O'Connor
1926	Miss Myrtle Anderson
1930	Rev. and Mrs. Glen B. Rhodes
1931	Miss Jennie R. Greider
1949	Classroom-gymnasium building erected
1951	Elsie Apling, R.N.
1952	Rev. and Mrs. C. D. DeCan
1956	Dormitory and dining-room building completed
	Professor and Mrs. Willard Trepus
1957	Willard Trepus, principal of school
	Supervision of Kentucky Mountains Mission churches transferred to Kentucky and Tennessee Conference
	Rev. and Mrs. M. C. Bidwell
1958	Executive council created to handle affairs pertinent to the school. Marked spiritual advance under ministry of Rev. M. C. Bidwell, pastor of the Oakdale church

MEXICAN MISSIONS

1917	Nella True
	Rev. B. H. Pearson
1925	Adelaide N. Beers
1926	Mabel Meinhardt (Mrs. Willard Dickson)
	Mrs. B. H. Pearson
1931	Mexican Provisional Conference organized at Chino, California
1933	Rev. Harry O. Harper
1935	Mrs. Harry O. Harper
	Miss Evelyn Hadsell (Mrs. C. D. DeCan)

1939 Harry O. Harper, Principal, Nogales Bible School
      Rev. and Mrs. Ernest Keasling
1941 Rev. and Mrs. Reuel Walter
1943 Rev. and Mrs. Chester Chesbro
1945 Willard Dickson
1946 Nogales Bible School, new campus
      Miss Mildred Leatherman
      Rev. and Mrs. W. R. Thompson (transfer from Dominican Republic)
1949 Rapid expansion. Several new churches
      Light and Life Christian Day School opened
1950 Mrs. Leona Bownes
1954 Rev. and Mrs. David Fenwick
1956 Rev. and Mrs. Philip J. Calkins (transfer from Florida Spanish Mission)
      Rev. and Mrs. Donald M. Vesey (transfer from Paraguay)
      New work opened in Colorado and Mexico
1957 Evangelist Edward Wyman spent entire year in revival meetings in Mexico, California and Arizona
      Light and Life Christian Day School expands to include kindergarten
      Conference contributions exceed Board appropriations
      Field divided: Pacific Coast Latin American, and Mexican Missions
1958 Board authorized purchase of property in Hermosillo, Mexico
1959 Work opened in Tucson, Arizona, and Hermosillo, Sonora, Mexico
      Rev. and Mrs. F. Burleigh Willard (transfer from Dominican Republic)
      Mary Current, R.N. (transfer from South Africa)
      Miss Ruth Zimmerman

NORTHERN ONTARIO MISSIONS

1943 Rev. and Mrs. Elmer Goheen
1950 Rev. and Mrs. Ross Lloyd
      Miss Kathleen Garland (Mrs. James O. Parker)
1955 Rev. and Mrs. J. A. Tanner
1956 Rev. and Mrs. C. M. Bright
1958 Rev. and Mrs. J. W. Joice

PACIFIC COAST JAPANESE MISSION

1911 Mrs. Guy Bodenhamer
1913 Bertha Ahlmeyer, Port Los Angeles
1915 A small work among Japanese at Berkeley, California, originally Nazarene, became the Japanese Free Methodist Church of Berkeley
      Miss Lillian Pool (Mrs. Clyde J. Burnett) was its missionary and pastor for eight years
1918 Mrs. D. H. Thornton, Los Angeles
1929 Rev. Clyde J. Burnett appointed by General Missionary Board as superintendent
1932 Provisional conference organized
1934 Miss Alice E. Fensome
1935 Florence Dillon, R.N.
1939 Mission conference organized
1942 Japanese population moved to inland camps

262

1948   Pacific Coast Japanese Conference made gift of $1,602.42, known as the Harry F. Johnson Memorial Fund, to be used in reconstruction of Free Methodist work in Japan
1953   Dr. and Mrs. Llewellyn Davis
1956   Berkeley and Venice complete extensive building programs without Board assistance
1957   Japanese Light and Life Hour broadcast on XERB, a 50,000 watt station

SASKATCHEWAN INDIAN MISSION

1952   Board approved limited support
        Rev. and Mrs. Lloyd Robertson
1953   Church building completed
1954   Church organized among Cree and Soto Indians
        Basement parsonage under construction
1957   First camp meeting held

TEXAS LATIN-AMERICAN MISSION

1949   Rev. and Mrs. S. R. Tarin
1952   Houston Free Methodist Church purchased for Latin-American work in Texas
        S. R. Tarin, superintendent and pastor
1955   Kindergarten opened at San Antonio
1957   Mission reports over one hundred members

MISSIONS Discontinued

CEYLON

1906   Mrs. K. C. B. (Kitty Wood) Kumarakulasinghe

INDIAN MISSION—Gallup, New Mexico (Navajo)

1929   Rev. and Mrs. C. R. Volgamore
        Services begun in Indian homes
1930   Miss Beryl Manyon
1952   Mission closed

ITALIAN MISSION—Melrose Park, Illinois

1924   Rev. Simon V. Kline appointed to work among 2,000 Italians in Melrose Park. Services held in homes, then in remodeled store building
1925   Mission organized
        Rev. Angelo Previte appointed pastor
        Manual training, Bible study, added to program
        Rev. Anton Traina appointed pastor
1932   Rev. Simon Kline reappointed superintendent
1934   Rev. Simon Kline appointed pastor
1947   Mission transferred to Illinois Conference

LIBERIA

1885   Miss Mary E. Carpenter
        Rev. and Mrs. A. D. Noyes

MASON CITY, IOWA (foreign-speaking people)
1927 Miss Ida O. Helgen, pastor at Mason City, became interested in immigrants. After two years she was appointed full-time missionary
Sunday school, children's and mothers' meetings held
Food and clothing distributed to poor
Contacts especially with Greeks and Mexicans
1930 House rented for mission purposes and dedicated

NORWAY
1894 Mr. and Mrs. S. V. Ulness

PANAMA-CANAL ZONE
1910 Rev. and Mrs. F. W. Amsden
1922 Rev. and Mrs. Burton Beegle
Miss Emma Corson (Mrs. B. H. Pearson)
1930 Miss Elaine Hilborn
Miss Florence Hilborn

MISSIONS INSTITUTIONS
SCHOOLS
(Other Than Elementary)

Monitor's School (a teacher training school), Kivimba, Ruanda-Urundi. A union project.
Mweya Bible School, Mweya, Ruanda-Urundi. A union project.
Protestant Alliance Home Economics School, Muyebe, Ruanda-Urundi. A union project.
Youth Bible School, Inhamachafo, Portuguese East Africa.
Evangelists' School, Inhamachafo, Portuguese East Africa.
Nurses' Training School, Inhamachafo, Portuguese East Africa.
Nurses' Training School, Massinga, Portuguese East Africa.
Nurses' Training School, Greenville, South Africa.
Lundi Mission Bible School, Lundi, Southern Rhodesia.
Baker Memorial Bible School, Transvaal, South Africa.
Holiness Bible School, Assiut, Egypt.
Holy Light Bible Seminary, Kaohsiung, Formosa.
Union Biblical Seminary, Yeotmal, India. A union project.
Lay Leaders' School, Chikalda, India. A union project.
Osaka Christian College, Osaka, Japan.
Light and Life Bible School, Butuan City, Philippines.
Theological Seminary of the Free Methodist Church of Brazil, Mairipora, Brazil.
Evangelical Institute, Santiago, Dominican Republic.
The Bible School, Free Methodist Mission, Asuncion, Paraguay.
Nogales Bible School, Nogales, Arizona.
Oakdale Christian High School, Oakdale, Kentucky.

MEDICAL UNITS
Kibuye Hospital, Kibuye, Ruanda-Urundi.
Nyankanda Leper Colony, Nyankanda, Ruanda-Urundi. A union project.
Kibogora Dispensary, Kibogora, Ruanda-Urundi.
Muyebe Dispensary, Muyebe, Ruanda-Urundi.

Dispensary and Maternity Hospital, Inhamachafo, Portuguese East Africa.
Dispensary and Maternity Hospital, Massinga, Portuguese East Africa.
Greenville Mission Hospital, Greenville, South Africa.
Lundi Clinic, Lundi, Southern Rhodesia.
Chikombedzi Clinic, Nuanetsi, Southern Rhodesia.
Dispensary (on campus of Baker Memorial Bible School), Transvaal, South Africa.
Umri Mission Hospital, Umri, India.
Dispensary (on campus of Osaka Christian College), Osaka, Japan.
Dispensary (on campus of Evangelical Institute), Santiago, Dominican Republic.
Medical Clinic, Free Methodist Mission, Asuncion, Paraguay.

FOOTNOTES

CHAPTER I. THE FRONTIER 1860-1900
Section 2. A Missionary Church

1. B. T. Roberts, "Gospel to the Rich," *The Earnest Christian*, February, 1865, pp. 60-63.
2. The same.
3. B. T. Roberts, Speech before General Conference, *General Conference Daily*, October 16, 1890, p. 107.
4. B. H. Roberts, *Benjamin Titus Roberts*, p. 16.
5. The same, p. 17.
6. The same, p. 294.
7. B. T. Roberts, *The Earnest Christian*, January, 1865, p. 7.
8. *Book of Discipline*, Free Methodist Church, 1955, Paragraphs 13, 14.
9. A. A. Phelps, "The Mission of the Free Methodist Church," *The Earnest Christian*, February, 1861, p. 48.
10. B. T. Roberts, *The Earnest Christian*, January, 1860, pp. 5, 6.
11. B. H. Roberts, *Benjamin Titus Roberts*, pp. 241, 242.
12. The same, p. 267.
13. The same.
14. The same, pp. 244, 245.
15. The same, p. 261.
16. E. P. Hart, *Reminiscences of Early Free Methodism*, p. 151.
17. The same, p. 53.
18. The same, pp. 71, 72.
19. The same, pp. 72, 73.
20. Minutes, General Conference, Vol. VI, pp. 10, 11.
21. Minutes, General Conference, Vol. I, p. 87.
22. The same, pp. 152, 153.
23. K. S. Latourette, *History of the Expansion of Christianity*, Vol. VI, p. 177.
24. B. H. Roberts, *Benjamin Titus Roberts*, p. 454.
25. *Book of Discipline* of the Free Methodist Church, 1874, p. 102, Par. 2.
26. Conference Minutes, 1882, p. 53.
27. The same, p. 63.
28. Conference Minutes, 1890, p. 106.
29. Minutes, General Conference, Vol. I, p. 31.
30. Minutes, General Missionary Board, Vol. II, p. 116.
31. *The Free Methodist*, January 14, 1880.
32. *The Free Methodist*, December 24, 1868.
33. *The Free Methodist*, May 27, 1869.
34. Minutes, General Missionary Board, Vol. I, pp. 8, 9.

35. The same, p. 8.
36. C. B. Ebey letter to T B. Arnold, December 4. 1889.
37. Minutes, General Missionary Board, Vol. I, p. 11.
38. The same, p. 14.
39. The same, p. 15.
40. The same, p. 19.
41. The same.
42. The same, p. 21.
43. Conference Minutes, 1882, p. 33.
44. Conference Minutes, 1885, pp. 71, 72.
45. Conference Minutes, 1887, p. 137.
46. Conference Minutes, 1889, pp. 44, 45.
47. The same, p. 128.
48. B. H. Roberts, *Benjamin Titus Roberts*, p. 534.
49. Editorial, *The Earnest Christian*, November, 1865, p. 163.
50. B. Winget, *Missions and Missionaries*, p. 7.
51. B. H. Roberts, *Benjamin Titus Roberts*, p. 373.
52. E. P. Hart, *Reminiscences of Early Free Methodism*, p. 2.
53. The same, pp. 60, 61.
54. *The Earnest Christian*, March, 1860, p. 75.
55. *The Earnest Christian*, October, 1865, p. 127
56. Minutes, General Missionary Board, Vol. II, pp. 459, 460.
57. The same, p. 460.
58. Minutes, Board of Directors, Vol. I, pp. 216, 217.
59. The same, p. 320.
60. *The Earnest Christian*, June, 1864, pp. 181, 182, quoted from *Church Guardian*.
61. *The Earnest Christian*, September, 1864, pp. 158, 159.
62. T. B. Arnold letter, October 17, 1888.
63. *The Earnest Christian*, August, 1865, p. 65.
64. *The Earnest Christian*, July, 1865, p. 32.
65. E. P. Hart, *Reminiscences of Early Free Methodism*, p. 141.
66. D. W. Thurston, *The Free Methodist*, August 6, 1868.
67. Elias Bowen, *History of the Origin of the Free Methodist Church*, pp. 292, 293.
68. B. H. Roberts, *Benjamin Titus Roberts*, p. 339.
69. The same, p. 309.
70. The same, p. 264.
71. The same, p. 263.
72. *The Earnest Christian*, December, 1864, p. 185.

CHAPTER I

SECTION 3. Education

1. *The Earnest Christian*, January, 1860, pp. 21-25.
2. The same, p. 21.
3. *The Earnest Christian*, June, 1860, pp. 168, 169.
4. *Free Methodist Hymnal*, 1910, No. 466.
5. Colossians 1:13.
6. B. H. Roberts, *Benjamin Titus Roberts*, p. 349.
7. James Truslow Adams, *Epic of America*, p. 276.
8. The same, p. 286.
9. The same, p. 279.
10. The same, p. 282.
11. James Truslow Adams, *Album of American History*, Vol. III, p. 423.
12. Minutes, General Conference, 1882, p. 125.
13. This was approved by missionaries in Africa: Minutes, General Missionary Board, Vol. I, p. 121.

14. *The Free Methodist*, April 30, 1868.
15. W. T. Hogue, *History of the Free Methodist Church*, Vol. II, p. 326.
16. Minutes, General Missionary Board, Vol. III, pp. 54-56.
17. Kenneth Scott Latourette, *History of the Expansion of Christianity*, Vol. IV, pp. 418, 419.
18. D. W. Abrams, *The Free Methodist*, July 28, 1880.
19. Elias Bowen, *The Origin of the Free Methodist Church*, pp. 292, 293.
20. Minutes, General Conference, Vol. II, p. 125.
21. II Corinthians 8:3-5.
22. W. T. Hogue, *History of the Free Methodist Church*, Vol. II, pp. 348-352.
23. The same, p. 352.

CHAPTER I

Section 4. General Evangelists

1. Minutes, General Conference, Vol. I, pp. 280, 281.
2. Illinois Conference report, *The Free Methodist*, January 16, 1868.
3. W. T. Hogue, *History of the Free Methodist Church*, Vol. I, p. 353.
4. R. Newton Flew, annual address of conference to Methodist societies of the Methodist Church in Great Britain, 1947.
5. James H. Nicholls, *Evanston: An Interpretation*, pp. 115-120.
6. *The Christian Century*, September 2, 1959, p. 1007.
7. Quoted in *The Christian Century*, November 17, 1954, p. 1395.
8. B. T. Roberts, *The Earnest Christian*, January, 1860, p. 32.
9. Minutes, General Missionary Board, Vol. II, pp. 118-125.
10. The same, p. 125.
11. The same, pp. 125, 126.
12. The same, p. 126.
13. The same, pp. 208, 209.
14. The same, p. 211.
15. *General Conference Daily*, June 20, 1907, pp. 61, 62.
16. Minutes, General Missionary Board, Vol. II, p. 377.
17. Gaius Glenn Atkins, *Life of Cardinal Newman*, p. 87.
18. Minutes, North Michigan Conference, 1889, p. 47.
19. Minutes, Michigan Conference, 1890, p. 108.
20. E. P. Hart, *Reminiscences of Early Free Methodism*, p. 141.

CHAPTER II. OVERSEAS VENTURES, 1885-1910

Section 1. Africa

1. James Truslow Adams, *Epic of America*, p. 303.
2. Minutes, Genesee Annual Convention, 1861, p. 5.
3. Minutes, New York Conference, 1878, p. 7.
4. Minutes, Iowa Conference, 1883, p. 41.
5. *The Free Methodist*, August 27, 1884.
6. The same, p. 5.
7. The same.
8. W. T. Hogue, *History of the Free Methodist Church*, Vol. II, p. 242.
9. *The Free Methodist*, June 24, 1884.
10. Minutes, General Missionary Board, Vol. I, pp. 34, 35.
11. The same, p. 36.
12. The same, pp. 162-66.
13. *The Free Methodist*, March 18, 1885.
14. *The Free Methodist*, January 7, 1885.
15. *The Free Methodist*, January 14, 1885.
16. *The Free Methodist*, January 28, 1885.

17. The same.
18. *The Free Methodist*, February 11, 1885.
19. *The Free Methodist*, April 15, 1885.
20. The same.
21. *The Free Methodist*, October 7, 1885.
22. Conference Minutes, 1885, p. 186.
23. Conference Minutes, 1886, p. 169.
24. Conference Minutes, 1887, p. 69.
25. The same, p. 75.
26. Conference Minutes, 1885, p. 135.
27. *The Free Methodist*, February 18, 1885.
28. *The Free Methodist*, March 11, 1885.
29. *The Free Methodist*, August 18, 1886.
30. *The Free Methodist*, February 18, 1885.
31. *The Free Methodist*, March 25, 1885.
32. K. S. Latourette, *History of the Expansion of Christianity*, Vol. V, p. 402.
33. *The Free Methodist*, August 26, 1885.
34. *The Free Methodist*, May 26, 1886.
35. *The Free Methodist*, November 18, 1885.
36. *The Free Methodist*, August 26, 1885.
37. *The Free Methodist*, November 18, 1885.
38. The same.
39. *The Free Methodist*, January 20, 1886.
40. Grace Allen, as reported to Byron S. Lamson.
41. *The Free Methodist*, November 25, 1885.
42. The same.
43. *The Free Methodist*, January 20, 1886.
44. *The Free Methodist*, June 9, 1886.
45. *The Free Methodist*, May 26, 1886.
46. *The Free Methodist*, June 9, 1886.
47. *The Free Methodist*, July 14, 1886.
48. W. W. Kelley letter to T. B. Arnold, August 11, 1886.
49. Harry Agnew, *The Free Methodist*, October 27, 1886.
50. *The Free Methodist*, December 29, 1886.
51. Quoted in *The Free Methodist*, May 27, 1885.
52. The same.
53. *The Free Methodist*, December 16, 1885.
54. *The Free Methodist*, January 20, 1886.
55. *The Free Methodist*, July 7, 1885.
56. *The Free Methodist*, July 28, 1885.
57. *The Free Methodist*, September 8, 1886.
58. *The Free Methodist*, September 22, 1886.
59. Minutes, Board of Directors, Vol. I, p. 126.
60. The same, pp. 127, 128.
61. The same, p. 125.
62. Minutes, General Missionary Board, Vol. I, p. 65.
63. Minutes, General Missionary Board, Vol. II, p. 332.

CHAPTER II
SECTION 2. India

1. K. S. Latourette, *History of the Expansion of Christianity*, Vol. IV, pp. 178, 179.
2. James Truslow Adams, *Epic of America*, pp. 309, 310.
3. K. S. Latourette, *History of the Expansion of Christianity*, Vol. VI, pp. 137-56.
4. Minutes, Illinois Conference, October, 1880, p. 28.
5. Minutes, General Missionary Board, Vol. I, p. 25.
6. *The Free Methodist*, March 21, 1883.

7. Minutes, General Missionary Board, Vol. I, p. 40.
8. *The Free Methodist*, October 28, 1885.
9. Julia Zimmerman letter, November 20, 1885.
10. W. E. Herden letter to T. B. Arnold, November 22, 1885.
11. *The Free Methodist*, December 30, 1885.
12. Louisa Ranf letter, January 4, 1886.
13. Louisa Ranf letter, February 20, 1886.
14. The same.
15. The same.
16. The same.
17. The same.
18. M. H. Freeland, *Our Missionary Martyrs*, pp. 88, 89.
19. The same, p. 116.
20. E. F. Ward letter, October 7, 1886.
21. *The Free Methodist*, January 6, 1886.
22. M. H. Freeland, *Our Missionary Martyrs*, p. 105.
23. E. F. Ward letter, February 27, 1888.
24. Phebe E. Ward letter, April 30, 1889.
25. Conference Minutes, 1889, 1891.
26. Celia Ferries letter, November 25, 1891.
27. Engraved on the tombstones.
28. Minutes, General Missionary Board, Vol. II, p. 92.
29. H. L. Crockett letter, August 23, 1900.
30. M. C. Clark letter, February 5, 1904.
31. V. G. McMurry letter to B. Winget, September 13, 1900.
32. *The Christian Century*, September 2, 1959.
33. The same.

CHAPTER II

Section 3. Latin Lands

1. K. S. Latourette, *History of the Expansion of Christianity*, Vol. IV, p. 415.
2. The same, pp. 438, 439.
3. Minutes, Board of Directors, Vol. I, pp. 2-17.
4. Minutes, Board of Directors, Vol. I, p. 224.
5. J. W. Winans letter, May 5, 1908.
6. The same.
7. J. W. Winans letter, September 4, 1909.
8. W. C. Willing letter, June 15, 1908.
9. Minutes, General Missionary Board, Vol. IV, p. 100.

CHAPTER II

Section 4. Japan

1. C. B. Ebey, *The Free Methodist*, December 27, 1904.
2. *The Missionary Review of the World*, January, 1897, p. 53.
3. The same, p. 55.
4. Letter, *The Free Methodist*, October 31, 1894.
5. Hogue, *History of the Free Methodist Church*, Vol. II, pp. 283, 284.
6. Carrie T. Burritt, *The Story of Fifty Years*, pp. 88-90; Byron S. Lamson, *Lights in the World*, pp. 79-81.
7. *The Missionary Review of the World*, January, 1907, p. 57.
8. Byron S. Lamson, *Lights in the World*, p. 81.
9. W. F. Matthewson letter, February 15, 1904.
10. A. Youngren letter, March 29, 1904.
11. A. Youngren letter, July 5, 1906.

12. W. F. Matthewson letter, June 29, 1906.
13. A. Youngren letter, July 5, 1906.
14. W. F Matthewson letter, June 29, 1906.
15. A. Youngren letter, October 7, 1909.
16. Frank Warren letter, November 6, 1926.
17. Minutes, General Missionary Board, Vol. IV, p. 204.
18. H. H. Wagner letter, December 9, 1932.

CHAPTER II

SECTION 5. China

1. *The Missionary Review of the World*, January, 1897, p. 46.
2. Clara Leffingwell letter, April 19, 1900.
3. C. A. Leffingwell, *The Free Methodist*, December 6, 1904.
4. W. A. Sellew, *Clara Leffingwell, A Missionary*, p. 245.
5. C. A. Leffingwell letter, May 25, 1905.
6. The same.
7. The same.
8. The same.
9. W. A. Sellew, *Clara Leffingwell, A Missionary*, p. 281.
10. The same, p. 282.
11. Minutes, Board of Directors, Vol. I, pp. 89, 90.
12. The same, p. 106.
13. The same, pp. 192-194.
14. The same, pp. 259, 260.
15. John Green, M.D., letter, April 9, 1934.
16. *Praise and Prayer*, December, 1934.
17. John Green, M.D., letter, July 27, 1935.
18. The same.
19. Minutes, General Missionary Board, Vol. IV, pp. 164, 165.

CHAPTER III. WOMEN VENTURE IN WORLD MISSIONS, 1890

1. General Conference Journal, 1890, pp. 137-140.
2. B. T. Roberts letter, August 17, 1890.
3. C. B. Ebey, Missionary Secretary, report to General Conference, 1890. Minutes, General Conference, Vol. II, pp. 137-140.
4. The same.
5. *The Free Methodist*, October 3, 1894.
6. *The Free Methodist*, August 16, 1886.
7. *The Free Methodist*, December 31, 1868.
8. *The Free Methodist*, February 17, 1870.
9. *The Free Methodist*, March 11, 1869.
10. *The Free Methodist*, September 2, 1869.
11. Mrs. J. S. MacGeary letter, December 3, 1889.
12. Ella M. MacGeary, *General Conference Daily*, June 12, 1907.
13. Mariet Hardy Freeland, *Our Missionary Martyrs*, p. 50.
14. Minutes, General Missionary Board, Vol. I, pp. 17, 18.
15. The same, p. 35.
16. The same, p. 57.
17. Emma Freeland letter, June 23, 1891.
18. The same.
19. *General Conference Daily*, June 13, 1907.
20. *The Free Methodist*, June 7, 1893.
21. *The Free Methodist*, March 22, 1893.
22. *The Free Methodist*, April 26, 1893.

23. The same.
24. The same.
25. *The Free Methodist*, February 13, 1893.
26. *The Free Methodist*, January 4, 1893.
27. The same.
28. *The Free Methodist*, November 1, 1893.
29. *The Free Methodist*, November 15, 1893.
30. *The Free Methodist*, August 23, 1893.
31. *The Free Methodist*, October 11, 1893.
32. *The Free Methodist*, May 9, 1894.
33. The same.
34. Pastoral address, General Conference 1894, *General Conference Daily*, October 10, 1894, p. 5.
35. *General Conference Daily*, notice by Missionary Secretary, October 20, 1894.
36. *General Conference Daily*, October 22, 1894.
37. *General Conference Daily*, October 23, 1894.
38. The same.
39. *The Free Methodist*, November 14, 1894.
40. The same.
41. The same.
42. The same.
43. The same.
44. The same.
45. Minutes, General Missionary Board, Vol. I, p. 331.
46. The same, p. 256.
47. Report, Ruth L. Cochrane, Vice-president and Stewardship Secretary, 1960.

CHAPTER IV. INDEPENDENT VENTURES

1. *The Free Methodist*, May 6, 1885.
2. I. D. Parsons, *KINDLING WATCH-FIRES*, pp. 67, 71.
3. *General Conference Daily*, October 25, 1894, p. 227.
4. Minutes, General Missionary Board, Vol. II, p. 311.
5. The same, pp. 446, 447.
6. *The Free Methodist*, June 23, 1880.
7. *General Conference Daily*, October 20, 1890, p. 186.
8. The same.
9. I. D. Parsons, *KINDLING WATCH-FIRES*, p. 77.
10. B. T. Roberts letter, July 31, 1885, quoted in *KINDLING WATCH-FIRES*, pp. 36, 37.
11. Minutes, General Conference, Vol. II, p. 205.
12. The same, p. 259.
13. The same.
14. The same.
15. *The Free Methodist*, October 31, 1894.
16. W. T. Hogue, *History of the Free Methodist Church*, Vol. II, pp. 198, 199.
17. Acts 1:8.
18. E. F. Ward letter, April 29, 1891.
19. Minutes, Board of Directors, Vol. I, p. 66.
20. Letterhead *circa* 1890.
21. Applicant's letter, March 29, 1890.
22. *The Free Methodist*, February 13, 1889.
23. *The Free Methodist*, May 29, 1889.
24. *The Free Methodist*, May 15, 1889.
25. *The Earnest Christian*, December, 1865, p. 190.
26. *The Earnest Christian*, January, 1865, pp. 32, 33.
27. *The Free Methodist*, January 7, 1880.

CHAPTER V. WORLD WAR I—THE LARGER CONCERN, 1918-1930

1. James Truslow Adams, *Epic of America*, p. 393.
2. E. B. Sherman, "Things Are in the Saddle," *North American*, December, 1921.
3. W F. M. S. Corresponding Secretary, Conference Minutes, 1919, p. 406.
4. Conference Minutes, 1920, p. 363.
5. Minutes, General Missionary Board, Vol. I, pp. 122, 123.
6. Minutes, General Missionary Board, Vol. IV, p. 136.
7. Minutes, General Missionary Board, Vol. III, p. 236.
8. Minutes, General Missionary Board, Vol. IV, p. 304.
9. September 14-21, 1926. Conference Minutes, 1926, p. 342.
10. Minutes, General Missionary Board, Vol. III, p. 143.
11. Brochure, Annual Meeting of the Missionary Board, November 12, 1889.
12. Minutes, General Missionary Board, Vol. I, p. 162-66.
13. *The Free Methodist*, November 20, 1889.
14. Questionnaire, Robert P. Wilder, January 19, 1889 (Student Volunteers).
15. Minutes, General Missionary Board, Vol. I, pp. 153-55.
16. Price list of C. and M. A. Store, 1919.
17. Minutes, General Missionary Board, Vol. III, p. 205.
18. Minutes, General Missionary Board, Vol. IV, p. 1.
19. Minutes, General Missionary Board, Vol. III, p. 143.
20. Minutes, General Missionary Board, Vol. IV, p. 270.
21. Minutes, General Missionary Board, Vol. III, p. 295.
22. Minutes, Board of Directors, Vol. I, p. 42.
23. Minutes, General Missionary Board, Vol. III, pp. 63, 64.
24. The same, p. 222.
25. *Book of Discipline*, 1955, Par. 144, 145.
26. Ecclesiastes 3:11.
27. Minutes, General Missionary Board, Vol. IV, pp. 370, 371.

CHAPTER VI. THE DEPRESSION YEARS, 1930-1944

SECTION 1. The 1885 Plan

1. J. W. Haley report, August 25, 1932.
2. The same.
3. The same.
4. The same.
5. J. W. Haley letter, June 27, 1933.
6. The same.
7. The same.
8. J. W. Haley letter, July 3, 1934.
9. J. W. Haley article "On to Congo," n. d.
10. Numbers 14:8.
11. Conference Minutes, 1934, p. 259.
12. J. W. Haley letter, November 26, 1934.
13. H. F. Johnson letter, January 11, 1935.
14. J. W. Haley letter, November 29, 1934.
15. J. W. Haley letter, December 3, 1934.
16. J. W Haley letter, January 19, 1935.
17. The same.
18. The same.
19. H. F. Johnson report, Conference Minutes, 1935, p. 261.
20. J. W. Haley letter, August 27, 1935.
21. J. W. Haley letter, December 22, 1935.
22. J. W Haley, Annual Report, July, 1937.
23. H. F. Johnson report, Conference Minutes, 1937, p. 282.

CHAPTER VI

Section 2. Two Huts on the Lundi

1. Ralph Jacobs letter, April 22, 1930.
2. The same.
3. Ralph Jacobs letter, August 25, 1930.
4. The same.
5. Ralph Jacobs letter, September 29, 1930.
6. Ralph Jacobs, Report on Inhambane Conference, July, 1933.
7. The same.
8. Ralph Jacobs, Report on Inhambane Conference, March 8, 1939.
9. Ralph Jacobs letter, March 28, 1939.
10. Ethel M. Jacobs letter, April 12, 1939.
11. Ralph Jacobs letter, April 25, 1939.
12. Harry Johnson letter, May 31, 1939.
13. Ralph Jacobs letter, June 21, 1939.
14. The same.
15. Ralph Jacobs report, July, 1944.
16. The same.
17. The same.
18. Ethel Jacobs letter, March 1, 1940.
19. Ethel Jacobs letter, April, 1941.
20. Minutes, General Missionary Board, Vol. V, p. 225.
21. Minutes, Board of Directors, Vol. III, p. 219.

CHAPTER VII. POST-WAR EXPANSION, 1944-1960

1. *The International Review of Missions*, January, 1941, p. 3.
2. See Covenant and Charter of the United Nations.
3. *The Free Methodist*, December 22, 1959.
4. Pearl Schaffer letter, April 9, 1948.
5. John Schlosser letter, April 12, 1948.
6. Geneva Sayre letter, January 6, 1949.
7. Geneva Sayre letter, September 20, 1948.
8. Geneva Sayre letter, December 1, 1949.
9. Geneva Sayre letter, January 26, 1950.
10. *The Free Methodist*, August 10, 1954.
11. The same.
12. *The Free Methodist*, October 30, 1956.
13. The same.
14. *The Free Methodist*, August 1, 1950.
15. Matthew 11:4, 5.
16. Romans 6:23.
17. I John 1:9.
18. Matthew 4:23-25.
19. Matthew 7:24, 25.
20. Melvin Pastorius, M.D., A Report, 1959.
21. Newspaper, Nagpur.
22. W. B. Olmstead, Quadrennial Report, June, 1931.
23. B. S. Lamson, *Lights in the World*, pp. 85, 86.
24. Romans 1:16.
25. Romans 10:13.
26. *News Bulletin of the Near East Christian Council*, Eastertide, 1959, pp. 23-25.
27. Minutes, General Missionary Board, Vol. I, p. 182.
28. *The Free Methodist*, January 30, 1951.
29. B. S. Lamson, Quadrennial Report, 1947.
30. Forward Movement Objectives 1960-1964, India, 1959.

CHAPTER VIII. WORLD FELLOWSHIP OF FREE METHODIST CHURCHES

1. *The Free Methodist*, October 29, 1957, p. 7.
2. *East and West Review*, April, 1954.
3. Donald McGavran, *The Bridges of God*, p. 109.
4. Author unknown.
5. Walter H. Talcott (?), *Free Methodist Hymnal*, No. 352.

INDEX

Abrams, D. W., 34-35; plea for funds for mission college, 35; 50, 51, 52, 54, 55, 63, 65, 66-67, 130-31
Abrams, Miss Helen, 128, 251
Adamson, Rev. and Mrs. Frank, 169, 248, 259
Adamson, Rev. and Mrs. Merlin, 248
Adamson, Miss Myra, 126, 248
Africa, 19, 20, 34, 35, 38, 44, 47, 50, 52, 53-68, 71, 72, 75, 77, 96, 99, 100, 101, 113-14, 118, 126, 127, 129-31, 134-45, 148, 154-56, 157, 159, 162-77; Lamson visit, 190-201; 203, 205, 209, 210, 211, 214, 215, 216, 219, 220, 226, 228, 237, 238, 246, 247; see also Belgian Congo, Liberia, Portuguese East Africa, South Africa, Southern Rhodesia, Transvaal
Agnew, Rev. G. Harry, 53, 54, 56, 57-62, 63, 120, 145, 162, 169, 211, 257
Agnew, Mrs. G. H. (Susie Sherman), 257
Agnew, Mrs. G. H. (Lillie Smith), 257
Ahlmeyer, Miss Bertha, 126, 262
Alaska, 139
Alberta Conference, 46
Albion, New York, 18, 44, 68, 139
Alcorn, Miss Gertrude, 254
Alexander, Dr. Merton and Dr. Arlene, 248
Alexander, Rev. and Mrs. T. W., 253
All-Africa Church Conference, 237
Allee, Miss Mata D., 254
Allen, Miss Grace, 120, 126, 127, 246, 257, 258
America; beginning Civil War, 11; 12, 47, 48, 49; frontier, 49; 61, 63, 71, 72, 74, 78; American church life, 82; seeking a frontier, 90; 91, 94, 106, 109, 141, 142-43, 160, 161, 162, 163, 168, 180, 181, 188, 191, 195, 202, 207, 211; world citizen, 223; 225; see also United States, North America
American Bible Society, 12
American Board of Commissioners for Foreign Missions, 12, 57, 58; missionaries evacuate, 61; 92, 114, 117, 144, 145, 194
Amsden, Rev. and Mrs. F. W., 264
Anderson, Rev. and Mrs. A. M., 258
Anderson, Miss Myrtle, 128, 256, 261
Anet, Dr., 162
Anglican, 42, 201
Apling, Miss Elsie, 257, 261
Apling, Miss Emma (Mrs. T. H. Gilpatrick), 253
Apple Orchard Convention, 15
Appleton, C. Floyd, 104-5, 249
Area Secretaries, 159
Arizona, 38, 45, 91-92, 218
Arkansas, 45; Little Rock, 245
Arksey, Rev. Laurence, 172, 258
Arksey, Mrs. Laurence, 258
Armstrong, Miss Mae, 127, 198, 257, 258
Arnold, I. R. B., 138

Arnold, Rev. T. B.; managed orphanage, 37; 49, 50, 51, 52, 53, 56, 63, 65, 68, 71, 72, 76, 116, 119, 144, 148-49, 150
Ashcraft, Rev. E. P., 109-12, 182, 250
Ashcraft, Mrs. E. P., 109-11, 250
Ashcraft, F. H., 92
Asia, 180, 209, 210-11, 223, 238
Asia Fellowship Conference, 235, 238-39, 256
Asquith, Herbert, 142
Asuncion; see Paraguay
Atkins, G. G., 42-43
Audio-visual aids on mission field, 221-22, 229-30
Avery, Miss Doane, 251
Avery, Miss S. Belle, 251
Awaji; see Japan
Aylard, Miss Gertrude (Mrs. W. F. Matthewson), 255

Backenstoe, Dr. W. A., 151-52, 257, 259
Backenstoe, Mrs. W. A., 257, 259
Baker, A. W., 169
Baker, Rev. F. L., 158
Baker, Rev. and Mrs. John, 261
Baker Memorial Bible School, 260, 264; dispensary, 265
Bands; see also Pentecost Bands; 27, 40, 41, 42, 43
Barkley, Miss Emma (Mrs. P. C. Bennett), 252
Barnes, Miss Grace, 78, 127, 254
Barnes, Miss Grace (Home Missions, 1911), 139
Barnhart, Mrs., 119
Barth, Karl, 241
Barton, M. L., 177
Bates, Rev. and Mrs. Gerald, 249
Baulke, Miss Louisa (Mrs. Torance Alexander), 252
Beare, Tom, 109-12, 250
Beare, Mrs. Tom, 111, 250
Becker, Miss Ella (Mrs. J. E. Cochrane), 254
Beckwith, Miss Berdina, 188, 248
Beegle, Rev. and Mrs. Burton, 264
Beers, A., 37
Beers, Mrs. Adelaide, 119, 138, 261
Beers, President and Mrs. Alexander, 101
Belgian Congo; Kibogora, 126, 207, 216, 233-34, dispensary, 248, school, 248; Kibuye, 126, 169, 199, 201, hospital, 248, 249; Muyebe, 126, 167, 199, 200, school, 248, dispensary, 248, 249; Nyankanda, 126, 215, 249; Usumbura, 126, 162-63, 215, 248; Ruanda-Urundi, 161-70, 249; 162-70, 188; Leopoldville, 190, 201; 191; Lamson visit, 199-201, 202; R-U Alliance, 201; medical, 207, 212, 215; R-U literature and literacy, 220; 228, 233; Kivimba, 264; Chronology, 248
Belgium, 141, 144, 162, 165, 202

275

276

Johnson, Rev. and Mrs. James, 248
Johnson, Rev. and Mrs. Warren, 259
Joice, Rev. and Mrs. J. W., 262
Jones, Miss Anna, 253
Jones, Bishop Burton R., 45, 46, 159
Jones, Miss Edith F., 127, 182, 183, 250
Judson, Mrs. Adoniram, 115
Junior Missionary Society, 115, 122-23, 159
Junker, Rev. and Mrs. James, 249

Kaifeng; see China
Kaifeng Bible School, 106, 109, 127, 183, 211, 250
Kakihara, Paul, 91-2, 93, 98, 100, 255
Kansas, 21, 23, 35; mission college for colored, 36; 37; Central Academy and College, McPherson, 37; 38, 44, 45, 118, 138, 189
Kawabe, T., 92, 93-4; St. Paul of Japan, 94; 97-8, 255
Kayero (Congo), 169
Keasling, Rev. Ernest, 251, 262
Keasling, Mrs. Ernest, 262
Kelley, Rev. W. W., 50; appointed missionary, 54; 56, 57, 58, 59, 60, 61-62, 93, 117, 157, 162, 257
Kelsey, W. M., 22, 138
Kendall, Rev. and Mrs. F. C., 252
Kenny, Rev. and Mrs. Lorne, 252
Kenny, Rev. and Mrs. Roy, 249
Kent, Dr. Lois E., 255
Kentucky, 38, 46, 126, 128; Mountain Mission, 139, 144; 209; Chronology, 261
Kessel, Rev. and Mrs. G. C., 259
Kibogora; see Belgian Congo
Kibogora Dispensary, 126, 207, 264
Kibuye; see Belgian Congo
Kibuye Hospital, 126, 207, 264
"Killer" Tribe, 186, 218
King, Rev. and Mrs. C. Wesley, 249
King of Urundi, 169
King Tappa, 51, 52, 65, 130-31
Klein, Rev. and Mrs. Matthias, 255
Kline, Dr. and Mrs. Frank, 254
Kline, Rev. and Mrs. Phillip, 259
Kline, Rev. Simon V., 263
Knapp, Eunice, 114
Kobe; see Japan
Korea, 97, 98, 179
Kragerud, Ole, 258
Kresge, Mr. and Mrs. Luther, 192, 259
Kuhn, Dr. Esther F., 126, 248, 249
Kuhn, Professor Harold, 212

LaBarre, Miss Margaret, 191, 259
LaDue, T. S., 19, 23
Lake Njela; first Portuguese East African station, 58
Lake Nyassa, 53, 57, 162
Lake Tanganyika, 53, 57, 62, 162
Landin, Miss Ruth, 126, 128, 261
Lane, Rev. George, 13, 115

Languages; Tonga, 59; Marathi, 75; Visayan and Manobo, 185; English, French, Portuguese, 191; Korkoo, 220
Latin America, 82-90, 127; evangelism, 214, 215, 216-18; literature and literacy, 220; 226, 238
Latourette, K. S., 57-58
Latshaw, Miss Adelaide, 127, 257, 258
Laubach, Dr. Frank, 208, 210, 220
Law and Gospel, 136
Lay Leaders' School, Chikalda, 264
Laymen; witnessing, 11; in apple-orchard meeting, 14-15; 27, 34, 57, 69, 99, 104; Light and Life Men's Fellowship, 159; 215, 218, 228, 231, 232, 238
Leatherman, Miss Mildred, 128, 262
Leffingwell, Miss Clara, 101-4, 106, 126, 152, 250
Lehman, Stanley, 249
Leininger, Miss Kate, 183, 250, 251, 253
Leise, Rev. and Mrs. H. R., 250
Lewis, L. G., 144
Lianga (P. I.), 186
Liberia, 35, 51, 65, 66, 68, 75, 113, 116, 130, 135, 136; Chronology, 263
Life Boat, The, 136
Light and Life Bible School, Butuan City, 257, 264
Light and Life Men's Fellowship, 159
Lights in the World, 125
Limpopo River, 58
Lincoln, Rev. A. Y., 257
Lincoln, Mrs. A. Y., 114, 257
Lind, Abraham, 254
Lindsay, Miss Naomi, 253
Literacy and literature; Kelley in Portuguese East Africa, 59; Ward and the Korkoos, 75; 208, 210-11, 219-22, 230, 231, 253
Livingstone, David, 20, 47
Lloyd, Rev. and Mrs. Ross, 262
Lloyd-George, David, 47
"Lobolosa," 154
London, 74, 147, 148, 162
Longhurst, Miss Sarah, 252
Los Angeles Pacific College, 109
Louisiana, 36, 45
Lower Ping Tung; see Formosa
Lundi; see Southern Rhodesia
Lundi Mission Bible School, 211-12, 264
Lundi Mission Clinic, 127, 206-7, 265
Luffy, Miss Mary (Mrs. S. C. Crawford), 255

McClean, Miss Clara (Mrs. F. C. Kendall), 252
McClish, Rev. and Mrs. Glade, 250
McCready, Rev. and Mrs. Burton, 248
McGavran, Donald, 237
MacGeary, Rev. J. S., 107, 144, 156
MacGeary, Mrs. J. S., 115-16, 118-19, 120, 121
Mackey, Joseph, 19
McMurry, Rev. and Mrs. V. G., 81, 254

281

www.ingramcontent.com/pod-product-compliance
Lightning Source LLC
Chambersburg PA
CBHW051820040426
42447CB00006B/299